Snake Music

a Detroit Memoir

by

J. Patrick Reilly

Lulu Publishing

Published by Lulu.com Publishing.
www.lulu.com

Library of Congress Cataloging in-Publication Data
Reilly, J. Patrick
    Snake Music: A Detroit Memoir

ISBN 978-1-105-92512-2

First Edition

Preface

When they closed his casket, I thought that would be the last time I would cry for Daddy. I was thirteen. Life for our family could only improve without him. Weren't all the problems in our family his fault? Hadn't he been a lazy drunk who initiated angry shouting matches with Mama? Didn't he push Mama into her "attacks", when her life hung in the balance? Didn't he withdraw into his own private world, ignoring his wife, his home, and his children in the process? Indeed, when they closed his casket, he was out of my life to the extent that I never grieved his passing, and eventually almost all memories of him faded away.

It was many years later, well into my adulthood, when I had children of my own, that I felt the need to search for Daddy. Who was he, and why did he act as he did? What were the forces that formed his attitudes and habits? Why was I so determined as a child not to be like him? And have I succeeded? As I pursued my search, only a few memories and pictures came back. I seemed to have done a good job of erasing them.

Somewhere, in an old dusty attic, I fantasized, someone might come across a book of Daddy's memoirs. What a treasure that would be! That fantasy compelled me to write my own story. Perhaps in the telling, I could come to understand Daddy. Perhaps I could provide my descendants and kin with some insight into their own family heritage.

I searched for Daddy in numerous talks with my sisters Kathleen and Helen, interviews with other family members, visits to old neighborhoods, research into old records and documents, but still he continued to elude me. Notwithstanding my failure to find Daddy, Mama came sharply into focus. It was she who exercised such power in our family, who so loved, inspired, instructed, frightened, and ultimately, so distressed me. Through it all, it was she who believed in me. My story cannot be told without Mama. So I have tried to tell her story along with mine.

When I told my friend Dick that I was writing my memoir, he asked: "Would it be the perfect truth?" I thought for a moment, and replied: "No, something higher—the *imperfect* truth." Dick looked puzzled. I explained that I was trying to relate the truth I saw as a child, without subsequent interpretation, even though I might want to say "but I now realize that it must have really been some other way." It is the imperfect truth that is our view of the world, the reality that forms our impressions and attitudes. So I have searched for that imperfect truth.

I have changed some names to protect privacy, and have invented others where my memory fails me. I have attempted to use the real names where possible. Some events are presented slightly out of order or merged with others for ease of story telling.

Contents

Preface   iii

Part I: The Child   1

1. Zoedy   3

2. Brinket   7

3. Grammy   13

4. Uncle Eddie   17

5. The Polish   21

6. Mama's Chicken   25

7. Daddy   29

8. The Birds and the Bees   37

9. Ad Altare Dei   39

10. The Skeleton Building   47

11. Mama Runs Away   52

12. The Legion of Mary   56

13. Grand Rapids   61

14. A Radio Flyer   67

15. Mama's Education   71

16. The Palace   74

17. Treasure Hunts   78

18. An Argument   83

19. The Musician   86

20. Dry Ice   90

21. A Pilgrimage   96

22. The Will   100
23. Kathleen Gets Ruined   101
24. A Fight   105
25. Kathleen Gets Defrocked   109
26. Discoveries   111
27. A New Friend   114
28. Shocking Games   118
29. Daddy Leaves   121
30. Three Rosaries   124
31. The Funeral   127

Part II: Man of the House   131
32. Man of the House   133
33. A Letter to Grammy   137
34. Eviction   139
35. Pinewood   142
36. Sister Emile   146
37. Charity   151
38. Paper Boy   154
39. An Attack   160
40. Nativity   166
41. Gene   172
42. Fever   176
43. The Explorers   178
44.. Free Tuition   185
45. Unsavory Adventures   187
46. Chair Talk   192
47. The Accident   195
48. Hospital Life   202
49. Mike   211

50.	A Birthday Disappointment	216
51.	Lure of the AuSable	219
52.	A Radio Hoax	222
53.	Mama's Treatment	227
54.	Crutches	232
55.	Mama Gets Courted	235
56.	Kathleen Escapes	240
57.	Return to Saratoga	242
58.	Used Crutches for Sale	246
59.	A Hangover	249

Part III: The Freshman | | **255** |

60.	The Freshman	257
61.	The Settlement	261
62.	Black Coffee	263
63.	Kathleen Returns	268
64.	Speedway 79	272
65.	Doo Wop	277
66.	Greener Pastures	281
67.	A New Fender	286
68.	An Engagement	288
69.	Tough Times	291
70.	YWCA	298
71.	Ballistic Missiles	303
72.	Licensed Practical Nurse	309
73.	Snake Music	311
74.	Big One, Small One	318
75.	Last of the Inheritance	325
76.	Mama's Graduation	328
77.	The Last Attack	330

78. An Unwelcome Opportunity   333

79. A Final Word   337

End Notes, Parts I – III   339

Part IV: Epilogue   345

  Pat   347

  Mama   348

  Kathleen   350

  Helen   351

  Daddy   352

Part V: The Ancestors   355

  Reflections   357

  Reilly   358

  Impens   366

  Rogoza   373

  Gryniewicz   377

Part I

The Child

♫♫♫♫

1.
Zoedy

One yard is for boys, the other is for girls. In between is a narrow no-man's land where only the nuns go. Dominik waves to his sister from the boy's yard. Helen, Helen, I see you. But little Helen Rogoza can't get to him because of the fence—it's like the one that Ma uses to keep the chickens in, only this one has stronger wire. Helen tries to climb over, but her hands only dig deeper into the wires. Sister Euphrasia takes her hand and leads her away, saying we don't climb fences here you naughty girl. She sees that Helen has wet her pants again, and she waves her finger and speaks in a scolding voice, but Helen can't understand her because she speaks the way so many other grownups do—not like Ma and Pa. Helen sees her big sister Mary and runs to hide behind her, peeking out from the side of her dress. Mary who protects her, who knows what to do, who is seven, who is big enough to stand up to Sister Euphrasia, big enough to hold the family together. Don't you talk to my sister that way, Mary says, she's only four. You have to take her to the potty, tell her to go pee-pee.

Ma sent Helen, her sisters Mary and Stella, and her brother, Dominik to this place in Rochester for children who don't have anyone to take care of them. Ma said she had to send them there after God took Pa away; she could only take care their baby brother, Edward. Pa had been sick for as long as Helen could remember. But she remembers how he had laughed and told her stories. After Helen had been in this place for three months, while she waited for Ma to come and take her home, God took away her baby brother Edward, the only child that Ma kept home, four months old when he went to heaven. Ma said that his babysitter didn't hear his cries when he pulled the table cloth that brought the kerosene lamp into his crib.

Tonight the Rogoza girls, Mary, Stella, and Helen will huddle together, thinking of Pa, who they miss so much, of Edward in heaven, of Dominik on the other side of the fence, and of Ma, who says they have to stay here until she finds a new Pa.

*   *   *   *

First the mad mommy came, then the sick mommy, then Zoedy. The mad mommy stuck out her jaw and showed her mad teeth. She smashed things against the walls and stamped her feet while she shouted in the language that Mama sometimes used with her sisters. When the mad mommy was here, I hid in the bedroom with my big sister Kathleen who was six, hugging her, hoping that the mad mommy wouldn't find us. All the while my little sister, Helen, who wasn't even two yet, screamed in her crib. I didn't mean to leave her alone, but I was only four, and I was too afraid to help her.

After the mad mommy went away the sick mommy came, lying in Mama's bed, ready to die. She moaned and called out to the Holy Mother to take her to God. Aunt Mary and Aunt Stella came to see Daddy. They all sat around the table in the kitchen, talking in quiet voices. They said Mama needed help, that someone would have to come to take care of her. "I know Julie needs help," Daddy said, "but there isn't any money. You know that I was on the dole last year, and I'm just now getting back on my feet." But the others said: "Jack, you just have to find a way."

Then Zoedy came. She took care of all of us, especially Mama and me. Her skin was a beautiful brown color, like the chocolates that Mama sometimes got from Saunders, and it seemed to shine like magic so that you could look deep into her body. She was big and strong, not sick and skinny like Mama, and she held me against her big warm breasts while she sang a song in a soft low voice that told me everything would be all right. She cleaned the house and gave me a bath in the washtub at night. She made dinner for all of us and took a tray to Mama in her bedroom. Each night she went away from our house after

Daddy came home from work downtown, but she always came back in the morning before he left.

I asked Daddy: "Why is Mama in bed?" "It's an attack," he said. "She'll get over it. She always does."

Just when Mama started to get better, Zoedy stopped coming. I told Mama how much I missed Zoedy, how she sang to me, how she took care of us. "We won't need her now, " Mama said. "God knows we can't afford that kind of help." But I still wanted her to stay.

I'm five now, and Mama is sick again. She's having an attack, and it's right when we are supposed to move from our house on Crane Street. Daddy, Uncle Bill, Uncle Stanley, and Uncle Salem put blankets and sheets together to make a stretcher for Mama because she can't walk by herself. "Don't you worry, Julie," Daddy says, "we'll get you there in no time." The men load Mama into the back seat of Daddy's car, and I'm afraid that they'll drop her, right when she's having an attack, and then she'll be a goner for sure.

Uncle Bill lets me ride in the front seat of the truck he borrowed for this move. All our stuff is loaded in the back. It is a million times better to ride in a truck than in a car, especially one with Mama having an attack on the back seat.

At Brinket Street, the men carry Mama into the front door of the house where we are going to live. It is a real house, all to ourselves, not an upstairs place like we had on Crane Street. Two bedrooms, a living room, a kitchen, and a bathroom. One bedroom is for me, Kathleen, and Helen. In the other bedroom the curtains are pulled to make it dark for Mama—the way it has to be when she has an attack. "Watch it boys, watch her head," Daddy says as they carry her in the bedroom. I peek in to see Mama lying on the bed. Her mouth hangs open, and she makes huffing noises like she is trying to get her breath.

The next morning Mama gets out of bed, looking sick and mad at the same time, and she starts unpacking boxes. "Are you better, Mama?" I ask. "God willing, I'll survive," she answers. "I'll just offer it up to Jesus in the name of the Holy Mother." Mama keeps working on the boxes, and I don't know if she'll die at any minute. I want her to be happy again and to take care of all of us, like she always does, except when she has an attack.

Pat (3 1/2), Helen (1 1/2), and Kathleen (5), ≈ 1940.

2.

Brinket

The siren screams from the firehouse up Brinket Street as I hide under the bed in Mama and Daddy's bedroom. Penny is in the closet, where she ran with her tail between her legs, whining and yelping. Mama says don't worry; it's only air raid practice so we can protect ourselves if the Germans try to bomb us. They want to bomb Detroit because we make so many things for the war. If there's nothing to worry about, why does the siren make that awful noise? And why do we practice blackouts and have to turn off our electric lights, cover our windows with dark curtains, and use candles to light the house? If any light shows from the edges of our curtains, a warden raps on our door with his nightstick and calls out *light showing, button it up folks.* Then Mama and Daddy scramble to cover up the crack with tape so the Germans won't find us with their bombs.

I like our home better when the sirens are quiet, like in the mornings when I sneak outside before everyone gets up so I can lie on the grass and have the bird songs to myself. I know the language of birds, and I answer back to them. Somewhere, far away, a morning bird always asks: *Who ee who? Who, who, who?* And I answer back: *Who ee who? You, you, you.* Big people can't understand birds and animals, but I can. I'm six years old.

I like our home much better when Mama fixes up the metal wash tubs for swimming in the summer. She fills them with water—one for Kathleen, and one for me, and puts them outside behind the house. We only have two wash tubs, so Helen gets one big dishpan to sit in and another smaller for her feet. She doesn't mind—she's only four—even though me and Kathleen get the best tubs.

In the summer, on really hot days, they open up the fire hydrant on Holcomb street; the water sprays high in the air, and comes down like rain. The kids run in the hydrant rain wearing their bathing suits or underwear; the real little kids wear their birthday suits.

There's only one water faucet in the house, and that's in the big white sink in the kitchen. When it's time to take a bath on Saturday, Mama heats the water on the stove and pours it in a wash tub set up on a table in the bathroom. The cleanest kid goes first, then the next cleanest, then the dirtiest, which Mama usually says is me. If Kathleen or Helen has to use the bathroom while I am sitting in the tub, I cover my privates with a wash cloth because it just isn't right to let your sisters see how boys are made.

When Mama uses these tubs to wash the clothes every week, she heats the water on the black iron stove in the kitchen. The stove has one part for wood or coal and another part with gas burners. When we use coal to heat the kitchen in the winter, Mama sometimes puts in pieces of broken glass. The burning coals melt the glass, and when we sift through the ashes, we find glass animals, birds, and other wonderful shapes.

In the winter the windows are frosted on the inside and icy on the sills. On really cold days, Mama puts all the winter coats on top of the covers of our beds—one pile for me, and another for the bed where Kathleen and Helen sleep. When we get up in the morning, the coals in the living room stove are just barely alive. Then Mama or Daddy throw in fresh coal and pull the big lever back and forth to shake out the ashes and clinkers; my job is to bring in a bucket of fresh coal in the morning from the shed outside, take out the ashes and clinkers at night and dump them in the alley where the trash men will get them.

Mama saves our grease for the war so they can make soap for the soldiers. She saves our tin cans to help make tanks. We always fight to see who gets to smash the can on the kitchen floor. Mama uses ration buttons to buy things like meat and butter, and Daddy has coupons to buy gas for our car. You can get things without ration buttons from black markets. When the store people tell her she can get more than her share if she pays more, she gets mad and she says she won't buy from black markets.

I want the war to end, because I hate the ration buttons, and the air raid wardens, and the cards with gold stars in the windows of the houses where someone is fighting in the war, and the houses with their doors draped with black cloth if someone there has been killed. But most of all, I hate the sirens because they scare me so. After the sirens stop, I will crawl out from under the bed, and check on all my animals. Usually, I let Andy Panda sleep next to me, because he is my favorite. But tonight I'll let all my animals, Andy, Monkey, Leo Lion, and all the others sleep next to me so they won't be afraid.

In the morning Dolly Crakiola comes to our house with her little baby Angelica, like she does almost every day. She never bothers to knock. Dolly is skinny like Mama, has big frizzy hair, and her face goes all red when she's excited. Mama makes her a peanut butter and jelly sandwich, first spreading the peanut butter, and then the jelly. "Here's a sandwich for you, Dolly. "

"You put the peanut butter on first. I don't like it that way. I like it with the jelly on first."

Mama just turns the sandwich upside down. "There, now the jelly's on first."

Dolly eats her upside-down peanut butter and jelly sandwich. "I'm worried about Sharon. She is supposed to make her First Communion in May, but I can't afford the dress for her. I don't know what to do. I can't let her march up the aisle on her First Communion day without a proper dress."

"Don't you worry, Dolly," says Mama. "I'll see to it that Sharon will have a First Communion dress."

"How can you do that, Julie? You don't have two dimes to rub together."

"God willing, I'll make a dress, Dolly. You just leave it to me."

The next day Mama brings home pieces of white cloth and what looks like material for a fish net. "I got it all for two-fifty," and this will be her veil," she says, gently smoothing the fish net.

For several days she works at the kitchen table, cutting material, and sewing pieces together. She sews tiny sequins onto the fish net.

After a week, Dolly brings Sharon over. "Come with me, Sharon," says Mama. "I've got something special for you". She leads Sharon to the bedroom. In a few minutes Sharon comes out, wearing a white dress that hangs to her knees. Around her neck is a crucifix with a silver chain. Mama carefully puts the veil on her head, held by a hoop that look a saint's halo. It hangs in back of her dress down to its hem. "Oh! You look so beautiful. Hold your hands like this," and she claps Sharon's hands together, with her fingers pointed up to heaven. "You'll be the most beautiful girl in your first Communion class." Everyone laughs, and Sharon claps her hands like it's the best day ever.

The following week Dolly runs into our house with Angelica, who is screaming something terrible. "Julie, help me! I spilled hot water on her!" Mama gently takes Angelica from Dolly, rinses her in cold water, and pats her with a towel. Then she lays her on the table over a towel, spreads butter all over her little red body, and finally wraps her in a clean white sheet. She rocks Angelica and sings a soft song. Mama always knows what to do in an emergency. That's why so many neighbor ladies come over when they have a problem.

The next day Joe Crakiola brings a big basket of vegetables to Mama from his truck. "Oh! What wonderful vegetables," says Mama. She takes a carrot and snaps it in half. "Here, Pat and Helen Therese. Why don't you give this to Joe's horse. Make sure you hold your hand out flat," she says, pulling my fingers out straight. "This way the horse won't bite your fingers."

We run outside to where Joe has his wagon parked. I hold my breath while I feel the horse's scratchy lips and whiskers as he eats the carrot out of my hand. Then it's Helen's turn, but she looks away and covers her eyes while holding the treat in her hand. Joe climbs on his wagon and snaps the reins of the horse, and the horse starts clopping up Brinket Street. I want so bad to sit up with Joe, because it's the greatest thing in the world to be up so high with a horse pulling you along. When Joe gets to Holcomb Street he shouts his vegetable call.

"Heya! Heya! Heya! Fresha! Fresha! Fresha! Gidda you fresha vegable! Heya! Heya! Heya! He turns up Holcomb Street.

Joe's not the only one who calls in the neighborhood. Other men who come around have their calls too, like the fish man who shouts out his fish call in a high-pitched song: "Good fish! Gotta fish! Catch 'em all today!" says the fish man. The scissors and knife sharpener man has a dingy-lingy bell. And the hurdy-gurdy man comes with a music box that he plays by turning a crank. Mama always gives me a penny to give to the hurdy-gurdy monkey, who takes it from me with his little monkey fingers that feel like soft leather on my hand, and he brings his prize back to the man with the big handlebar mustache.

The milkman, the bread man, the ice man, and the sheeny man all have their trucks pulled by horses. My favorite horse belongs to the sheeny man, who has dark skin and drives a wagon on big wooden wheels like those on the stage coaches in the movies. As he goes down the alley, he blows a horn that sounds like a party horn. He pays for the junk we bring him, and he digs through the trash piles looking for treasures. He never notices how me, Kathleen and Helen run after his wagon so we can hitch a ride—how I hang on the back of his wagon, while Kathleen carries Helen, who tries to grab on too. But she's only four, and is just too little to hang on for long.

After Joe goes up Holcomb, Mama calls out to us. "Come in the house. We're going to play the skating game." She has already spread wax on the bedroom floor. Now she ties rags on our bare feet, so we can we skate on the wax. Before we can slide, though, we scuffle our feet like crazy to get the wax shiny. Mama skates like Sonja Henie, singing a tune as she goes.

When you are in love,
It's the loveliest night of the year.
Stars shimmer above,
And you almost can touch them from here.

Words fall into rhyme
Anytime you are holding her near.
When you are in love
It's the loveliest night of the year.

Kathleen takes a running start and slides a long way. Helen Therese and I hold hands and try a long slide, but we end up in a pile, laughing as we wiggle on the slippery floor.

We have the best fun playing games with Mama. She's a better mommy than any of my friends. I hope she never has another attack, because then she could die, and she'd be gone forever.

Pat (4), Helen (2), and Kathleen (6) on Brinket Street, ≈ 1941

3.

Grammy

Like most Sundays we all pile into Daddy's car for the trip to Grammy's house. We drive up Jefferson Street until we can see the bank on the corner; then we turn on Coplin Street to the big house with a porch raised high up above the sidewalk so anyone sitting there can see the whole neighborhood and whoever is passing by, where us kids like to sit in the summer and read comics. No one else sits on the porch, especially not Grammy or Lala. And Uncle Eddie can't because his muscles are wasting, and now he's in the hospital.

We climb up the stairs, and Daddy just opens the door and goes in—he can do that because it's his mother's house. As usual, Grammy sits in the living room in her big stuffed chair, smoking a cigarette and drinking a glass of beer poured from the bottle beside her. She's wearing the same old dark blue dress with white polka dots, and a hair net that makes her look extra old, especially since she never wears any makeup. She wears smelly brown rubber protectors on her thumb and finger to protect them from the cigarette smoke. Why would she put such a stinky thing on her fingers?

Grammy's dog, Jerry, runs up to us and yaps away. "Oh! My widow babycums," Grammy says to Jerry as she picks him up and raises him up so he can lick her face. "Sweetee poochee gimme mommy a widow kissey." I don't know why anyone would want to treat a dog like that. But Jerry isn't a regular dog you could be friends with, but a yappy little poodle that bites if you're not careful. We each go up to Grammy and get a peck on the cheek. Grammy holds Jerry, who keeps on yapping.

The next stop for us kids is Lala's room; she's our aunt. Kathleen knocks; it wouldn't be right to just go into a closed door, and this door is always closed. "Come in," says the voice behind the door. As usual, Lala lies on her bed looking sad, fat, and old, even though she's no older than Mama. The shade on the window is pulled, and a bare light bulb hangs from the ceiling above her bed, casting cold dark shadows in the dimly lit room. She wears her night gown and fuzzy slippers and is propped up by some pillows. A jumbo bottle of Goebel's sits on the table beside her. She puts down the detective story she has been reading. "Come give Lala a big kiss."

Kathleen goes first being as she's the oldest—nine years old—and she turns her cheek to Lala, who makes a kissing sound. I'm seven, so I go second, and I get a big sloppy beer kiss on my cheek. I know enough not to wipe it off until I leave the room. "Just wipe it off" Lala will say in a mad way. "Just wipe off my kiss." After Helen gets her beer kiss, we leave the room and Kathleen closes the door. Me and Helen rub the cold wet spots on our cheeks. Kathleen starts snickering, and that sets me and Helen into giggling fits.

"What are you kids up to," calls Grammy from her chair in the living room. "Nothing, Grammy," says Kathleen.

Our next stop should be Uncle Eddie's room just down the hall from Lala's, but he's not here anymore. He was always the best part of going to Grammy's because I liked his stories and the things he would teach us. He would lie in his bed, the covers showing the outlines of his legs in an always-bent position, and the shape of a cardboard box that protected his feet from the weight of the covers. Helen and I used to sit beside his bed for a game of *Old Maid*, our cards right next to his pee pot, with its long white nose, making a stinky odor that Uncle Eddie couldn't smell because his nose didn't work right, and he couldn't smell anything at all. I wished Helen would notice how stinky it was and empty it, but I'm two years older, so I had to empty it and rinse it out so I could concentrate on the card game. Uncle Eddie would sometimes would show us the Old Maid when he got it dealt in his hand, and Helen and I couldn't stand the suspense wondering who would get stuck with it and when.

After we're finished with Lala's beer kisses, Mama calls us into the kitchen. As usual, Grammy has made ham, boiled potatoes, and green beans. Lala comes out to eat dinner, but she wears her bathrobe and slippers. Why would Lala want to eat dinner in her pajamas and slippers like she's sick?

After dinner, we go to the living room, but Lala goes back to her room. We aren't allowed to play in the kitchen or dining room after dinner because we would need to put on another light, which would cost money, and Grammy is a poor woman. The living room is lit by a lamp behind Grammy's chair.

The two things to do at Grammy's house are reading comics from the big stack she keeps in a closet in the hall, and playing with the buttons that she brings out in a big button box. There are a million different buttons of all colors and designs. Some are glass, some are plastic, and some are metal. Some are as big as a quarter, and some are small as a Cheerio. We make houses with the big buttons, and pretend that the little buttons live there. Mama and Daddy sit on the couch across the room from Grammy's chair.

Grammy says we can have a snackey for dessert, and Helen and I run to the kitchen. We know the rules. We each can get one slice of bread with jelly on it, but not too much. Before I eat mine, I bring the bread slice back to Grammy for inspection. "That's too much jelly," she says. "I'm a poor woman, and I can't afford keeping you in jelly and sweets like there's no tomorrow." I run back to the kitchen to scrape some of the jelly back into the jar. I don't want to cross Grammy. She always says, "I never forgive and I never forget." Helen is still smearing jelly on her bread slice so I dip out an extra dollop of jelly and smear it onto her bread, giggling at the thought that she'll get in trouble with Grammy over this.

"Cut it out Pat. I'll tell Grammy you did it," she whispers as she scrapes some back in the jar.

Me and Helen eat our jelly bread and play with the buttons, while Mama, Daddy, and Grammy talk, and Kathleen reads a comic. Usually I don't pay attention to what they talk about, but this time I notice that they are talking about the war. Mama says something about President Roosevelt. My ears perk up when I hear Grammy laugh.

"Listen to Missus High and Mighty. And where would a Polack get such high falutin' ideas," she says, laughing.

Daddy laughs, and Mama does too, but I don't think she likes it, because her mouth is pulled in a funny way and her eyes are flashing. Sometimes Grammy makes jokes about Mama and calls her a dumb Polack, like when she pronounces a word like she does when she talks with her sisters. Mama usually looks embarrassed when that happens.

Daddy grabs the little chain that goes to a tiny pocket at the top of his pants and pulls out his gold Bulova watch. "Nine o'clock. Time to head home," he says.

Why does Grammy make fun of Mama, and why doesn't Daddy stick up for her? If I was big, like Daddy, I would say to Grammy that Mama's not falutin', and she's not high and mighty, and she's not a dumb Polack either.

Kathleen (7-1/2) and Catherine (Grammy, age 61) on day of Kathleen's First Holy Communion (1943).

4.

Uncle Eddie

The big room at Eloise Hospital is very scary. I hide behind mama's skirt, afraid that one of the men in white will lock me in a room like this, except it will be for seven year-old boys like me.

"Say Hello to uncle Eddie," Mama says.

I do, but my thoughts are on the other men in the big room. Twenty other strange-looking men in beds like Uncle Eddie's. The man in the next bed over, looking like he hasn't shaved in a week, stares at the ceiling, not moving. The man on the other side has the covers pulled aside, showing his white bony legs and the black bottoms of his bare feet. A man dressed in white goes up and down the soles of his feet using the blade of the knife as a scraper. Across the room, someone cries out that he wants to go home. Mama has brought a jar of cream, which she dips into with her fingertips, and then puts her hands under the sheets of Uncle Eddie's bed. "Lift yourself up, so I can get this on your back," she says, and she rubs her hands back and forth like she does when she puts Vick's on my chest when I have a cold. But what I smell isn't Vick's. It smells like someone has peed on the floor. I am too afraid to talk.

After our visit, we ride the streetcar back to our house on Brinket Street. Mama looks mad, like she looked last week when the man at the store tried to sell her butter without ration buttons. Her mouth makes a thin line, and her eyes look straight ahead across the aisle, right through the people sitting across from us.

"What's wrong with Uncle Eddie?" I ask.

"He can't move his legs; they are frozen in a bent position, and his muscles are wasting away. He used work as a janitor, and later went to the seminary to study to be a priest. But he had to come back home because his muscles wouldn't work right. And then he couldn't walk any more. After Grammy couldn't care for him anymore, she sent him to Eloise Hospital, where they keep people who can't afford better places, sometimes for a very long time."

Then her voice becomes angry. "Edward is coming home," she says. "He may be your father's brother, but he's a brother to me too. If it's the last thing I do on earth, God willing, he's coming home."

On Sunday Daddy drives us all to Grammy's house. After dinner we all sit around in the living room with Grammy. Kathleen reads a comic book near the light behind Grammy's big stuffed chair while me and Helen play with Grammy's button box. I can hear Mama and Grammy arguing.

"Edward has to come home," Mama says. "That place is no good for him. He has terrible bed sores. That is no place for your son."

"You know I can't take care of him," Grammy says. "I can't lift him out of bed by myself. And I can't afford to buy the things he will need. God knows I'm a poor widow without proper help. And just who do you think your are, Miss High and Mighty, telling me what to do?"

But Mama keeps at it. "We have to figure out a way."

On the way home, I help drive the car from my place in the back seat by working the window crank. Mama and Daddy don't speak. I can tell they're both mad.

After we get home, Me, Kathleen, and Helen get into our beds, me in my own, and the girls in the other bed. After I pull the covers over my head, I hear mad voices from the kitchen. At first it's just talking, then the voices get louder and louder.

"That's no way to talk to my mother."

"I don't care. Your brother has to come home."

"Damn you, Julie. Damn you to hell."

"You blasphemer, you. I'll not tolerate that."

"Shut your yap, or I'll shut it for you."

"Don't you dare raise your hand to me."

Doesn't Daddy know he can bring on an attack in Mama if he upsets her like this?

The next day Mama is at the kitchen table, writing something. I peek over the checkered table cloth to see what she's doing.

"I'm writing a letter to Ahntie Reet," she says, still wearing her mad face. Ahntie Reet's our rich aunt who lives in Grand Rapids, Michigan. "She'll help because Edward is her nephew."

The following week Daddy, Uncle Salem, Cousin Nell and Mama sit around our kitchen table, talking about Uncle Eddie. Uncle Salem knows everything—he can fix a radio or a car, he can put in a new light switch without getting shocked, and he can build almost anything he wants out of wood or metal. Daddy and Uncle Salem make drawings on a piece of paper, and they point to the lines and talk about them. After Nell and Salem leave Mama whispers something to me, like she's sharing a special secret. "Edward is coming home."

One day when we make the trip to Grammy's house, Mama looks very happy. "Edward is away from that awful place; now he is home," she says. "Ahntie Reet sent the money for his wheel chair, his bed, and everything he'll need. At Grammy's house the back bedroom has been fixed up for Uncle Eddie. Cousin Nell and Uncle Salem are there. Uncle Eddie lies in a big bed—the kind they had in the hospital with a crank to raise up the top of the bed and another crank to raise up the middle part where his knees are always bent like he's sitting. There are shiny pipes that look they're set up for a swing set going across his bed. But instead of a swing there is a contraption with pulleys and ropes.

"Look at what I can do," says Uncle Eddie, as he pulls aside the covers. He's not even wearing pajamas, but something that looks like a dress, and it's terrible because a man should wear pants and not a dress and I shouldn't be able to see his legs that look like a skeleton's covered with some pink skin and his knees frozen in a bent position because his muscles are wasting. On one toe grows something knobby, like the worst corn you ever saw in your life.

He props himself up with one elbow, and with the other hand slides a piece of canvas with some rings attached to it underneath his rear. He attaches ropes to the rings with some metal clips. The ropes run up to some pulleys, and the pulleys are attached to wheels that are on a little trolley that rides on one of the pipes. As he pulls on one of the ropes, he slowly rises up from the bed with his arms jittery and shaking, and I think he's going to let go and fall to the bed and break his skeleton bones, but little by little his whole body goes sideways until he is right over a wheel chair beside the bed. Then he slowly lowers himself right on to the wheel chair. Everybody is laughing and clapping. Grammy is laughing too. Even Aunt Lala comes out of her room, laughing, and that is something she almost never does. But especially Mama is laughing. She goes over to Uncle Eddie and gives him a hug.

"Thank you, Julie," he says, looking into her eyes. I think he wants to cry. "You're a wonderful sister to me."

On the way home, Mama sits in the front seat of Daddy's car. I can tell that she is happy by the way she is humming something. I am happy too, because now we can visit Uncle Eddie every time we go to Grammy's. And I'm glad it was Mama who figured out how to get Uncle Eddie home. That will teach Grammy to call her a dumb Polack!

Uncle Eddie, age ≈ 38 (1951)

5.

The Polish

Ma had taken the Rogoza kids out of the orphanage after she married Pa Zalut. Mary, the eldest of the Rogoza kids and the one who speaks English the best, gives the information to the census agent of the year nineteen-twenty. Her new Pa is Albin Zalut; her Ma is Stanislawa—both immigrants from Poland. The Rogoza kids consist of: herself, Mary, almost ten years old; Dominik, eight; Stella, seven; Helen, five. Anna is a Zalut; she's one year old. The census taker shakes his head. Along with this family, twenty-two people—nine adults and thirteen children—are jammed into this house on St. Aubin Street in Detroit. And in this modern age, no less!

*   *   *   *

The great thing about Stitch's Bar is that nobody tells you you're making too much noise, because making noise is what everybody does here. We get to play hide and seek and can hide under the tables, behind the bar, in the back room, or down the basement without anyone telling us not to. I get to sip off the foam whenever Mama, Daddy, an uncle, or an auntie gets a new glass of beer—children aren't supposed to drink beer, but foam doesn't count. Besides me, Kathleen and Helen, our cousins are here: Donny and Jerry, Ritchie, and Dianne.

Stitch's Bar is what Uncle Stanley calls his place in Hamtramck, the Polish section of Detroit. Mama's bunch is here, everybody smoking cigarettes and drinking beer. Aunt Stella is behind the bar, looking like the Queen of Sheba with her long blond hair done up in a bun, and her long-sleeve blouse that covers up the burn scar she got on her arm as a little girl, smiling and joking with the men and ladies sitting on the bar stools. When she wipes the counter with a rag she looks like she's having the greatest fun in the world. "Pour me another boilermaker," says Daddy, and Aunt Stella dumps a shot of whiskey into his glass of beer.

"Come on over here," says Aunt Stella to Richie. "Give us some music on the juke box." She digs out nickels from the cash register, and dumps them into his hand. "And be sure to give us some polkas."

Richie feeds the juke box, which thumps out a polka tune.

I have a girl friend, she is a honey.
She only loves me, when I have money.

Mama and Aunt Mary spin around and kick up their heels, while the people in the bar clap their hands and make yipping noises in time to the music. Then Auntie Anna and Uncle Stanley join in, and before long, half the people in the bar are whooping and laughing and spinning their polkas on the floor. That's when all us kids start running in circles around the dancers, around the back of the bar, back on the dance floor, holding hands, spinning, running, jumping, falling, giggling, and whooping like wild Indians.

After the polka music finishes, I go up to Daddy, who looks like he's in a good mood. "Tell this man who you are, my boy," he says, pointing to the fat man on the bar stool next to him.

I know what Daddy wants, what makes him happy.

"I'm John Patrick Reilly, and I'm Irish."

That gets Daddy to whooping and slapping his thigh. "That's my boy," he says, handing me a nickel. "Eight years old, and smart as a whip."

I go to where Mama is sitting at a table with Aunt Mary, to try for another nickel.

"I'm John Patrick Reilly, and I'm Irish."

Mama smiles, and smoothes my hair. "Of course you are. But you're also half Polish, and don't forget the Dutch you get from Grammy's side."

"Does that make me a Polack, Mama?"

Mama's smile goes away. "No you're not a Polack. That's a bad word. You shouldn't ever call someone that."

I think I've gone over the line this time. There are bad words for all kinds of people: Italians, colored people, Jewish people, Germans, Chinese, and Irish too. If Mama ever catches anyone using one of these words at home, even if it's an Uncle or an Auntie, she gets really mad. "We don't use language like that in this house," she will say, while giving a mad look that makes you weak in the knees. But I remember the look Mama gets when Grammy says she is a Polack. Is it a sin to say Polack?

On Saturday night we go to Uncle Bill and Aunt Mary's house on Berry Street. It's the greatest place in the whole world, because it's out in the country where you can run around and play. Outside there is an outhouse that smells as bad as the yucky ditches that line the dusty dirt streets. Uncle Bill built the house himself with crooked windows and doors that never seem to shut right. We'll stay overnight tonight; me, Kathleen and Helen will go upstairs to a loft, where we'll sleep as cozy as bugs in a rug on mattresses spread on the floor, along with cousins Donny and Jerry,

They're playing poker around the table in the kitchen—Daddy, Mama, Aunt Mary, Uncle Bill, and Uncle Joe and Aunt Rose too. Us kids are playing war games. Even Laddie was let off his chain so he could join in too. Jerry says him and Donny are bad guys, and me, Kathleen, Helen, and Laddie are good guys. We all run around in the dark, and as I run through the field to Berry Street, the ground suddenly disappears, and I land with a splat into a drainage ditch. I stand up in the muck, with my legs sunk in right up to my knees, making smucky sounds as I work first one leg out, then the other. The worst part is the putrid smell.

When I walk into the house, everybody howls with laughter, but I don't know what's so darn funny. Aunt Mary says "Hey, look at what the cat dragged in," and Uncle Bill says, "Let's hang him on the clothes line and hose him off," and everybody laughs even harder.

"Mama, I'm yucky," I cry, but Mama and the others only laugh harder. "I'll get you a pair of Donny's pants," says Aunt Mary, "but first go outside and clean yourself off with the hose." As I let the screen door slam behind me, I hear everybody inside laughing and making loud noises as they slap their cards and chips on the table.

I finish hosing off the muck from my pants and shoes, and I wash my hands and face in the cold water. I walk back in, stomping my feet to shake off the water. Big clouds of smoke rise from the table in the kitchen from the cigarettes that everybody smokes. Daddy rakes in a pile of chips. Just then Aunt Mary jumps up, and puts an arm lock around his head, mussing his hair with the other hand, saying "I love you Jacky boy, you rich, handsome brute." Daddy's face gets red as a beet, and Mama laughs and claps her hands. Then I laugh, and so does Kathleen, Helen, Aunt Mary, Uncle Bill, Donny, and Jerry. We're all laughing, and I'm glad Mama and everybody on her side is Polish, because the Polish have all the best fun.

Mama & sisters. Standing L—>R: Aunt Dolly (Dolores); Jenny; Anna; Lilly; Mama; Stella. Kneeling: Aunt Mary.

6.

Mama's Chicken

My first stop on Brinket Street after coming home from school is usually the bathroom. But this time is different. Mama has stopped me short of the bathroom, and speaks to me in grave tones.

"Son, before you go in the bathroom," she says, "there is something I have to tell you."

Mama calls me *son* when she wants to tell me something really serious, like someone is very sick, or maybe has died. She calls me *Patrick* when I am in trouble, and *John Patrick Reilly* when I am in big trouble. Usually, she calls me *Pat*.

"What is it, Mama?" I ask, fearing the worst.

"There's something special in the bathroom. Come, let me show you."

We tiptoe to the bathroom door. Mama puts her finger to her lips, making a shushing noise, like there's a big secret that just me and her are going to share. She smiles, and opens the door a crack, letting me peek in. I am amazed to see a feathered creature staring at me; it's definitely a chicken. I can see that Mama has set out some newspapers, a dish of chopped up vegetable scraps, and a bowl of water.

I look at the chicken, then over to Mama who has the look that she gets when I've just opened a special Christmas package.

"It's the chicken I bought from the poultry market this morning," she says. I know the place well because Mama sometimes takes me there. The market has rows of cages of chickens, most of them wearing white feathers. I remember the sounds of clucking and the smell of chicken poop. At the poultry market, you can buy a live chicken, and have it slaughtered and dressed. A dressed chicken is actually undressed, because it looks embarrassingly naked with all its feathers gone. But for a cheaper price, you can dress it yourself, and that's what Mama usually orders. "I'll dress it myself," she always says. "I just want you to slaughter it," and the poultry man takes one of the excited cluckers by the feet to the back room. Later he comes back with a package wrapped up in brown paper and hands it to Mama.

Mama fills me in on what happened. "When I got home from the poultry store this morning, I put the package in the ice box, in a place near the ice to keep it cold and fresh. Later I pulled the package out of the icebox, placed it on the table, and unwrapped it. What happened next made my heart skip a beat. Up jumped an obviously healthy chicken, which immediately started to walk around on the kitchen table. Apparently, the poultry man had missed the jugular vein. The jugular vein is the main one going in the chicken's throat. If you want to kill a chicken, you have to cut and drain the jugular vein."

"What are you gonna do with it Mama?"

"Well, I thought I would ask Mr. DiAngelo to slaughter it for us," she says. "He knows how to do that sort of thing." I remember seeing the slaughtered chickens hanging by their feet on the back porch of Mr. DiAngelo's house, which I can see from our back yard 'cause he lives only three doors up Holcomb Street. "But he won't be able to get to it until Saturday, and that is two days off. In the meanwhile, we will just have to make the chicken comfortable."

I like to stay in the bathroom for extra long periods, when I can sit with the chicken, play with it, and pet it. Helen takes her dolls into the bathroom and spends extra long times there too. Kathleen named the chicken *Matilda*. Mama cleaned up the red stains on Matilda's neck feathers and tied a little bandanna there. And Penny keeps sniffing at the bathroom door, wagging her tail, and making little whiny sounds. Daddy mostly grumbles about Matilda, saying things like: "A man can't do his business with that stupid chicken staring at him."

Mr. DiAngelo comes to the house on Saturday, and takes Matilda away, holding her by the feet, which seems like a very impolite way to hold a chicken, or any other animal for that matter. Later, me, Mama, and Helen go outside and look towards Mr. DiAngelo's back porch from our back yard. Something white hangs upside down by its feet. At first it appears to be flapping around. Finally it just goes still. I look over at Helen, and see that she is crying. I try to hold back my tears.

On Sunday afternoon, Mama prepares a dinner of roast chicken, mashed potatoes, and vegetables, just like a feast on thanksgiving. We all just stare at the chicken. Nobody speaks or makes a move to cut into it.

"I don't want any," Kathleen says. "I'm just not hungry for chicken." Then me and Helen chime in, saying we won't eat Matilda either. Even Mama says she can't eat her. But Daddy says to Mama, "cut me a piece of chicken. I'm plenty hungry." That's when all three of us kids throw a holy fit. "You can't eat it," we all say, almost in unison, "that would be cannibalism," and "that's heartless," and "that's mean", and the like. Finally Daddy slams down his fork and knife and shouts out in a mad voice.

"Well hell's bells. A man can't have a decent meal in peace in his own house. Hell's bells." Finally he gives in, saying, "If it will keep everyone from all that hollering, I'll skip the chicken. I don't give a hoot if I starve to death."

That evening me and Mama cross our yard to take a platter of roast chicken up to Dolly Crackiola . "I thought you might like to have this," she says. "The family isn't feeling very well, and we couldn't eat it, and there's no room in the ice box to keep it."

"Oh, thank you, Julie" says Dolly. "You're a wonderful woman. We will really enjoy this fine roast chicken."

Mama , Kathleen,(6) Pat (5), & Helen (3)

7.

Daddy

We go to the twelve-thirty Mass on Sunday, which lets everybody sleep in late. Mama makes breakfast when we get home. I can tell Daddy is in a good mood by the song he sings while looking into Mama's eyes.

I'll be with you tonight in dreamland,
Under a starry sky.

I don't know what the song means, but whenever he sings it to Mama, he has a smile that says he knows some special secret. Mama doesn't smile but looks peeved. "Oh Jack, not in front of the kids."

That night, Mama tucks us in, gives us each a kiss, and turns off the light. The dark soon closes in, and Superman comes to carry me off to an adventure. Loud voices awaken me—moaning, like someone is getting hurt. Then a mad voice. Kathleen gets up, and goes past my bed toward the bedroom door.

"What's happening, Kathleen?"

"Mama's getting hurt, we've got to go help her."

I follow Kathleen across the living room to Mama's bedroom door, where the noises are coming from.

"No Jack! Stop! Leave me alone!"

"Oh, Julie! Oh Julie!" comes Daddy's voice.

Kathleen pulls aside the curtain that covers their bedroom door. From the light of a blackout candle I can see Daddy, naked as a jaybird, lying on top of Mama. Why is he hurting Mama?

"You leave my mother alone!" shouts Kathleen.

The moaning stops, and both Mama and Daddy suddenly look our way.

"It's okay, children," says Mama. "I'm okay. Just go back to bed. There's nothing wrong."

Daddy rolls off Mama, and pulls the blanket up to cover his naked body. "This is none of your business," he says.

"Please, go to bed," Mama says again.

The next day, after dinner, me and Helen get into a fight over a Batman comic book.

"It's mine, and you got no right to it."

"No! It's mine."

"Liar, liar, pants on fire."

"You shut up!"

"I was brought up, not shut up, and every time I look at you, I want to throw up." I grab for the comic.

"Mama! Pat's calling me names," whines Helen, as she pulls the comic away from my grasp. That's when I hear Daddy come up to us, all riled up. "Damn it! Damn it!" he says as he pulls off his belt. I know what this means, and I run behind the stove, where Daddy follows, and he backs me up against the wall with nowhere to run.

Whap! Whap! Whap! Daddy's belt lands in sharp blows, while I scream, "No Daddy, No. Please don't hit me. I'm sorry, Please!" But he only swings harder, drawing his arm way above his head, bringing the strap down with a hard swing, saying over and over: "Damn it to hell! I'll teach you a lesson." His face is red as a beet, and a vein sticks out on his forehead just above one eye, like a little rope even redder than his face. His mouth is drawn back, and he shows his angry teeth, like a snarling dog.

I keep screaming, and dancing like the cowboys do when the bad guy shoots bullets at their feet. All this dancing seems to be working, because all the blows land on the wall or floor, where they make sharp cracking sounds. Daddy keeps missing me, and he doesn't realize it. If I keep on screaming, he'll think he's connecting.

Finally, he's done with me, and he goes for Helen, who was watching in horror as I got my beating.

"Now it's your turn, Damn it to hell! I'll teach you kids to bicker!"

I run to the bedroom, and shut the door, hoping Daddy will forget about me, but I can still hear the crack of the belt and Helen's cries. Finally, Helen comes into the bedroom, still screaming. The two of us keep this up for a respectable period of time, then we both change to quieter whimpers. I look at Helen, who started all this trouble. Tears run down both her cheeks.

"Did he get you?" I ask.

"No, he missed me."

"Me too." Its lucky for both of us that Daddy is such a bad shot, because he hardly ever connects.

Daddy doesn't like it when we argue. He calls it bickering, which me and Helen do lots of. We bicker about who gets to read the back of the cereal box at breakfast, about who got the bigger slice of dessert, about whose turn it isn't to wash the dishes, about what radio program to listen to, about wanting to read a comic the other guy is reading, about whose comic it is, and about who started the bickering in the first place. But the way he argues with Mama at night after we go to bed is much worse than any bickering we ever did. Then the two of them will be screaming and hollering, while Daddy says a lot of bad things. I don't know why he is so mean to Mama. Doesn't he know he could make her have an attack? And why doesn't he pay attention to us kids. As far as I'm concerned, he could go to work and never come back.

Daddy works downtown as a bookkeeper for General Motors. On some weekends he brings home his ledgers, which are books full of rows of words and tiny numbers all lined up in a column on one side of the page. He adds these up in his head by touching the back of his fountain pen to each number, going down the page, mumbling numbers under his breath. Finally, when he gets to the end, he writes down a big number in ink. He doesn't have to use a pencil, because he never makes a mistake in adding the numbers. He learned how to do this by going for two years to the University of Detroit, which is a very fancy college. If Daddy is so fancy, then why is it that he never has enough money to buy me a bicycle?

I don't know why I can't have a bicycle—all my friends have one. Daddy said that we had to get a letter from the chief of police saying that it's okay for us to have one; otherwise, we will have to do without. We heard that so many times, that once we decided to do something about it. Me, Kathleen, and Helen went to the McClellan police station, Kathleen in the middle, and me and Helen on each side, holding her hand. The three of us marched up the concrete steps, through the glass door that we bravely soaped on Halloween, and up to the front counter where a policeman with a dark blue uniform and shiny brass buttons sat.

"We want to see the chief of police." Kathleen said.

The man at the desk studied us for a while, and said with a serious look, "And what would you children be wanting with the chief of police?"

"It's private business," Kathleen answered. "We have to see the chief of police, and no one else".

The desk man looked at us for a while longer with a smile, like he wanted to laugh at us, to make fun of us. He got up and went through a door behind his desk. After a while, he came back and led us into another room, where another policeman sat behind a giant desk filled with papers. "These children have some important business to discuss with you," he said.

Kathleen explained how we needed a letter saying that we can have a bicycle before Daddy will let us have one. But the chief just smiled and shook his head.

"I'm sorry, but I can't write a letter like that. You will just have to convince your father to give you permission." So that was that, and we still don't have a bicycle.

Daddy comes home late a lot, and although Mama and us kids have dinner by ourselves, she leaves out a plate for him. Sometimes it's because he has to work late, but usually it's because he's at Glick's, the bar where he goes after work. I always thought it must be a real fancy place because he goes there so often. But one time, Mama and I came downtown on the streetcar, and Mama pointed at a little place with a neon sign in the window saying *Glick's*, not the fancy night club I thought it would be like in the movies, but a crummy little brown-brick building. Why would Daddy want to spend so much time at such a dump?

After dinner, especially when he has been to Glick's, Daddy usually goes to the living room and stretches out full length on the floor, takes off his wire-rimmed glasses, puts them face up on the floor and goes to sleep. It's amazing that no one ever steps on his glasses.

On weekday mornings he gets up before anyone else, and has his usual breakfast of coffee and cigarettes. When I get up, he is usually sitting at the kitchen table, wearing just his undershirt and boxer shorts, smoking and drinking coffee, one foot on the chair with his knee pulled up, and the other foot on the floor. He doesn't say anything, not even good morning. If he speaks to me at all, it's because he's angry about something.

Before he goes to work, Daddy usually jumps up from the table and runs into the bathroom, where he makes gagging and puking sounds behind the closed door. He must be throwing up all the poison he puts into himself at Glick's. After he's done puking, Daddy gets dressed for work, puts on his pants, black wing-tip shoes, a starched white shirt and a blue tie with little polka dots. Mama fixes him a starched shirt for every day of the week. She usually does these on Tuesdays, which is her ironing day, when she makes up a solution of starch and water, dips the collars and cuffs into it, and rolls them into tight cylinders to put on the ironing pile. After he's dressed, Daddy goes to work, looking like he must be the most important person at General Motors, maybe even the most important man in all Detroit.

But it's not just Daddy's way of dressing that makes him look special. The really important thing about him is his gold Bulova watch, which he keeps in a special little pocket at the top of his pants. When he wants to look at his watch, he pulls on a little gold chain, and out comes the watch. When Daddy pulls out his watch, you know that it's time to do something, maybe something important.

Daddy had a chance to move to a fancy job in General Motors when they asked him to be a supervisor at a branch in California. He discussed it with Mama, who said without a second thought, "I'll pack my bags, and be ready to go tomorrow. I'd love to go out west." But Daddy said he had to think it over.

I dreamed that we'd go to California by making a covered wagon out of our car, and we'd stop at all the cowboy ranches along the way. Like in a Roy Rogers movie, there would be cactus plants and the skulls of dead steers, and Indians on their horses would watch us from the tops of the bluffs. Maybe Daddy would buy a shotgun to keep us safe from the wolves, coyotes, and mountain lions we'd run across along the way. Finally we'd make it to the ocean, and there would be a million orange trees, so you could pick the ripe fruit from the trees on the side of the road.

A few days later Daddy said that he couldn't take the job because Grammy would need him, that he couldn't desert his poor widowed mother.

I'm in the kitchen eating a bowl of corn flakes on Saturday morning. Mama wipes the table with a wet rag. "I want you to do a little chore for me. Go into your father's bedroom and get his socks and bring them to the hamper in the bathroom. Be careful not to wake him."

I drop my spoon and swallow my corn flakes but I have to swallow hard, because I'm in for the worst job Mama could ever give me. I tip toe into Daddy's bedroom, and there, next to the door, are his shoes, black and shiny, looking like they're ready for the most important man in the world. But inside is something awful, something I can't stand to touch, can't stand to smell. I hold my breath, reach into each shoe with just the tips of two fingers, and pull out two black stockings, long and kind of silky. I hold my two arms out as far from my nose as I possibly can and I walk back to the kitchen on the way to the bathroom, I just have to take a deep breath. That's when the smell comes to me, strong and horrible, and it make me go *Urk! Urk!* That's when the milk and corn flakes go on the kitchen floor, making a puddle of throw-up, where I drop the sock.

"I'm sorry Mama. I couldn't help it. The smell was so bad. I had to throw up. It just came out."

"Don't you worry, Pat," she says, while giving me a hug, and pulling me away from the puddle. "It wasn't your fault. I should never have given you that job. I know how much you hate it. I'll clean it all up. You can just go out and play."

On Sunday I'm stretched out on the floor reading the Sunday comics. Daddy sits on the couch, reading the news. It suddenly pops into my head that I might be able to draw a cartoon character. I'll try Mickey Mouse. As I look at Mickey's face in the comic strip, my pencil moves on a sheet of school paper, making a curved line where the back of Mickey's head is supposed to be, then it makes two circles at the ears. The pencil draws the stuck out part of a nose, big wide eyes, the pupils in the eyes, the mouth, the whiskers. There on my paper is a perfect image of Mickey Mouse, somehow magically drawn by my own hand.

"Look, Daddy! Look! I drew Mickey Mouse."

Daddy looks at my cartoon. "Uh huh. That's nice," and he turns back to his newspaper, like he really doesn't care about this marvel. So I run to the kitchen.

"Mama, look at what I did. I made a picture of Mickey Mouse."

Mama takes the paper from my hand, handling it like it's a picture of the Blessed Mother. "Oh, it's so beautiful. My son, the artist."

The following Sunday I take a stack of cartoons to show Uncle Eddie. "The work of a true artist," says Uncle Eddie.

In another month it's my ninth birthday. My most special gift comes from Uncle Eddie—an artist's set of drawing pens. I'm so excited with this gift, I can't stand it. I show my pen set to Daddy. "Now I know what I want to be when I grow up, I say. "A scientist and a cartoonist." But Daddy says "you can't be both. You have to choose." Why do I have to choose? Why can't I be everything I want to be? And why doesn't Daddy care?

When I grow up, I'm not going to be like Daddy. Not in a million years. I won't be lazy, and I'll wash my feet. I'll have a bike, and I'll ride it everywhere. But I won't be like him.

Daddy at White Fish Lake

8.

The Birds and the Bees

"I'll tell you a real secret," says Kathleen, "something I found out." She waves me to come into the bedroom; she shuts the door to make sure no one else can hear. "I know what married people do," she whispers. "You wouldn't believe it. Its the most awful thing imaginable. I'm never going get married."

"So tell me. What do they do that's so terrible?"

"I can't tell you. You'll have to get Mama to explain it to you. Ask her to tell you about the birds and the bees."

I forget all about our talk until one day when me and Mama are riding the Kercheval street car from downtown. It's crowded, and we're standing in the back, holding on to the poles that go from the floor to the ceiling. The tall people hold on to straps hanging from the ceiling; everyone sways back and forth together. Just then it pops into my head.

"Mama, tell me about the birds and the bees."

Mama bends down, and puts her finger to her lips. "Shush! I'll tell you later when I get a chance."

A few days later I'm home alone with Mama, when she calls me into the bedroom and shuts the door. She sits on the edge of the bed, and pats it with her hand, motioning me to sit along side her. I can tell already this is going to be something really serious. "Son, I'm going to tell you about the birds and the bees."

She starts explaining the most amazing story. She says that when people get married, they love each other, and that makes them want to have a baby. They start hugging and kissing. After a while, the man gets the idea to put his thing into her thing, only Mama uses names for the things, which wouldn't be right for me to repeat. When his thing is in her thing, a seed comes out, which finds an egg inside her stomach, and joins up with it. From that egg and seed a baby starts to grow inside of her. She explains that this is God's plan so that there will be new people in the world, and that God makes it feel good as a reward for the man and woman for doing His will. I don't know why she is telling me all this stuff, because all I wanted to know about was the birds and bees.

"Did you and Daddy do it?"

"Yes. That's how you and your sisters came into this world."

"Do you still do it?

Mama stops for a moment, as though she is thinking how to answer that question. She looks away from me, and her face seems to go all white. Then she turns to me. "Yes son," she says, like she's ashamed. "We still do it."

Later that night, after going to bed, I think about the things that Mama told me. It's all just too fantastic to understand. I wonder why it should feel good, and what makes the seed come out, because I have never seen any seeds come out of my thing. I wonder if people know they will have to do this before they get married, because if everyone knew they had to, probably no one would want to get married, and there wouldn't be any more babies in the world.

I fall asleep, thinking about this new secret, thinking that I won't be able to tell my friends these things, because maybe nine-year-old boys aren't supposed to know this—it was only because of Kathleen I found out. And besides, who would believe it anyhow?

9.

Ad Altare Dei

It's not easy to be a Catholic, to belong to the one true church. Like the saints, we have to be willing to be slow roasted over hot coals or shot full of arrows to defend our faith—something a Protestant never has to worry about because God would never send a Protestant to hell just because he didn't stick up for his false religion. To get to heaven, you have to be baptized in the one true faith. But, lucky for them, Protestants can get to heaven through baptism of desire, which means that if the Protestant wasn't so ignorant, he would want to run to the nearest priest and get himself baptized a Catholic. Because of baptism of desire, a good Protestant can still get to heaven, but his place there won't be as neat as a Catholic's. In my house there are many mansions, God said. The fanciest ones are for the saints, next come the popes and other holy people, then come all the really good Catholics. The crummy mansions are for Protestants who got baptized by desire.

The hardest part of being a Catholic is that we have way more mortal sins than the Protestants do, and it's the mortal sin that will send you into hell if you die without confessing it. It's a mortal sin to go against any of the ten commandments, just like for Protestants, but Catholics can also commit a mortal sin by eating meat on Friday, or by skipping Mass on Sunday or a holy day of obligation. It's a mortal sin for a Catholic to pray in a Protestant church, or to get married without a priest. And it's a double mortal sin to receive communion with a mortal sin you didn't confess. That's how you can tell all the sinners at Sunday

Mass. When it's time to go to communion, they sit back in the pew, with the shame written on their faces.

Our house is holier than any other one in Annunciation parish because Mama is not just a Catholic, she's an extra special one, just one notch down from a saint. I want to be holy, like Mama.

"You can be an altar boy," Mama says. That's how you can get close to God. In the fourth grade you are allowed to become an altar boy."

An altar boy. Yes, that's what I want to be. I'll wear the long black robes and white lacy tops while helping the priest at Mass, and I'll wear the red robes on high Masses, and I'll hold the golden plate underneath people's chins during communion, and I'll say the Latin prayers, and run back and forth in the sanctuary where nobody is supposed to go except for priests and altar boys, and everybody, even Daddy, will think I'm great.

I see Father O'Hara at the Annunciation Church rectory, and he gives me a book to study. To be an altar boy, he says, I have learn how to serve at Mass. But first I have to learn the Latin responses for the Mass. When I learn these, he will instruct me in the rest.

I sit on a wooden kitchen chair at the living room stove. A red glow from the coals shows through the little mica windows. My bare feet are propped against the warm metalwork on the lower part of the stove. It's warm and cozy, and I forget about the wind whistling outside as it blows the snow in swirls, and about the cold breezes blowing up from the cracks in the floorboards behind the furnace in the places where the papers Mama has placed for insulation have been knocked aside. Daddy had already explained how to pronounce the Latin words, something he learned when he was an altar boy. Now I am trying to make them my own.

Priest: Introíbo ad altátre Dei.
Server: Ad Deum qui latíficat, juventútem meam.

I speak the words again and again, first reading them, then trying to repeat them without looking while mama reads along in the book, correcting me when I say something wrong. I don't know what these words mean, but I know they are the holy language that God himself speaks. When I pray in Latin, the words go directly to God, right to His ears. These are the words that will make me holy, like Father O'Hara, like Mama.

The hardest part is the *Confiteor Deo*, because it is a very long prayer to be spoken entirely by the altar boys, without any hints from the priest. I feel a warmth in my chest as if holy waves come out of my body as I speak the words, the same feeling I get after receiving communion at Mass.

> *Confiteor Deo, omnipoténti, beátae Maríae semper Vírgini, beáto Michaéli Archángelo, beáto Joánni Baptístae, sanctis Apóstolis Petro et Paulo, ómnibus sanctis et tibi, Pater: quia peccávi nimis cogitatióne, verbo, et ópere, mea culpa mea culpa, mea máxima culpa. Ideo precor beátum Maríam semper Vírginem, beátum Michaélum Archángelum, beátum Joánnem Baptístam, sanctos Apóstolus Petrum et Paulum, omnes Sanctos, et te, Pater, oráre pro me ad Dónimum Deum nostrum.*

In a few weeks, I have learned all the Latin responses and go to see Father O'Hara. When he tests me on my Latin I proudly remember it all. Then he instructs me on the art of serving. He takes me first into the sanctuary, the holy place beyond the marble gates in front of the church where only priests, altar boys, and other special people, are allowed, and then to the sacristy in the rooms behind the altar. The sacristy is where the priests keep their vestments, lectionaries, chalices, wine, and other things needed for Mass. An adjoining room has all the stuff for the altar boys—cassocks and surplices in various sizes, and candle lighters and snuffers placed on long poles so we can light or snuff out the tall candles that are placed high up on the altar. He shows me how to prepare the water and wine before Mass; these will later be consecrated by the priest to become the blood of Jesus. The hosts, which only the priest himself can handle, will become Jesus' body after the priest consecrates them. My favorite duty is when I'm supposed to ring the little hand bells during consecration.

Father O'Hara says he will post the weekly schedule for servers just inside the door of the sacristy behind the altar, and the list will also appear in the *Annunciation Record* each Sunday: two altar boys for each Mass, four Masses on weekdays, and five on Sundays. You might get assigned one particular Mass for each day of the week, one on a Saturday, or else one on a Sunday.

I'm supposed to serve my first Mass with Mikey Morrison at six-thirty on a Saturday morning. Me and Mama make the walk to Annunciation Church.

"Why doesn't Daddy come to see me serve, Mama?"

"Oh, you know your father. He likes to sleep in on Saturdays."

"But it's my first Mass, Mama."

"Just don't think about it. If there was a herd of wild elephants in the bedroom, it wouldn't wake your father on a Saturday morning."

But all I can think is that Daddy could get extra grace from going to Mass when he doesn't have to, and he could see how great I am up on the altar.

When we get to the church, Mama goes in the front door, and I go around to the back so I can enter through the sacristy door. I check out the cassocks in the closets where these long black robes are arranged by size. Even the smallest size seems to be way too long. I pick a white surplice, clean and starchy, to put over the cassock. Father O'Hara is in the next room, getting ready to put on his vestments.

"Ready for your first Mass, Pat?"

"Yes Father, I am."

"You'll do just fine. Now I have to put on my vestments and say my prayers. You and Mikey can wait at the sanctuary door."

When Father O'Hara appears behind us, holding on to his chalice, that's the signal for Mikey to pull the cord that rings a bell and signals the whole church that the altar boys and the priest are about to enter the sanctuary. The people stand as we walk toward the altar, first me and Mikey, then Father O'Hara, and everyone is admiring how smart I look. I take a peek to beyond the sanctuary rail to see Mama in the front pew, just where I knew she would be.

Oh, how I want Mama to see me ringing the bells on my first Mass, but when it's time for consecration, it's Mikey who gets to do it. At communion time, the people line up to the front of the church and take their turns kneeling at the sanctuary rail. My job is to hold the golden paten below the chin of the recipient so I can catch any crumbs that might fall off the consecrated host. This is necessary because even one crumb has the entire body of Jesus in it. It is a terrible responsibility to catch these crumbs. If I miss even one, that would leave Jesus just lying on the floor, maybe until one of the altar ladies sucks him up in the vacuum cleaner. It wouldn't be a sin if it was accidental, but I can't stand the thought of Jesus sitting there inside the dark vacuum cleaner bag with all that dirt.

The first ones to get communion are the nuns. Each nun closes her eyes when it's her turn, and sticks out her tongue to receive the host. Even Sister John Marie, the meanie of Annunciation, looks peaceful and holy. But her teeth are full of fillings. Are nuns allowed to go the dentist? After the nuns, the first person to receive is Mama. Usually she's the last person in the whole church to receive Communion, but today she's the first after the nuns, and I know it's for me.

Tommy Smith and I are both called out of class to be acolytes at a funeral High Mass, like they have when somebody important dies. The funerals on school days are great because the funeral Mass is always held after the regular ones, and we get pulled out of school for the service. For the High Mass, in addition to the two regular servers, they use four acolytes who each carry a pole with a candle on the end covered by a red glass. Counting the two servers, that gets six of us out of school at once.

As the service goes on we are kneeling in the sanctuary with our backs to the people, holding on to our candle poles. These High Masses are really long, and there are endless prayers, making it hard to just pray and think about God or about the dead person in the casket just outside the sanctuary. Big gobs of candle wax have dripped out onto the pole. By working the wax between my fingers, I can soften it and mold it into eyes, ears, a nose and a mouth stuck on the pole. Soon Tommy, who is kneeling besides me is doing the same. I turn my pole so that Tommy can get a look at the wax face with the long crooked nose on my pole. That sets him into a case of the giggles. His shoulders shake as he snickers and snorts while trying to keep the giggles bottled up. The red candle glass swings back and forth, but Tommy doesn't notice that the candle flame is licking the glass. All this time the organ is playing a sad funeral song, and the organist is singing something mournful in Latin. Father Carroll comes over to Tommy, and positions himself so that his vestments hide his hand as he gives a twist to Tommy's ear. Just then the glass cracks from the heat, and red glass scatters on the sanctuary floor. That stops the giggles, and Tommy now kneels up straight with a dead candle on his pole. I'm glad that I am innocent in all this mess.

Today us altar boys are in the back of the sacristy, preparing for a Solemn High Mass. These Masses, which only happen on very holy occasions, take a bunch of priests and a whole procession of altar and choir boys. Someone starts a blow gun war with one of the fancy candle snuffers on the long brass poles. The brass handles are hollow inside with a hole just big enough for a wooden match. I place a match in one end and blow into it. If the match head lights when it hits a joint half way down the pole, a flaming dart will shoot out. I take cover behind a rack of white silk surplices, the fancy ones that we use for solemn high masses. A flaming match flies from the end of a brass pole sticking out of the cassock closet where Jimmy is hiding. It hits the rack of silk surplices, quickly making flames. We both run to the rack, slapping out the flames, leaving only a little bit of charred marks on one surplice. With a little bit of luck, maybe the black mark will come out when the nuns do the wash. Just then Father O'Hara comes into our room and says its time to start the mass. We march out holding our hands flat together, fingers pointed to heaven.

One of my jobs today is to hold the lectionary for the priest at one point in the Mass. Father O'Hara had selected me for this job, saying it would be a great honor. The lectionary is a really giant book, containing huge print and all the words for the prayers and the musical score for the chants. At ordinary Masses, these books are kept in holders on the altar. But this is a fancy Mass, and at one part the book has to be held by an altar boy. When the time comes, Father O'Hara takes the book from the altar and hands it to me, nodding to the visiting Monsignor to remind me where to take it. Although it looks light as a feather when Father O'Hara holds it, it weighs a hundred pounds when he hands it to me. I carry it to the Monsignor who stands in front of me with his two open hands and his arms spread a little apart, and he begins to chant the long Latin prayers that go with a solemn High Mass. My arms get tired, and the book starts to droop. Monsignor pulls the book back into position while he continues the chant. The book droops again. My arms ache, and I know that I will soon drop the book, and it would be a great sacrilege that would ruin the whole Mass, and would surely offend God. Monsignor keeps pulling the book up, and it keeps drooping. Finally I push up the book from my outstretched arms and place it on my head, right where he can read it. Just then Father O'Hara comes over and takes the book, and holds it in the proper position for the Monsignor. He gently motions with his head for me to go over to the side of the altar. He doesn't seem mad, but did I commit a venial sin? Do I have to ask forgiveness in confession for letting God down like this?

I like being an altar boy, to help the priest say Mass and serve communion, to say the Latin prayers for all the people to hear, to help out at evening novenas and on special holy days. I like getting out of school for funerals on weekdays, and to serve at weddings on Saturdays. I like all the friends I have made. I feel like I'm someone special, and it's a great honor to serve God. But the best part is Father O'Hara, who thinks I'm the best altar boy ever, and who talks to me like I wish Daddy would.

Tom Smith (9), Pat (10), and Penny

10.

The Skeleton Building

Kathleen pulls my arm to get me to come to the far side of the living room, out of earshot of Mama.

"Tomorrow we're going to the skeleton building," she says in a low voice. "Mary Ann's coming." That's her best girlfriend.

"Is it haunted?"

"No. But it's something special. Don't tell Mama."

"Why not?"

"Never mind. You'll find out."

Later, when I go to bed, I think about a great adventure that I'm going to have tomorrow. It will be a holy day when I won't have to go to my fourth grade class, but not a holy day of obligation when we have to go to Mass. I keep thinking about skeletons and haunted houses.

The next morning me and Kathleen pack lunches of peanut butter and jelly sandwiches. We put our lunches in cloth bags with drawstrings that Mama had made for our hikes.

Helen notices that something is going on, something that she wants to be part of.

"I'm going too."

"No, you're not. You're too little," I say.

"Mama, I want to go with Kathleen and Pat. Tell them I get to go too."

"No, Mama. She can't come. She's only in the second grade. We're going too far. Tell her she can't come."

"Yes I can."

"No you can't."

This is the part where Helen's forehead makes those little bumps just before she's going to cry, the look that always gets Mama to feel sorry for her.

"Can't you two be nice to your little sister? Couldn't you bring her along?"

"Aw, Mama. Not this time. Mary Ann's coming over, we're going all the way to Belle Isle. It's too far for her. She just couldn't keep up," says Kathleen.

"I'll tell you what, Helen Therese. If you stay with me, we'll make some nice cupcakes together. Then we can eat them ourselves while your brother and sister are away."

Helen seems to perk up at this news. A knock at the door signals that Mary Ann is here, and it's time for our getaway. We grab our lunches and run to the door. Mama says be careful, and be back before the street lights go on. We assure her that we will be careful. But we don't tell her that first we want to stop at Scripts School on our way to Belle Isle.

We walk the two blocks to the Scripts schoolyard and stand near the school building. Being as this is a Protestant school, they don't get off on holy days like we do. So all the Protestant kids are sure to be at their desks.

We form a circle, and start to sing.

Old Mac Donald had a farm, ee-ii ee-ii oh.
And on his farm he had a cow, ee-ii ee-ii oh.
With a moo-moo here, and a moo-moo there,
Here a moo, there a moo, everywhere a moo-moo.
Old Mac Donald had a farm, ee-ii ee-ii oh.

We pick up the volume as we circle and dance. Now we are all laughing and twirling, skipping and laughing. Mary Ann starts to sing louder. Kathleen spins like a top while dancing around a bigger circle.

When we get to the part about the donkey, we all burst into hilarious laughter. Tears roll down my cheeks as I shout at the top of my lungs.

With a hee-haw here, and a hee-haw there,
Here a hee, there a haw, everywhere a hee-haw.

At the second floor window a Protestant head looks out, then another. We sing and laugh all the harder. I don't care that we have to go to school for an extra week in the spring to make up for the holy days. Now I'm free while the Protestants have to be locked up in their Protestant school.

Now that our singing has done its job, we hold hands and skip across the school yard, hoping that the kids in the window are still watching. We walk across Kercheval, then another four blocks down to Jefferson Street. At Jefferson we turn right and walk another half mile. Mary Ann points to a structure off in the distance.

"That's the skeleton building," she says.

I've seen it many times on my hikes to Belle Isle, but this is the first time I've paid attention to it. It's a tall building that was never completed. Something about the war stopped the construction. There are girders but no walls. I count the floors—one, two, three, four, five, six, seven, eight, nine, ten. It has ten floors.

"We're going to the top," says Mary Ann.

When we reach the skeleton building, I see that there is no fence or signs saying *Keep Off*. We cross through the place where the wall should be and onto the concrete pad that is the first floor. Trash litters the floor, along with the remains of some burnt wood where someone once had a fire. At one end is a square enclosure with an opening.

"That's the elevator shaft," says Mary Ann.

I look up the shaft to see a dark tunnel that reaches to the very top. At the other end of the room is a set of wooden stairs to the second floor. Mary Ann leads the way up the half-rotten, creaky stairs. We go to the edge of the second floor and look down to the ground. It's not very far—nothing scary about this. Like the bottom floor, this floor is made of concrete and is full of holes where you can see the floor below. Kathleen leads the way up to the third floor. I have to be careful on the broken stairs.

Now we are on the third floor, looking at the staircase leading up to the fourth floor. The first two stairs are missing entirely. I look at Kathleen; then to Mary Ann, then down into the space of the missing stairs where I can see the floor below. When I look just at just the right angle, I can see all the way to the bottom floor, and it gives me a shiver.

"What do we do now?" I ask

"No problem," says Mary Ann. "We just jump—like this." She jumps the space up to the third step. "Come on, it's easy," she says.

Mary Ann goes up a couple more stairs. Then Kathleen makes the jump. I look again through the missing stairs, and then up to the two girls who are laughing and waving to me to make the jump.

"Don't be a chicken," they're saying. I don't want to go any farther, but I don't want to be a chicken. One slip, and I'd be smushed like a bug on the floor below. But I can't let two girls show me up, even if they are two years older than me. I swallow hard and jump, landing perfectly on the good stair. My heart is pounding, but I won't let them know it.

We make our way like this up to the ninth floor, where the stairs just end. The bottom of the tenth floor is mostly missing. Lining the walls above the open space are tiers of what looks like steps for the bleachers at Briggs stadium. At the very top, way above the highest bleacher level is a platform, and on the wall above the platform are many initials painted by kids who have proved their bravery.

"How do we get up there?" I ask.

"You have to climb the girders" says Mary Ann.

The girders have lots of bumps from rivet heads. It looks like you could probably get a grip on these with your hands and feet. We talk about whether we should . "No, we shouldn't go up," announces Kathleen. "That would be dangerous." Now when Kathleen says something is dangerous, it's dangerous! Thank goodness this is as far as we go. Besides, Mama would be very upset if one of us fell off.

I go to the edge of the building and look down—a long, long way down. I have to hold onto the girder because something is trying to suck me off into the empty space.

After we eat lunch we make the trip down the stairs, which is much easier than going up, especially the places where you have to jump broken stairs.

When we get home, Mama offers us a cupcake, still warm from the oven.

"How was your day at Belle Isle?"

"It was fine, Mama." We don't tell her where we actually went, because that might upset her, and that could bring on an attack.

11.

Mama runs away

Helen Rogoza sits on his lap—shy Helen who always hangs back, who gets overlooked, who is too afraid to assert herself, who often stays in the background, hoping to avoid a beating from Ma. She enjoys his fussing over her and his funny games. The others don't really need as much attention as she does. Her sister Mary, a Rogoza, knows how to stand her ground; everyone fusses over pretty Stella, also a Rogoza; her brother, Dominik, is strong enough to take care of himself. The Zalut children who came after Ma married Pa Zalut, get plenty of care from the Rogoza girls. Helen loves the attention he gives her - the tickles, the jokes, the stories, the little gifts. She shifts her position, confused about what is happening. He must not realize what he is doing, and she is too timid to say anything. He sets her down, places a sweet in her hand, and whispers into her ear You must never tell anyone. This will be our special secret.

*　　　　*　　　　*　　　　*

Kathleen had to put things right, to kill the ugly rumors already circulating around school, to draw a curtain around the shame. Mama had run away.

"Of course she hasn't run away," she lied to Sister Emile. "She's only gone to visit our relatives. Don't pay any attention to Helen, she has gotten things all mixed up, just like a third grader. Mama will be back in just a few days, and Daddy is taking care of everything."

Kathleen tells me this story at recess in a harsh whisper. I can tell she's really mad, thinking about how she'll give Helen a piece of her mind when she gets home from school. Helen had to go and tell Sister Michael Marie in her third grade class: My mama has run away, that little rat had said, and we don't know where she is. The rumor had spread to Kathleen's sixth grade, where Sister Alma asked her about Mama, and to my fifth grade too. This is how it all started.

Yesterday when I came home from school, Mama was nowhere in sight, but Daddy was already there, home early from work. He told us that Mama was gone and he didn't know where she was, or when she would come back. She had just packed her bags that morning and left. I remembered the screaming and shouting the night before. There shouldn't be have been anything special about that; it happens all the time. But this time it was special. Mama has run away. But I know she'll come back. She could never desert us—not in a million years.

I know it's Daddy's fault. The night before Mama left he came home late with the Glick's smell on him again, and they started to argue right after he finished the supper she had left out for him. And the arguments picked up again after we went to bed, late into the night. Yesterday morning, after we left for school, she packed her bags and just left. Daddy said that Mama has to cool off, that she would be back real soon. In the meantime, we would just have to get along by ourselves. I tried to put my meanest stare into Daddy's eyes, to let him know that I blame him for making Mama run away, for treating her so mean. But he just acted like he didn't notice.

We sit around the dinner table without speaking, eating the awful dish of macaroni and cheese that Kathleen made. She already gave Helen a tongue lashing for telling the sisters and the kids at school about Mama. Helen will just have to go back tomorrow and tell them that she got things mixed up. She looks down at her plate, not eating, sticking out her bottom lip, like she's ashamed for what she has done. Daddy lights a cigarette from the red ash of a still glowing butt. After dinner he goes into the living room, stretches out on the floor next to the couch, and goes to sleep. Kathleen washes dishes while Helen and I dry. Afterwards, Kathleen, Helen, and I sit around the kitchen table, talking about Mama, why she left, where she went, and when she will come back. Nobody has any answers, but we all know this: Mama will come back.

On Saturday, the fourth day after she left, Mama walks in the front door, with a suitcase and a bag of packages, all smiles like she just came back from a vacation. I rush to hug her, but Kathleen gets there first, and Helen grabs hold of a leg. Daddy comes up and throws a bear hug around the whole bunch of us—something he almost never does. He doesn't speak, but his eyes shine like he's got a speck of dust in them. Mama says she's sorry she had to go so suddenly to East Rochester, New York; her grandmother was sick, and she needed to be with her. She gives me a box with a toy truck inside. Kathleen gets a scarf, and Helen gets a barrette with little diamonds in it. Daddy looks on with a little smile, not saying a word. And then Mama goes up to him, and they hug, and the next thing I know, they're kissing, and I can't believe my eyes, because hugging and kissing are things Mama and Daddy never do to each other.

Mama tells us the story of her adventure.

"I took a street car to Detroit Grand Central Station, and then took a train all the way to Rochester, New York. They had food on the train, and bathrooms too. The seats reclined, and there was a foot rest so you could sleep on the seat if you wanted to. I struck up a conversation with a woman I met on the train, and we had a long talk. Eventually she told me she was going to Rochester to kill herself. But I told her about the power of prayer, and how God looks out for all his children. How you should never give up hope. We talked and talked all the way to Rochester. I think the Holy Mother put me on that train for a special purpose."

That evening, Kathleen pulls me aside and whispers a secret.

"Mama's psychic, didn't you know?"

"What's that."

"She knows things. She finds people in trouble, people who want to commit suicide, and she helps them."

On Monday everything is normal again. Kathleen tells Sister Alma how Mama had to help her sick grandmother. Sister said what a good woman your mother is, someone who looks after her poor old grandmother, someone who is always willing to sacrifice herself for others.

Now Mama's home for good. Daddy will be nice to her, and she'll never run away again. She won't have any more attacks, and we'll be the happiest family in the world.

12.

The Legion of Mary

"I want you to come with me," Mama says, "so you can see God's work in action." So I March down to the Parker Party Store with Mama, Mrs. Wagner, and Mrs. O'Brian.

"Oh Jesus," says Mr. Parker as we come in his store. "It's the Legion of Mary again." Mama marches in with a determined look, flanked by her two fellow legionnaires, both large and big-breasted women who make Mama look skinnier than usual. Mama stops at the magazine stand in front of the store, picks out a few magazines and a couple of paperback novels, and brings them to the glass counter in the middle of the store where Mr. Parker stands behind the cash register next to a snack counter with little round stools.

"Good afternoon ladies," he says with a wide tight grin, making it look like he had just banged his elbow and he doesn't know whether to laugh or cry. "And what can I do for you fine ladies today?"

"You know darn well why we're here, Mr. Parker," says Mama, who is clearly the boss here. "We're here on God's business."

"And what would that business be?" asks Mr. Parker, but I can tell he already knows the answer.

"Smut," says Mama, like she's spitting. "This filthy smut," she says, slapping the terrible evidence for all to see onto the counter. One of the paperbacks bears the title *The Secret Lover* and shows a picture of a woman in a very tight slinky dress with a slit up the side, and with pointy bulges on her chest. She is smoking a cigarette held in a long cigarette holder. A magazine called *Stag* has a cover showing a woman with pouty lips bending over so that you can look way down into her blouse and see what you're not supposed to.

"The last time we were here you said you would remove all this filth," says Mama. "Now it's still here."

"But I did," protests Mr. Parker. "All the magazines we had last month are gone. These are all new ones, but I don't know anything about them being smutty."

"Don't play games with me, Mr. Parker. I know smut when I see it," Mama says.

Now Mrs. Wagner speaks up. "As the president of the Legion of Mary, I can tell you, Mr. Parker, we won't stand for this filth in our neighborhood. We'll give you just one more week to get rid of this trash. If you don't, we plan to hold a prayer vigil here every day. Our volunteers are ready to be on their knees on the sidewalk right in front of your store, praying the rosary every day from the time you open up till the time you close. And we'll keep it up until we get results."

"I'm very sorry if the books offend you ladies, but it's what my customers want," chances Mr. Parker.

"One week," reminds Mrs. Wagner. "We'll be back with the prayer brigade in one week." With that, me and Mama, Mrs. Wagner, Mrs. O'Brian turn sharply, and walk out of the door, and down the street, satisfied that the wishes of the Holy Mother will be respected, or it will be holy war with the Legion of Mary.

The Legion always seemed like Mama's business, but she invites me to join, and I decide to try it for a while. At my first meeting all the ladies of the Legion sit around a long table and discuss different ways to spread God's word in the Holy Mother's name. I am the only kid there—a fifth grader. Everyone else is a grown-up lady, except for Father O'Hara, who is the Legion's spiritual sponsor. A resolution is passed that I should take back-copies of *Our Sunday Visitor* and *The Michigan Catholic* to the old folks home on Pennsylvania Street. After the meeting, Father O'Hara says that if I want to be a member, I have to meditate on the Hail Mary every night for fifteen minutes.

When I get home, I tell Mama that I don't know how to meditate. She goes with me into my bedroom, closes the door, and we both get down on our knees beside the bed, like we were going to say our night prayers. "First let's pray the Hail Mary," she says.

> *Hail Mary, full of grace, the Lord is with thee. Blessed art thou amongst women, and blessed is the fruit of thy womb, Jesus [we bow our heads]. Holy Mary, mother of God, pray for us sinners, now and at the hour of our death, Amen.*

"Now we will meditate on each word. *Hail* means hello, it is the greeting of the angel who came down to carry God's message while Mary was praying. We will think about the angel, with his white flowing garments, and Mary kneeling beside her bed, just like we are doing now. We will think how Mary was afraid at first, but the angel managed to make her calm and trusting."

And so we go through the entire prayer, word by word, thought by thought. When we finish, Mama looks at the clock and says: "Fifteen minutes. You see that's really not so hard to do."

Mama is much holier than the mothers of my friends. She is especially dedicated to Mary, the mother of Jesus. She says her favorite color is blue because that was the color worn by Mary. That's why so many of her clothes are blue. She makes sure we always wear a scapular. That's a square piece of cloth on a string that has been blessed specially by a priest, and it's something one of the saints said that Mary wants us to wear around our necks. Most of my friends wear a metal scapular on a chain, but Mama says that you don't get as much grace as you do when you are wearing a real cloth scapular. So we all wear cloth scapulars; no cutting corners in our family! In addition, just to be safe, I also wear a chain around my neck with a metal that says *I am a Catholic. In case of an accident, please call a priest.* If I'm bleeding to death on the street, it's a priest I want, although I hope his blessing would keep me going till the doctor got there.

Mama is extra safe and extra holy, so she wears a scapular with a lot of separate cloth pieces arranged like the pages in a book. Each scapular is for a different saint and has a different color—a blue one for the Holy Mother, a brown one for Saint Francis, a green one for Saint Theresa, and so on. Mama doesn't insist that I wear that type all the time, and she is satisfied that me, Kathleen and Helen keep our multiple scapulars tied to the bed post at the head of our beds so, God willing, we won't die in our sleep in a state of sin. Mama also wears a rope with a series of knots in it tied around her waist, just like the monks do, but hers is hidden beneath her dress. She also wears a crucifix around her neck.

Saturday nights are when Mama usually goes to confession to Father O'Hara. That's the best time to go, since you don't have much chance to commit any new sins before communion the next day. Most people are in and out of the confessional in a few minutes. But Mama is usually in there for at least a half an hour, while the other people in line for Father O'Hara look at their watches and shuffle in the pews. What does she do that is so bad that it takes her such a long time to confess her sins and pray her penance?

At Mass, she is usually the last one to go to communion. After she receives the host, she walks slowly in tiny steps, with her rosary threaded around her clasped fingers, taking an eternity to get back to her pew, while Mass goes on, and the rest of the congregation can see how holy she is.

We keep a little altar in Mama's bedroom with a statue of the Sacred Heart, and some candles in little red glass holders which we light for special prayers. I found the statue sticking out of some trash in the alley, and took it home to Mama since it would have been a sacrilege to leave Jesus in the alley that way. She took it to a man who fixed the broken nose and hand, and repainted it just like new. We kneel in front of the statue when we pray the rosary, which is most every night. She has probably said a thousand times *the family that prays together, stays together*. Another one of her favorite expressions is *If I've told you once, I've told you a thousand times*. Well, when it comes to praying, Mama reminds us about it more than a thousand times.

We have a holy water crucible at every doorway within the house. That's a little container we nail to the wall and fill with holy water. Every time you go from one room to another, you are supposed to dip your finger in the water, and make the sign of the cross. My prayer book says that each time you make the sign of the cross, you get three years indulgence, and seven years if you do it with holy water. It pays to save up lots of indulgences, because this will let you work off purgatory time. Purgatory is where you go for punishment for your sins when you die. If you die with a mortal sin on your soul that didn't get confessed, you go to hell straight away. But for mortal sins forgiven in confession and also for venial sins you still have to burn in purgatory, but maybe only for a few hundred years rather than for all of eternity like in hell. I hope I can get rid of my purgatory time faster than it can add up, but it's hard to know if you're ahead. Although we know how much credit we get from indulgences, no one tells us how much time we have to burn in purgatory for saying a bad word or having an impure thought.

Every night Mama sprinkles holy water in every room of the house. Sometimes I'll still be awake at night, and I'll see her open my door, sprinkle my room with holy water, and then make the sign of the cross in the air like the priest does when he's blessing everybody at Mass. She uses extra powerful holy water that she got from Mrs. Wagner who got it from a friend who went to Canada and got it from a holy woman. This is not ordinary holy water, which has to be blessed by a priest, and when it's gone, you have to get a new batch blessed. The special holy water is so powerful, that if you start to run low, you can put just one drop in a jar filled with ordinary water, and the entire jar of water will become holy. I wonder why Mama doesn't put a drop of it in the ocean, and make the whole world holy. Maybe that would stop wars and other bad things in the world.

Mama at White Fish Lake

Peace and Joy for the
holiday season, and the new
year.

From Pat and Lyn Reilly
December, 2012

13.

Grand Rapids

Mama has to have another operation to stop her attacks. They keep finding more bad parts to take out of her. She says this time she is going to ask the doctor to put in a zipper, rather than sew her up, so it will be easier to take out another part the next time. While she recovers, I get to stay with my cousin Dick Maloney in Grand Rapids, Kathleen goes with Ahntie Reet, our rich aunt who also lives in Grand Rapids, and Helen is condemned to stay with Grammy.

Daddy drives me and Mama to Detroit Grand Central Station, downtown, where I'll catch a train to Grand Rapids and stay with cousin Dick Maloney. The station is like a palace, with high ceilings and huge glass windows. A voice from a loudspeaker echoes like you hear on the spooky Inner Sanctum radio show, but it's impossible to understand what it is saying, and I wonder how anybody can find their train from the jumbled announcements. Mama and Daddy take me through a door, which leads to a place full of train tracks, and waiting trains.

"You'll be taking the streamliner," says Mama. "When you get in Grand Rapids, your Uncle Bert and Aunt Helen Maloney will meet you."

When the train starts up, I see Mama through the window, waiving like crazy, and then she's gone from sight. At first I see houses and buildings out the window, then trees. We're on our way to Grand Rapids, with no one to tell me what I should or shouldn't do, and I'm not the least bit scared. I love to stand between the cars, in the place where they are connected together. I can hear the ticka-ticka-ticka-tacka of the wheels as I watch the scenery go by. There's a bathroom on the train, and when I flush the toilet, I can see the track rails flying past through the hole that the toilet makes. I go back to my seat, where I read the book that Mama gave me for this trip: *The Tin Woodsman of Oz,* which tells about the adventures of a man made out of tin, his friends, witches, goblins, balloon men, and all kinds of magical people

Cousin Dick and I are in his parent's bedroom. His dad, Uncle Bert, is at work, and his mother, Aunt Helen, has gone out for a chore. "Can I trust you alone for a few minutes while I run up to the store?" she had asked. "Oh yes," we assured her, "we'll be just fine."

Dick shows me his father's shotgun that was standing in his parents closet just minutes ago. It has a long black barrel, cold and hard, held in a polished wooden stock, so smooth that I want to pet it like a sleeping cat, but I'm afraid that this cat might suddenly awaken to become a snarling animal that scratches and bites. Dick got a box of shells from his dad's dresser drawer. The shells are red, with a yellow brass end with a little round spot right in the middle where, Dick says, the striker hits, making the shell explode into a spray of pellets. There is a little metal door on the side of the gun, which you can push in and let it spring back. "This is where the shell goes, like this," Dick says, as he shows how the shell just fits into the little door. He teases the door with the shell a few times, making it open and spring shut. It all seems so beautiful, and yet so frightening.

Suddenly, the door snatches the shell from his fingers, and clicks shut. We look at each other, not speaking. Dick's eyes are open wide, like he didn't expect this to happen. He probes the door with his finger, forcing it open, but the shell is nowhere in sight. "What are we going to do now?" I ask. "Can you get it out?"

"I dunno. I'm trying." He pokes the door a few more times with his finger, but this does nothing useful. He turns the gun over, shakes it, and looks again into the door, but still the shell hides somewhere inside.

"Let me try." I take the gun from his hands and turn it over, looking for a secret release mechanism, being careful not to point the end of the barrel at Dick or myself. I can't find any way to get the shell out, so I hand it back to Dick.

"We've got to get it out," he says. "If my dad finds out, he'll kill me."

We stare at the gun, and discuss our options. We decide that our best bet is to aim the gun out the window and pull the trigger. We talk about where to aim the gun so we won't shoot out the neighbor's window, how we'll hold it in place, who will pull the trigger, and how to keep the recoil from breaking someone's shoulder. Eventually we decide that's not a good idea because the gun will make such a big noise that someone will surely hear it and tell on us. So we do the safest thing. We put it back into the closet, and close the door. Dick puts the box of shells back into the dresser drawer. We agree that we'll just have to keep a tight lip about this. Probably, when hunting season starts in the fall, his dad will find the shell in the gun, and think that he forgot to remove it from the previous season.

We can't afford to get into any more trouble, especially since the Vernor's incident. Here's what happened. Every evening we all sit around the kitchen table and drink Vernor's ginger ale. They keep the stash of pop bottles in the basement fruit cellar. Last week, when Dick and I were downstairs fooling around, we looked in the fruit cellar, and saw the bottles lined up like little soldiers. We couldn't resist opening a bottle of Vernor's that was just sitting there on the shelf with an opener right there along side it, begging to be used. When the cap just seemed to fall off, we had to drink the pop, or else the bubbles would go flat.

After that, we debated what to do with the empty bottle. Just put it in the trash I said, under some garbage. But Dick said that wouldn't work, because his mother counts the bottles, and she would know that one was missing. So we hit on a perfectly good solution. Between the two of us, we filled the bottle with fresh pee, exactly the golden color of Vernor's ginger ale, and Dick put the cap back on by hitting it with the palm of his hand. He put the bottle at the end of the line, where we thought it would be the last to be used, and by then his mother would lose count, and we could empty it. But it didn't happen that way.

A few days later, we got called into the kitchen by Aunt Helen. "Sit down, young man," she said to Dick. "And you too," she said turning to me, glaring like she was going to stab me with the daggers coming out of her eyes. Right then I knew we were in trouble over something, but I wasn't sure what. Maybe it was about the dirt bombs we were throwing that morning. Or maybe it was over the toilet paper parachutes Dick was sailing down to me from the upstairs bathroom window.

"I found a bottle of Vernor's," she said, "with something in it. Who wants to explain it to me?" She looked over at Dick, who was staring at the table cloth. I wanted to blurt out that it was all his idea. But I kept quiet. Maybe it's better to play dumb. "Well," she said, as if expecting somebody to own up, "how many bottles did you do that to?" Then she turned straight to me.

"Just one," I mumbled.

"Yeah," Dick joined in, "only one. We just couldn't help it. We were in the basement, and we had to pee. We couldn't make it to the bathroom, so we had to do something."

That seemed like a perfectly good explanation, but Aunt Helen Maloney didn't buy it. She gave us an angry lecture about being trustworthy and respectful of other people. I listened, all the time staring at the little patterns in the table cloth. I think its all blown over by now, but ever since then, when we sit around the kitchen table in the evening, Dick and I share a Vernor's while the others drink Coke.

Uncle Bert and Aunt Helen Maloney take me to visit Ahntie Reet, who lives in Grand Rapids in a big fancy house with three floors plus a basement. In her living room is a big grandfather clock that makes a slow tick tock that you can hear all over the first floor. On the wall there is a cuckoo clock, with a little bird that comes out when the clock strikes the hour. Behind the house there is a gigantic garage that can hold two cars and a tractor, and there is still room for another car. All our other aunts are called *Aunt* or *Auntie,* like Aunt Mary, Aunt Stella, or Auntie Anna. But Ahntie Reet is *Ahntie,* maybe because she is so rich that it wouldn't be right to call her a plain *aunt* or *auntie.* Everybody acts all respectful when they're around her, like she's mother superior or something. Mama says no one wants to get cut out of her will. I don't mind going to her house, because she gives us money to buy ice cream and other treats. But I wouldn't want to stay there for a long time like Kathleen does, because it's just too boring there.

Baby Helen—that's Daddy's sister—used to live with Ahntie Reet, but now she has her own apartment in Grand Rapids. When Baby Helen was little, Ahntie Reet asked Grammy to let Baby Helen live with her, because she couldn't have children of her own. She surely wouldn't have asked for Lala, who was not as pretty and happy. Grammy said okay, and so Baby Helen came to live with her rich aunt until she grew up. That was probably a good thing, because Baby Helen didn't get to be a sourpuss like Lala, and maybe she will be rich some day like Ahntie Reet.

Uncle Phil lives with Ahntie Reet. He has fruit orchards, and sometimes Dick and I get to visit his farm, playing in the hay loft, and riding baskets down the roller tracks inside the barn. He's not my real uncle, because Ahntie Reet was married once before to a man named Mr. Anway. When he died, she became rich, because Mr. Anway had a lot of money from a furniture company he owned. Uncle Phil's last name is Klenk, which makes me think of the clinkers we get out of our coal furnace. He is skinny, has an old wrinkled face, and never smiles or jokes. I think he is so sour because he eats lettuce with plain vinegar every afternoon. He got me to try it once, but it just made my face pucker up, like his.

Grammy says that Uncle Phil is going to hell and will drag Ahntie Reet there too because he is a Protestant, and he insisted they get married in a Protestant church. That means they are not really married, and are living in sin. Every time I look at Uncle Phil, I feel sorry for him because his face is so sour, and when he dies, he will go straight to hell, and will never know what it's like to have a good time alive or dead. But I think that Ahntie Reet will go to heaven because she gives us money for treats, and she can make a good act of contrition before she dies.

After four weeks with the Maloneys, Uncle Bert puts me on the train. When I step off the train in Detroit, Mama and Daddy are there to greet me. Mama wears a big smile, and gives me hug and a kiss. She looks skinnier than usual, and her eyes seem to be sunken in her head. Daddy takes my suitcase, and we walk to the car. Mama walks slowly, like it's a great effort. On the way home, she tells me about her operation. "They took out my female parts," she says. "Just be glad you weren't born a girl, so you don't have to worry about such things." I tell Mama and Daddy about my adventures with Dick. How we made model airplanes, went to the park, got three dips of ice cream for a nickel, delivered newspapers, went to the doctor, dug a big hole, made a fort, went swimming, went to Uncle Phil's farm, rode in a basket down the rollers in the barn, climbed up in the hay loft,

slid down the hay pile, swung from a rope, climbed trees, worked Chinese puzzles, played baseball, collected fireflies in a jar, drank pop every evening. I don't tell about Vernor's ginger ale or the other troubles Dick and I got into. And I especially don't tell how I learned to ride Dick's bike. If Daddy finds out about that, he won't let me come to Grand Rapids anymore because he doesn't want me riding bikes. That part of my adventure will be my secret.

Dick (11) and Pat (15) Maloney,
Grand Rapids ≈ 1948

14.

A Radio Flyer

After school us boys form a circle around the yo-yo man to watch him do tricks with a new kind of yo-yo that *sleeps*. When he throws it down, it just stays there spinning magically; it wakes up with a jerk, and then rolls up like a regular yo-yo. He shows us loop-the-loop, around the world, walking the dog, rocking the cradle, eating spaghetti, and all the other yo-yo tricks. He says that he uses a *Duncan* yo-yo that costs forty cents.

When I pass by Joe's Grill on Kercheval, I can taste the frying hamburgers just from their wonderful aroma. They cost fifteen cents. A Captain Midnight ring goes for fifty cents. A cap gun is a dollar, and caps cost ten cents a pack. A baseball costs seventy-five cents, and a baseball glove is two dollars. A bat is a dollar. Roller skates are two dollars. Comics cost ten cents. A spy glass costs a dollar fifty. A bag of marbles goes for fifty cents.

How can I ask Mama for money to buy those things? She barely has enough money to buy food for our family. Just the other day she came home with a bunch of bruised vegetables from Joe's vegetable truck. She said that she could cut out the bad spots from the potatoes and apples, and they would have to last us for a week. *Money doesn't grow on trees* she always says.

My friend Raymond told me about the working boys at the Am-Pee store on Kercheval. Every Saturday they line up outside the store under the sign: *Atlantic & Pacific Food Store*. When a lady comes out with bags of groceries in her arms, she puts them into one of the boys wagons, and he carts them to her home. Raymond says you get tips that way and can make good money.

I don't have a wagon, but my eleventh birthday is coming up, and I ask Mama for a Radio Flyer wagon. My birthday falls on a Saturday this year—March nineteenth, nineteen forty-eight. On this day, like on my birthday every year, Mama takes me on a special outing. We ride the street car to downtown, a magical place of tall buildings and millions of people all rushing one way and the other. We have a birthday dinner at a real restaurant in the basement floor of Hudson's. My birthday is the only time I have ever been to a restaurant, but Mama says she can afford it once a year for me. A waiter comes and asks us what we want, just like we are somebody special. I order frog legs—something you will never get at home. They are so delicious and the meat just melts in my mouth. After the dinner we go to a movie at the Fox theater, a palace with glass chandeliers hanging from the ceiling, red carpets, and ushers who wear fancy red uniforms with gold braids and brass buttons, and little round hats. In the lobby there are red carpeted stairs going to an upper balcony. We see a movie about ships and adventure. When we get home, mama has a present for me. It's not a Radio Flyer. I don't tell her how disappointed I am.

A couple of weeks later Kathleen runs up to me; she's all excited. "I found a wagon thrown away in the alley. Maybe it's what you need for the Am-Pee store." She takes me down the alley that goes in back of our house. Underneath a pile of junk, cardboard, and tree branches, partially hidden, is an old wooden wagon. We clear the junk away and pull it out for inspection. It appears almost workable, with four wooden wheels and cracks in the sides. As we roll it home, one of the wheels acts kind of gimpy, making the wagon lurch from side to side as it rolls along.

When we get home, we are able to fix the wagon with some nails and a good scrubbing. Next Saturday I will try my luck at the store.

On Saturday morning four boys are already lined up in front of the Am-Pee with red Radio Flyers. "Where did you get that piece of junk?" one of them says, pointing to my wagon, which gets them into fits of laughter. I swallow and try to ignore their snickering and carrying on and watch to learn the routine. This is how it works. You get at the end of the line of wagons. When a lady comes out with groceries, the first one in line goes up to her, and says, *Need any help ma'am?* If she puts the groceries in your wagon, you are hired.

Finally it's my turn to be first in line. My heart beats with excitement as a lady comes out holding two bags of groceries. "Need any help ma'am?" I say in a very professional tone, trying to hide my excitement. She looks at me, then at the wagon, then back at me again. I know she is going to pass me up. My wagon isn't good enough. She is going to choose one of the other boys with their fancy Radio Flyers. But she walks over to me and puts her bags into my wagon. As we roll along, she asks me about my wagon. I tell her it is just temporary; I am saving to buy a Radio Flyer.

When we get to her house, she gives me twenty cents—that could buy four candy bars. By the end of the day I'm going to be rich beyond my dreams.

By supper time, my tips from several deliveries adds up to a dollar fifty—more money than I've ever had before. This calls for a celebration, a special treat of something that I can only get doled out in stingy amounts at home: a jar of olives for twenty cents, which I will eat entirely and drink the juice before going home, and save the rest of the money for a new wagon.

After a few weeks, I have saved four dollars and fifty cents. I give the money to Mama and ask her to buy me a new Radio Flyer. She takes the money and gives me a big hug. "Don't you worry, Pat," she says. "You'll get your wagon." The following week I take my place in line at the Am-Pee with a brand new Radio Flyer—a wagon shiny and bright red like a fire truck, with black tires with deep grooves for treads, one that sails down the sidewalk without a single rattle or shake, one that is powerful enough to hold a person, or a whole load of grocery bags.

In another month I have a new Duncan yo-yo in my pocket as I walk into Joe's Grill. Since I started to work at the Am-Pee I have bought a hamburger every week from Joe's, had it heaped with pickles, and slathered with mustard. "Hide the mustard," Joe says, laughing. "Here comes the mustard kid." He makes a motion like he is going to gather up all the mustard dispensers on the counter. Joe knows how I like my hamburgers. The other customers seated at the counter are laughing too. They surely are admiring me—a boy who comes here every week to buy what he wants with his own money. I reach into my pocket and pull out a dime and a nickel and slap them on the counter, making a clinky sound.

"One hamburger, Mister, with plenty of pickles."

My new savings account is at the Detroit National Bank, just a block down from the Am-Pee. The pass book has a blue cover that is tough enough to last a long time, but soft enough that it flexes when you rub it against your face, soft enough to slip right

under your pillow at night. It has a smell like new ink. And the best part is what is says inside: three dollars.

It's great to be a working boy, to have my own money, to hear the sound of jingling in my pocket, to feel the weight of it. Most of all I like being independent, not to have to ask Mama for money, to be able to just walk up and buy what I want. I will always work, and will never have to ask anyone for money ever again.

Pat, (age ≈ 11)

15.

Mama's education

Ma stirs a big pot of stew with a large wooden spoon. Please Ma, please, begs Helen Rogoza, I want to go back to school. I'll do my chores after school, and I can do the laundry on Saturday. Ma stops stirring, pulls the spoon from the pot, raises it like a club, and advances to the sobbing girl. You want lessons? I'll give you a lesson. Here's your teacher right here, she says, waving the spoon while Helen retreats into the next room.

       *   *   *   *

Me, Mama and Helen are in Stoller's Used Book Store on Kercheval. My Radio Flyer wagon is parked outside, red and shiny, waiting for an important job. Lining the walls inside are shelves way higher than my head, filled with books of all colors, many looking ragged and old. Mama looks over the shelves of books, while me and Helen study the comic books at the tables in the back of the store, near the desk where Mr. and Mrs. Stoller sit side by side, looking like ancient chubby little dwarfs at least fifty years old, and not much bigger than I am. Their desk is lit by a little lamp with a green glass shade. This is where the business of Stoller's is conducted, where they check over the comics that you bring in to trade, or where you pay outright for the used comics or books that you want to buy. Although the Stollers look odd, no one would dream of making fun of them, not because you don't want to loose your comic trading privileges, but because they are fair and honest, and especially because they are nice to all the kids who come here.

A new comic costs ten cents at the regular magazine stores. But Stoller's has used comics, which you can buy for a nickel each, or you can trade two of your comics for one of theirs. The used comics are on four long tables: one has only love and romance comics, one has funny ones, one has crime and horror, and another has beat up comics. You start a trade by bringing your stack of comics up to the desk where Mr. or Mrs. Stoller will flip through the pages of each one to make sure there aren't any torn or missing pages. Sometimes they don't notice a missing page, and will count that comic as a good one. I always feel a little ashamed when that happens, but I usually just bite my tongue and keep quiet. I don't have to confess the torn comics, because it's not a sin if you didn't actually lie about it. After checking, they will say something like: "You can take three comics from table one, and two from table two." If you brought in love comics, you can choose only from the love table. I never get any of those because they're just plain dumb. And I never get any of the horror comics because Mama would throw a fit if I brought one home. But I do read them every chance I get when I'm at one of my friends who has those kind of comics.

Mama is interested in regular books, not comic books, and she picks out only the really hard to read ones. Her book reading started when she met with Sister Providentia after class one day when I was in the fifth grade. *I want to be educated,* Mama had said, *would you please teach me?* She told Sister that she had only gone up to the sixth grade. It was then that Sister Providentia started Mama on a reading program. Mama came to school on one day every week, and met with Sister for an hour after our classes. At first Sister started her on the books that we use in the sixth or seventh grade. But after a while, she said that she needed to get Mama into harder books, like the ones they read in high school and even in college. After that Mama started to bring home all kinds of hard books on every subject you can imagine. You can hardly pronounce the titles of some of them, and most of them sound boring, like *Plutarch's Lives,* and *Plato's Republic,* and *Confessions of Saint Augustine.*

Mama has been coming to Stoller's ever since she got started with Sister Providentia. She likes to come with me since I got my Radio Flyer, because now she can bring home a big stack in the wagon. Sometimes she brings in the old books from home that she has already read, and trades them in for some others.

She started working crossword puzzles soon after she started working with Sister Providentia. Mama says it helps her vocabulary. She bought herself a Webster's Dictionary, which she keeps in the kitchen next to the table, and by now the pages are all worn and dog-eared. At first she did only the easy puzzles that are in the daily *Detroit News*. Then she started on the really hard ones in the Sunday paper. Those puzzles don't have any black boxes at all, and you have to figure out where to put them.

Lately Mama has been using big words, and sometimes she pronounces words in a fancy way, like when she says ha-where and ha-what, because she says you should pronounce the *H*'s.

Mama goes up to Stoller's desk and plunks down a stack of books. She has picked out *Selected Works of William Shakespeare, History of Western Civilization*, and *How Green Was My Valley*. Mrs. Stoller looks inside the front cover of each book to determine the price. "This one is seventy five cents, fifty cents for this one, and forty cents here," she mumbles as she goes through the books, "that comes to a dollar sixty five." Mama pulls out her change purse, peels out two bills, and hands them to Mrs. Stoller. I have traded some comics for others: Batman, Superman, Plasticman, and Captain Marvel. Helen has traded her comics for Little Lulu, Donald Duck, and Mickey Mouse.

Outside, we load up the wagon with Mama's books and our comics. Mama sings a song under her breath as she walks ahead of me, holding hands with Helen, to our home on Brinket Street. I follow pulling our important load in my Radio Flyer that all the people passing by can admire.

16.

The New Palace

At the end of the summer, Daddy finds us a new house. Daddy, Uncle Bill and Aunt Mary, and Dolly and Joe Crackiola load stuff into the truck that Uncle Bill borrowed for our move from Brinket Street. Mama says that our new house is furnished, so we leave some things for the Saint Vincent de Paul, like our junky, old couch.

I look around the old house, in our bedroom at my bed where I played tunes on the brass bars of the headboard, in the living room at the metal furnace that warmed me in the cold winters, at the place beside the couch where Daddy would sleep on the floor, then in the kitchen with its cast iron stove where Mama would make glass animals in the hot coals, and finally in the bathroom where Mama had kept the chicken. I take one last look outside at the dirt yard, remembering the many failures I had trying to grow grass from tufts I brought in and planted, and in back of the house where Mama set up our laundry tubs for swimming. Next to the alley is the rickety old coal shed where I did my coal chores in the winters, and where we built the fort in the summers. Just beyond the alley is the grassy place where I would lie in the early mornings to listen to the morning doves and chirpy birds before anyone else got up. I run over to Holcomb street to say good-bye to my friend Raymond and to Mr. and Mrs. Fochey. I'm going to miss this place. But that won't last long, because we're going to move into a fancy furnished palace on Pennsylvania Street.

The ride to Pennsylvania Street is just a few blocks down Kercheval from Brinket. Our new house looks like a mansion from the outside. It is mostly brick with some white trim, and has a set of steps leading to a big porch that goes all across the front of the house, just like Grammy's house. There is a door at each end of the porch. One is for our house; the other is for the people who live in the flat upstairs.

Daddy opens the front door, and we run inside to a magic fairyland filled almost from floor to ceiling with the most wonderful things, and with a cleared path running from room to room. The first room, after we pass through a small side hall, is the living room, which is piled with boxes nearly to the ceiling. Against one wall is a giant upright piano that we can barely get to because of all the stuff piled around it. There are tall columns of books stacked around the piano. I open one of them to discover that it is a medical book, as are the other books in this stack. Kathleen and Helen join me in shouting our glee and amazement about our new home. Helen tries out the piano to discover that it actually works, making thunderous low booms and piercing high clinks. Daddy shushes her, saying it will bother Mama.

The next room is the dining room with a big table heaped high with bottles of pills and other medicines. Against one wall are straw hats forming a sloping mountain from the floor right up to the ceiling. One wall of the dining room has two doors, each going to a bedroom. The other wall has a large bay of windows with a seat filling in the space across the bay. There is no hope of opening the lid on the window seat to see what is inside because of all the stuff piled on it.

Two bedrooms are off the dining room, and, like everywhere else, it is piled with a thousand boxes on the floor, and stuff piled in great heaps on the dressers and chest of drawers. "This room will be for Daddy and me," says Mama, pointing to the first room, "and that one will be for the girls,' and she points to the other room.

After the dining room is a large kitchen that has spaces without piled-up stuff, so that you can just barely get to the sink on one wall, and to the cabinets lining another wall. The sink is large, with two faucets, one marked *H* for hot, and the other *C* for cold. Could this place actually have hot water? There are two doors next to the cabinets. One goes to a bathroom, and inside is the most wonderful thing of all—a lovely white bathtub, just like Grammy's, on little feet that look like closed fists, with two faucets—one for hot, and one for cold. I can't believe the luxury of this place. Baths in Mama's laundry tubs will be a thing of the past from now on.

The door next to the bathroom leads to a bedroom. "This will be your bedroom," Mama says. "The other one off the dining room will be for Kathleen and Helen." I stare in awe at my new bedroom—just for me, without any sisters to bother me. Like the other rooms, it has boxes stacked on boxes, but the bed is mostly free of litter. There is a chest of drawers and a door to a closet against one wall. And most wonderfully, there is a writing desk with a sloping lid on hinges. When I pull the lid open, it becomes a writing surface, and inside there are little compartments and drawers. Right in the middle of the opened desk is a human skull. It looks like the top part of the head has a cut around it. I pull off the top of the skull to discover a pair of gloves inside. I know that I am going to like this place.

At the other end of the kitchen is a short hallway that leads to a back door, and to another door that has a set of stairs leading to a basement that can be lit up by flipping a light switch at the top of the stairs. We tip-toe down the stairs, not knowing what spooks or crazy killers may be lurking down there. At the bottom of the stairs is a huge room so packed with stuff that it makes the upstairs look empty. Lining all the walls, for the full length of the basement are wide shelves packed solid with cardboard boxes, cigar boxes, metal pans, clothes, hats, and every imaginable item. But there is no way that you can get to the shelves, because the floor is packed solid with fairly big items, like bird cages, a wash machine, motors, a Victrola, and millinery forms. Hung from the ceiling are more bird cages, old lanterns, and other items. There is a narrow path that lets you go to certain critical parts of the basement like wash tubs in front, and a coal furnace in the back. Next to the furnace is a gas water heater, which would explain the hot water taps upstairs. At the very back of the basement is a coal room that has a little metal door going to the outside for coal deliveries.

That night I go to bed in my own bedroom in a palace on Pennsylvania Street, but I can't sleep for a long time. I keep thinking of treasures yet to be discovered, of my own special bedroom with my own writing desk with a human skull inside, of the ways that I can use this desk for homework, drawing cartoons, and writing about my chemistry experiments. We are surely going to be the happiest family that ever lived.

17.

Treasure Hunts

We have been cleaning up our new house on Pennsylvania Street for three months now, and the place is starting to appear livable. It's so sad that the piano is gone. Daddy said it would just make too much noise, and nobody could play it anyhow.

The house used to be owned by the Hall brothers, who lived here with their mother. One brother was a doctor; the other a dentist. After their mother died, the brothers slowly went crazy. They began collecting things, and became hooked on nutrition. Towards the end they would eat only vitamins and pills, and they finally both starved to death. They left an estate without a will.

After the last Hall brother died, their relatives had to figure out how to divide up their estate. Charley Earl, who Daddy knows from the Holy Name Society, is a lawyer for the Hall estate. He said we can live here for two months free of rent if we cleaned it up ourselves, and we can keep anything in the house we want. But Mama says that if we find anything really valuable, we have to save it for the estate. The valuable things we put in one section of the garage out back, which Mama keeps locked and forbids us to go into; the other section of the garage we can use. She decided that the medical books are valuable, and these have been put out back. Before the books were put away, I spent hours searching through them, looking at all the pictures of people with strange diseases that I never knew even existed. When Mama wasn't looking, I found pictures of naked people. I really miss all these medical books, and sometimes I look through the window of the garage and dream about the stacks of books inside, and the people with their strange diseases.

The first thing we do to clean up is to throw out the heaps of stuff on top of the tables, which is mostly vitamins and medicines. Then we throw out all the food stored in the kitchen cupboard and basement pantry, including boxes and canisters of grains and flour full of worms, and cans that are so old that some are puffed out like they are going to explode. Even Daddy joins in on the cleaning and sorting after he comes home from work.

After that the cleaning process gets slower. Mama assigns us each a box to go through when we get home from school. She tells us to look through the stuff in the box, to throw out what is no good, to put in one box what is good but not valuable, and in another box what is good and valuable, such as all the doctor's and dentist's instruments. To sort out my assigned box, I have to think carefully about everything.

A strange looking device has a handle sticking up that you hit and it springs back.

"What's this?" I ask Mama.

"That's a cherry pitting machine."

"Is it good to keep?"

"Yes, we will save that."

I find another machine with a hand crank. "What's this?"

"That's an apple peeling machine."

"Should we keep it?"

And so it goes. I find a toy machine gun that shoots fire from a flint. This one I decide to keep for myself. Helen finds some old dolls, which she decides to keep. Kathleen finds a stereoscope viewer and a box of pictures that go in the viewer. Each picture has two scenes, one for each eye. When you look in the viewer, you see mountains and canyons as if you are right there. We put the throw-away boxes in the alley. The sheeny man comes by every day with his horse-drawn cart rather than just once a week as usual to sort through the trash we put behind the garage.

Downstairs there are boxes full of wax sheets separated by fine paper. Mama says these are for making dental impressions. I discover that this wax is great for all kinds of experiments and games. I can melt it to make different shapes, candles, or cover things with it. I form some hollow wax balls, fill them with water, seal up the holes, and bury them in the back yard in a tin box along with some other things. Next year I'll dig them up to see if it is possible to keep water for a whole year this way.

One of the things that Mama has saved for herself is the washing machine. This one has a motorized wringer instead of the crank wringer she used on Brinket Street. She says the wringer has a safety feature so that if your hair or arm gets caught, you hit a release lever on top, and the wringer will pop open. This information has given me nightmares where Mama's arm gets caught in the wringer, but she can't quite reach the release lever.

We have cleared enough stuff from the basement so that we can get from one end to the other. At the very end of the basement is a window that leads to a opening under the porch, which is sealed off from the outside by lattice work. You can see out through the lattice holes, but you can't be seen from outside. Sometimes I hide there, waiting for someone to come by on the sidewalk. "Hello mister" I call out to a passer-by, who stops and makes a bewildered look around, wondering if he is hearing ghosts.

The Bartons live upstairs. Mr. Barton has a cocker spaniel named Jiggsie who lives under the back porch on a short chain. No one ever comes down to play with him, or to clean up his poop, which is all around him in white cigars that have been drying for months. Mr. Barton told me that he got Jiggsie for hunting. He says that he will give him one trial hunt, and will shoot him if he fails. I often sit under the porch with Jiggsie in a place where I have brushed aside the poop. I try to explain to him that he has to do a good job of hunting. Sometimes I just sit with him, scratching behind his ear, without even speaking. I think that I am the only friend that Jiggsie has.

Mr. Barton is really mean. Once Mrs. Barton invited me to come upstairs with her. There was Mr. Barton in the kitchen, holding his baby grandson upside down by his foot. He held a lit cigarette just an inch away from the baby's bare foot. The baby was screaming and his mother started to scream as did Mrs. Barton, but no one made a move to stop Mr. Barton, who was making a high-pitched laugh. I ran down the stairs and I will never go up there again.

A great thing about our new home is that we are only four blocks from school, and on nice days we can roller skate all the way to school without having to cross any busy streets. We use roller skates with steel wheels that we clamp to our shoes. Me, Kathleen, and Helen skate down the middle of the street because the side walk has too many cracks. The last block is down hill, which we coast at high speeds. At school, I hang my skates in the coatroom behind the black board in front of our sixth grade class room.

While treasure hunting in the basement, I find some glass tubes as big around as my finger and about a foot long. It doesn't take long to figure out that I can shoot spitballs made from wadded up toilet paper soaked in water, and I can shoot these really far from the open window of the girl's bedroom. Helen comes in, and watches me plaster a spit ball on the back of the real estate office across the alley way that separates the side of our house from the backs of the businesses on Kercheval.

"Let me play too."

"Here, Helen. Take this tube, and do like I do."

Splat! One of her spit balls hits the brick. Spat! Another hits the window. Pretty soon she is almost as accurate as I am. We play that you get one point each time you hit the window. After about a half hour the window is plastered with spit balls from top to bottom, with lots more spitballs stuck on the window frame and the side of the building. We get tired of this game, and leave her bedroom.

A little while later Mama calls out to me from Helen's bedroom: "John Patrick Reilly, come in here."

I go into the bedroom to see her pointing out the window in the direction of the real estate office. "What's the meaning of this?"

"It's nothin', Mama. Helen and I were having a spit ball contest. It was her idea," I say, thinking this response is perfectly logical being as this all occurred from her bedroom window.

I expect that I am in for some big punishment. But Mama doesn't say anything. She just marches out of the bedroom with a determined look on her face. Next thing I see her stride across the alley with a bucket, rags, and a window squeegee, wearing a bandanna on her head with little rabbit ears where it is tied at her forehead. Then she cleans the window from the outside, as well as the side of the building. After that she goes in the back door of the office, comes out after a while, and marches across the alley back to our house.

"What did the people say?" I ask.

"Nothing, really," she says, laughing. "I cleaned the inside windows too. They just thought that I was the cleaning lady." Helen and I join Mama with laughter, and I'm thinking: *No punishment. Hey, this is great! I'm going to love living here in our palace on Pennsylvania Street.*

Helen (age 10) at White Fish Lake (approx. 1949).

18.

An Argument

They moved to the farm where life is hard. The family grows with two more Zalut children: Anna, now eight years old; Joseph, six; Stanley, three; Joan, two; and Lilly, six months. The Rogozas are: Mary, sixteen; Dominik, fifteen; Stella, thirteen; and Helen, twelve. Helen's job is to care for the toddlers with diapers, feeding, laundry, and she loves to do it. She loves to feed the chickens and the rabbits too. But, like all her brothers and sisters, she has to watch out for Ma's stick. And if a stick isn't handy, it will be Ma's hand or fist, or whatever is in her hand. Helen gets a beating for being slow on her chores, for talking back, for asking questions, for arguing with her brothers and sisters, for getting up late, for forgetting to bring in the water from the pump outside, for not correctly hanging up the laundry, for wanting to read her book when she is supposed to be doing her chores.

She hears his footsteps as she hides behind the door. She knows what he wants. He's going to take her out to the shed to play piggy game—this little piggy went to market, this little piggy stayed home. It's a game—not a sin, he had said; you don't have to confess it. But the nuns said your body is the temple of the Holy Ghost. Had she been defiling it? If not, then why does Jesus stick in her throat when she receives Holy Communion?

*   *   *   *

Now that we're in our new house, everything is supposed to be better. But Daddy still goes to Glick's, and he still pukes in the mornings. Mama still has her attacks, and she and Daddy keep arguing. One night angry shouting wakes me.

"Don't you dare touch me, Jack."

"Damn you Julie, that's what married people are supposed to do."

The voices pull me into the kitchen, where I get a good view of Mama and Daddy in the dining room. Mama is in her night gown, facing me, holding a crucifix before herself, like the woman in the movies who keeps Dracula from biting her. Daddy stands in front of her, shaking his fist in the air.

"Damn you Julie! I ought to teach you a lesson."

"Don't you dare Jack. Holy mother, protect me. *Hail Mary, full of grace, the Lord is with thee. Blessed art thou amongst women* ...."

Before Mama can finish the *Hail Mary*, Kathleen comes out of her bedroom. Mama turns first to see her, then me. She lets the crucifix go down, while Daddy brings down his fist to his side and turns toward me, showing his red, sweaty face with the vein popping out on his forehead.

"Go to bed, children," Mama says, her voice suddenly calm. "I'll be all right." Daddy's angry mouth turns slack, and he turns and walks into his bedroom. After I go back to bed, there's no more screaming. I think I saved Mama this time.

The next day me, Kathleen, and Helen talk about what happened. "I was afraid Daddy was going to kill Mama," I say.

"I wish she would have hit him with that damn crucifix," says Kathleen. She'll have to go to confession for that!

"I don't like it when they fight so much, and I'm afraid that Daddy might hurt Mama, or that he would make her run away like he once did," Helen says.

"But that doesn't happen, and he never actually hits Mama," says Kathleen. "And she stays here to take care of us."

We try to figure out what to do to make things better. "We should each pray a rosary," offers Kathleen. "That might change Daddy."

The next day after school I stop in Annunciation Church. I go to the statue of the Sacred Heart, my special statue, just like the one

I rescued from a trash heap in the alley, the one that shows Jesus' burning heart outside his chest, and him pointing to it. I put in a whole quarter into the money slot, hear a loud clink that tells me my quarter has found its way to the money box, and I light a big candle—one that will burn for a whole week. I kneel and pray a rosary for Mama and Daddy, one that will surely count in heaven, because I'm saying it with all my heart to the Sacred Heart in Annunciation Church, and with a lit twenty-five-cent candle.

19.

The Musician

The Boy Scouts are the greatest thing of my entire life. We wear uniforms like soldiers, display our awards and medals, recite oaths and laws, march around, play games, and do all sorts of indoor and outdoor activities. I love the secret ceremony with candles and solemn oaths when I get inducted as a *Tenderfoot*. I love the camp out in Canada where we buy fireworks and sit around a giant fire at night and tell stories. I love the Klondike derby where we make a musher's dog sled, and pull it through Belle Isle, stopping at different stations where we compete in tests, like shooting a gun, cooking, estimating the height of a tree or the width of a river, and demonstrating first aid skills.

Mr. Rouse, our scoutmaster, talks to me and acts like he really likes me. He teaches me about wood lore, about first aid, about being a good scout, about being a good citizen.

The troop owns an old dented bugle that the boys play with at the meetings. Like the other Scouts, I can get a tooting sound, but not much else. The bugle draws me again and again, and I can't resist blowing it. Mr. Rouse notices my interest.

"Would you like to take it home and learn to play it, Pat?"

"But I don't know how to do anything but make some blapping sounds."

"Why don't you go to the library and take out a bugling merit badge book. I'll give you the name of a bugling counselor who can teach you, and later test you for a merit badge. And why don't we keep this a secret, until you learn to play. Then, one fine day, you can play at a ceremony, and we'll surprise the whole troop."

I go to a bugling counselor, who shows me how to read music and produce the notes. After a few weeks, he tests me on my ability to play the various bugle calls: *Taps, To The Colors, Revelry, Officer's Call,* and *Mess Call,* and approves my award of a bugling merit badge. Soon after that, Mr. Rouse holds a ceremony in the school gymnasium to promote someone to Second-Class Scout. At the end of the ceremony, I proudly play Taps while hiding behind the curtains of the stage, cracking half the notes, but still no one in Boy Scout Troop 31 will ever be able to deny that they heard *Taps* this day.

Now that I'm a musician, I use my earnings from the Am-Pee to buy a new plastic harmonica for twenty five cents at the Kresges' five and dime store. But something is wrong when I try playing a scale. Starting on hole number four, I can get a scale one note at a time: *doe-rae-me-fa-so-la-ti-doe.* But starting on hole number one, something is wrong with the scale: *doe-rae-me-so-so-ti-doe,* but *fa* is missing, as well as *la.*

"I want to see the manager," I say to the girl at the cash register, who walks away, and comes back a minute later with a man.

"Did you want to see me?"

I explain how I paid twenty-five cents for this harmonica just this morning, but when I got it home, I found that some notes were broken. "Please Mister, can you give me another one?" I ask, handing him the harmonica.

He looks at the harmonica, turning it over, like he can tell just by looking if it's good or not. He's not going to believe an eleven year old boy. He's going to say that I broke it myself, that I better get home, and not cause any trouble.

"Go ahead, and pick out another one," he says, pointing to the bin of yellow plastic harmonicas. I carefully go over them, looking for the perfect one.

"This one," I say.

As I walk down Kercheval towards home, I try the notes one by one. *Doe-rae-me-so-so-ti-do.* Hey! this one is broken too. There's no way he's going to believe me a second time. Maybe they're all bad. I'll just have to settle for a broken harmonica.

I start blowing in and out on different holes, hoping maybe some tune will jump out. After a while, I think I hear something familiar when I start on hole number four. *Doe-doe-rae-* sounds a little bit like the start of *My Country 'Tis of Thee*. I turn down Pennsylvania, and pass up our house, looking for the next note, playing over and over *doe-doe-rae*. I find the fourth note when I get to Jefferson Street, so that I've got *My-coun-try-'tis*. I turn right at Jefferson, looking for *of-thee*. Two blocks later, the harmonica plays the whole line, *My-coun-try-'tis-of-thee*. Now I look for *sweet-land*.

When I get to the Belle Isle bridge, I turn and cross the Detroit River, then to the Belle Isle zoo, the arboretum, the aquarium, the memorial, and the band shell. When I cross the bridge again, I can play all the way to *My-coun-try-tis-of-thee, sweet-land-of-lib-er-ty*.

Four hours after my second visit to Kresges', I run excitedly into the back door of our house, into the kitchen where the table is set for dinner. Mama looks annoyed. "Where have you been? It's way past supper time."

"Look at what I can do, Mama," I say, ignoring her question. Then I triumphantly play the entire song, note by note.

> *My country 'tis of thee,*
> *Sweet land of liberty,*
> *Of thee I sing.*
> *Land where my fathers died,*
> *Land of the pilgrim's pride,*
> *From every mountain side,*
> *Let freedom ring.*

"Oh! That's so beautiful," says Mama, with a smile that she gets when she's just heard *Oh! Holy Night* at Christmas Mass. "I just know, some day my son is going to be a great musician."

Now I know what I want to be when I grow up: A scientist, a cartoonist, *and* a musician, and nobody can tell me that I can't be everything.

Pat (age 12) plays the bugle at boy scout camp.

20.

Dry Ice

At recess, up Parkview a block from school, Frankie, Norman, and Dave crowd around Howard, staring intently at something he's holding. If Howard has something, it has to be cool. He's always the first to get all the really neat stuff, like a Captain Midnight atomic ring, or a Sergeant Preston decoder badge. He knows lots more than most of the kids in our sixth-grade class, even though he's usually stuck in the back with the other boys who are never called on to answer questions or give recitations. He's traveled to Chicago—that's in another state. He's seen what's inside a girl's blouse, and I'm talking about a girl with developments. He can make stuff that blows up with his chemistry set. He has a big stack of horror comic books. And he can do this great trick where he pushes out his two false front teeth that he got after breaking his own teeth during a basketball game. If Howard has something that the others want to see, it's something neat.

I push my head into the ring of boys to see Howard holding something in a cloth wrapper.

"Look at what I've got," he says.

On the cloth is a lump of white material that looks frosty in a magical sort of way. A misty vapor rises from it.

"What is it?"

"It's dry ice. It's very cold. You can freeze anything with it. You can even freeze a grape solid, and break it like a piece of glass."

"Where did you get it?"

"The ice cream man. I got it from him."

I decide that I must get of a piece of dry ice. I want to experiment with it—to freeze a grape, to freeze a bug, to find out what it can do.

The next day after recess, I go to the place where the ice cream man usually comes on warm days. He stands next to his cart, which is attached to the front half of a bicycle. I hold out a nickel.

"I want to buy a piece of dry ice."

He looks at me like he's going to say no. He'll say that dry ice is no thing for a boy. It's too special for the likes of me. But instead of saying anything, he lifts the lid of his cart and pulls out a small lump with a piece of paper. It looks just like the one that Howard had.

"You can't touch it," he says. "You have to wrap it in a cloth. If you touch it, it will burn you. Do you have something to wrap it in?"

I hold out my handkerchief, and he places the lump there.

"You don't owe me anything," he says. "Just be careful".

I walk back to school holding a great treasure—something magical. After school, I will find out what this can do. I fold the handkerchief around the lump, put it in my pocket, and go back to school.

The class after recess is history. Sister John Marie goes on about something really boring. She slowly makes her way up one of the rows of desks, wheezing like she is going to die at any moment. My thoughts are on the treasure in my pocket. After a while, my pocket starts to get really cold. Then my leg begins to feel more than just cold—it's starting to hurt. I remember the warning of the ice cream man—this thing will burn my leg.

I pull the handkerchief out and unwrap a lump that is smaller than the one the ice cream man gave me, and place it on my desk. Sister John Marie keeps talking and moving up and down the rows of desks. Soon she will come to my desk, and she will see the strange white lump and I will be in trouble for bringing it to school. I look around to see if there's some way to ditch this thing. The waste paper basket is way in front of the room—no way to get to that. But here is an obvious solution, right on my desk—my inkwell just sitting there in its hole on the front of the desk. I pop the lump into the ink well.

Now something strange starts to happen. A trail of white smoke rises out of the ink well like a miniature volcano. Sister will kill me when she sees this. But there is a way to fix this problem. There, next to the inkwell is the cork that caps it up. I quickly place the cork over the hole. At first, everything is fine. But then something really weird starts to happen. The cork starts to rise. I push it back down, but it just rises again. Ink starts to spatter out onto the desk from around the cork, as though there's air pressure inside the ink bottle. The ink makes little spattery designs all over my desk. This is really going to get me into big trouble. I pull out my handkerchief and wipe the ink spatters, but that just smears the ink around, making a bigger mess. Things are getting worse now. I feel the force of Sister John Marie's stare behind me.

"Patrick, what in heaven's name are you doing?" she demands.

Now the cork has popped out of the bottle, and the smoke is rising again.

"It's just dry ice in my inkwell, Sister," I say in my most nonchalant voice.

Sister John Marie gives me a stern lecture. Telling me how I have to have more respect for the school. What a bad boy I am. She writes out a note, folds it up, and gives it to me.

"Take this to Sister Alma's room. You are going to stay there for the rest of the day."

I know what this means, because it has happened before. Sister Alma teaches the seventh-grade class that my sister Kathleen is in—one grade ahead of me. I would rather be whacked, like some of the sisters do to us boys. I would rather be sent to spend an hour in the coat room like we are sometimes punished. There is only one humiliation greater than to be made to sit with the girls. It is being made to sit with your sister in the older kids' class.

At Sister Alma's class the door is closed. I knock lightly, hoping that no one will hear. Sister Alma opens the door and I hand her the note. She reads it and tells me to come into the class of bigger kids. There is a section for boys on the left, and a section for girls on the right, just like in our classroom. I scan the rows of girls, and meet Kathleen's gaze. She is staring daggers at me.

"You'll have to sit with your sister," Sister Alma says.

I walk along the rows of desks to where Kathleen sits. The seats are wide enough for me to slide in alongside her. She clenches her teeth and speaks in a whisper without moving her lips.

"Just wait till we get home. I'm telling Mama."

After school Kathleen runs ahead, but I walk slowly home. Maybe Mama will forget what Kathleen tells her by the time I get there.

When I get there, Mama asks what happened. I tell her about the dry ice. I tell her how much I wanted to experiment with it. How everything went wrong. How I tried to fix things, but they got worse.

"Some day you'll be a great scientist, I just know it." she says. "Just don't do anything foolish like this again and get yourself in trouble."

I assure her that I will never do that again. But Mama doesn't realize how many different ways there are to get into trouble.

It's my second week in Sister John Marie's class. She wheezes and gurgles as she goes on and on about something so boring that my mind goes everywhere else. I try experimenting with my ruler and a rubber band. I hook the rubber band around my finger, and then put the ruler in the loop. I pull down the ruler and grip it in my hand. When I relax my grip, the ruler springs out like an arrow from a bow, but by tightening my grip, I stop the ruler before it springs away. It is wonderful to feel the ruler slip through my hand, like it is a Buck Rogers rocket, and to see how perfectly I can stop it dead just as it is about to fly away. Well, not quite perfectly. I misjudge, and the ruler gets away from me, shoots down the aisle, and clatters to the floor in front of her desk. She stops talking and glares in my direction. The whole class is so quiet that you could hear a pin drop.

"Who did that?' she says angrily, looking up and down my row.

"I'm sorry sister, it was an accident," I try to explain. I can't tell her about the Buck Rogers' rocket, and how beautiful it all is.

"Bring that up here, young man," she says.

I pick up the ruler, go to her desk in front of the class, and hand it to her. "Put out your hand," she demands.

I stretch my right hand out flat. Then she begins to hit me with the ruler. Whack! Whack! Whack! Whack! Again and again. It seems like the hitting will never stop. Still I hold my hand out, afraid that if I pull it away, she will swing the ruler past my missing hand and hit herself, and I will be in even bigger trouble. Whack! Whack! The ruler keeps coming. I want to cry, to scream, but I hold it back. Just when I don't think I can take it any more, just when I think I will have to pull my hand away, the hitting stops. She seems to be trying to catch her breath, gurgling and wheezing, her face red and sweaty.

"I'm sorry I'm not healthier," she says. "I wish I had the strength to hurt you, but I just can't. Go back to your seat." As I go back to my seat, I look at my red, swollen hand, still stinging with pain. I blink to keep any tears from showing, to avoid a terrible humiliation—crying in front of class.

A few days later, just when I think the sixth grade is going to be the worst time of my entire life, Sister Providentia shows up. "I'm taking over the class for a while," she says. "We'll all have to pray for Sister John Marie, who is very ill."

That is my happiest day at Annunciation School, because Sister Providentia is my all time favorite nun. She's the one who has been tutoring Mama—the one I had in the fourth grade. She never hits anyone, and is always kind. But best of all, she told Mama she loves me. She said that even when I cause trouble, like when I brought a bottle of water in my pocket to drink during class and she thought it was medicine, or when I got around the no-candy rule by chewing during class on the toothpicks that I had soaked in peppermint extract, she doesn't think I am bad. She even likes the cartoons that I draw on the edges of my homework. "I love your son," she told Mama. "I think he's a fine and creative boy. With the right encouragement, he will go far." Still, I never got really good grades from her, mostly *B*s and Cs.

Sister John Marie doesn't came back, and I'm in heaven because we have Sister Providentia every day.

21.

A Pilgrimage

Dog's blood! Dog's blood — Cholera! Ma curses in Polish at Helen Rogoza, who cowers against the wall. You dirty bitch! Ma grabs her by the hair with one hand, slapping her face with the free hand. Helen wiggles away and runs to the other side of the room, her eyes wide with terror. Ma picks up the plate of butter from the table and throws it at Helen, but it misses and smashes against the wall. Ma grabs her by the hair again and turns her head to the wall. Look at what you've done, you filthy whore. Helen looks in horror at the creamy blob oozing down the wall. Ever since Helen told Ma the secret, the one he told her never to tell, the beatings have become more frequent and more fierce. When Ma is finished beating her, Helen will have to clean up the broken dishes and wash the butter off the wall. Then she can get to the laundry and her other chores.

*   *   *   *

In the spring, while I'm still in the sixth grade, Mama announces that she is going on a pilgrimage in Canada with Mrs. Wagner and Mrs. O'Brian to search for stigmatics. Stigmatics are holy people who relive the crucifixion of Jesus, and they are Mama's latest thrill in life. She goes nuts not just over stigmatics, but over anything from the One, Holy, Catholic and Apostolic Church: lighting candles before the statue of the Mother of Perpetual help, lighting candles before the statue of the Sacred Heart, scapulars, holy cards, holy water, holy people, holy medals, holy days of obligation, the days when you're not obliged but go to Mass anyway, novenas, evening devotions, confessions to Father O'Hara, long conferences with Father Snider and Father Mark, churches, cathedrals, the saints, the blesseds who are waiting to become saints, rosaries, sermons, indulgences, prayers, and prayer books.

"I'll be gone for two weeks, and Kathleen will be in charge of the cooking and the house while Daddy's away at work." Mama doesn't know what she's doing to us. Kathleen's cooking is so bad that I'd rather starve than eat it, and she's so bossy that we will never be able to shut her up if she thinks she's in charge. And Mama doesn't know how the three of us fight when we're left alone. Me and Helen put up a big fuss, but Mama says, "She's the oldest, thirteen years old, and plenty capable of taking care of the house." I look over at Kathleen, who sticks her nose up in the air, and puts on a phony smile.

On Saturday Mama has her suitcase packed; Daddy carries it outside and loads it in the trunk of the car. After the car is out of sight, I look over at Kathleen.

"Now I'm the boss," she says.

"You're not the boss. I don't have to take orders from you," I say.

"You heard Mama. I'm in charge, and what I say goes."

Then Helen joins in. "You're not my mother. I don't care what you say."

"You shut up," says Kathleen, who gives a shove to Helen. Then Helen shoves her back, and Kathleen again shoves Helen, who falls against me. So I give a shove to Kathleen. Pretty soon the three of us are shoving and slapping, and shouting insults.

By the time Daddy comes back, everything is calm. We don't tell him about our fight.

That night Kathleen makes macaroni and cheese, and it tastes yucky, just as I knew it would.

In the next days we get post cards from Mama showing pictures of cathedrals in Canada, and Mama writes notes about these wonderful holy places. Kathleen stays bossy and keeps cooking those lousy meals..

In two weeks Mama comes home all excited. She asks us to join her at the kitchen table—me, Kathleen, Helen, and Daddy too. She snaps open her suitcase, and starts pulling out pictures and brochures and telling us about all the cathedrals and churches she went to in Montreal, Quebec City, and other places in Canada. Then she starts her tale about the stigmatics she visited.

"Just outside of Quebec City was a holy woman, Madame Marie St. Clair. She knew just exactly when the stigmata would come to her; it always came at the same time and on the same day. There were probably twelve people crowded into her bedroom. She was laying in her bed, at first looking peaceful, almost asleep. Then the stigmata started. Madame Marie called out with every whip lash that Jesus got. She moaned in agony when they put the crown of thorns on his head, and again when Jesus fell on the ground. But the most terrible part came when they put the nails in the hands of Jesus. Her screams filled the whole room, and that's when blood came to her hands, right where the nails were hammered. I saw it with my own eyes. She opened her hands, and they were covered with blood, and there was an ugly nail wound right in the center of each palm And she cried out like this." And with that, Mama holds out her hands, with the palms pointing to heaven, and she lets out a horrible moan, one that is a million times worse than the howl of the wolf-man in the movies, and it gives me the most terrible scare.

Mama talks on and on, and none of us can even speak, because the stories are so amazing, and frightening too. She tells us how Madame Marie finally became exhausted, and all the pilgrims had to leave the room, how they prayed the rosary together. And before they left, everyone made a generous contribution to Madame Marie so she could spread God's holy word.

Madame Marie wasn't the only stigmatic they saw. There was Blessed Pierre in Trois Rivers, who carried the marks of the nail wounds in his hands, and when he received the stigmata, the blood would appear not only on his hands, but on his forehead, where the crown of thorns was placed on the head of Jesus. They saw a third stigmatic just outside of Saint Anne de Beaupré, a marvelous cathedral, and I wonder why it is that the Canadians get all the stigmatics and fancy cathedrals.

I think that Mama's trip to see all the holy people and places should have cured her sickness, should have made her more peaceful. But it doesn't happen that way. Soon after her return, she becomes angry, talking day after day of sin and eternal damnation. She explodes into a rage if anyone steps out of line. She smashes dishes on the kitchen floor. Then comes another attack.

22.

The Will

Near the end of the school year Mama and Daddy sit at the kitchen table, drinking coffee and talking about a very important paper: a will from Ahntie Reet who died last March, just before my twelfth birthday. I'm sitting at the dining room table, drawing cartoons and minding my own business while I listen to what they're saying. After Ahntie Reet died, her lawyers sat around with some of the family and had a reading of her will. Most of her money went to Grammy, and Lala got a thousand dollars. Her will said that if Grammy was dead, then a big chunk of her money was supposed to go to Uncle Eddie. Her house, furniture, and diamonds went to our aunt Baby Helen. Ahntie Reet was true to her word on that one. She had told Baby Helen that if she stayed loyal to her and didn't marry, she would get her house and diamonds when she died. Uncle Phil could live in the house until he died.

Included in the will was something that bothered Daddy a lot: *And to my worthless nephew Jack, I leave nothing.* Mama says that Daddy once sassed her, so she cut him out of her will.

"I don't care, Jack, if you don't get a cent of her money," Mama says. "You don't have to kow-tow to anybody, rich or poor."

I don't know why he sassed her. Everybody else always acted like she was the Queen of England, and you had to be all respectful because she had millions of dollars stashed around, and you didn't want to get cut out of her will. I'm glad daddy didn't kow-tow for Ahntie Reet's money.

23.

Kathleen Gets Ruined

As Mama and I are leaving from evening devotions at Annunciation Church, she spots a girl wearing a long white dress and a little veil. This is something that always turns Mama's head—a girl wearing what looks like a nun's outfit. Mama has to embarrass me by going up to her, and getting all sentimental over her outfit, like she just got a visit by the Holy Mother herself. The girl tells Mama that she is a student in the Saint Francis missionary order in Wisconsin, in training to become a full-fledged nun. She says that their order takes on young girls who go to school there as aspirants. I know all this impresses Mama, who feels that there is only one honor in a family greater than having a daughter become a nun, and that is having a son become a priest. Since I'm not interested in becoming a priest, Kathleen becoming a nun looks like a good bet for Mama. And she probably hopes that Kathleen might learn the meaning of obedience and humility as a bonus.

Mama writes to the order, and after a while an envelope shows up with information about the Saint Francis Order and an application form to enter school there. She fills out the form, and Kathleen writes a paragraph on why she wants to become a nun, saying all kinds of pious gobeldy gook, like she wants to save souls for Jesus in the remote corners of the earth. But when Mama's not around, Kathleen tells me the real reason she wants to become an nun,

"It's because of Tarzan. In the movies he swings on vines, and has great adventures in Africa. He has a woman friend named Jane who he is always saving from some danger. Most boys probably dream of swinging on the vines like Tarzan, while the girls want to be like Jane. But not me. I want to be like Tarzan, not a wimp like Jane. I know that my only chance to get to Africa and swing on vines is to become a missionary nun."

Mama makes a novena to try to persuade the Holy Mother to ask God to tell the head nun in the convent to take Kathleen. A few weeks later Kathleen gets a reply that she is accepted and could start school there in the fall. This news makes everybody happy, including Mama, who knows the power of a novena, and especially me, since I am glad to get rid of Kathleen, who has been getting awfully bossy.

At the end of August, Kathleen packs a suitcase, and Mama and Daddy take her to the train station for a trip to Chicago, where she is supposed to meet Uncle Frank Impens, Daddy's uncle who none of us had ever seen before, who will drive her to the convent in Milwaukee.

Not long after Kathleen leaves for the convent, Mama gets a letter from her. She says that Mother superior met her when she arrived at the convent, and took her to her assigned room. A few days later, when she was making her schedule for the semester, Mother Superior made a shocking discovery. Kathleen was supposed enter the eighth grade, not the ninth as they had supposed. This was a high school, not a grade school, and they had no classes for grade schoolers.

Kathleen says that rather than send her back to Detroit, Mother Superior got two old retired nuns at the convent to be her private tutors for the eighth grade. When they tested her, they made another surprising discovery—she could read only at the third grade level, and must have been bluffing her way through classes all these years. They said Kathleen would be given a lot of private attention. With this news, Mama says she plans to go to church so she can light a million candles at the statue of the Mother of Perpetual Help, and she will go to Mass every day for a week to thank Our Holy Mother for pulling strings in heaven and getting Kathleen all this special attention.

Two weeks before Christmas Kathleen comes home for a break. I tell her a great joke. "Why did the moron fall off the top of the Empire State Building?"

"I dunno, Why?"

"Because he was smoking a cigarette, and he threw off the wrong butt," I snicker. But instead of the hilarious laughter that I expect, Kathleen purses her lips with a real sourpuss look.

"Shame on you. Don't ever speak in such a dirty way again. That offends God," she scolds. "You should get down on your knees and pray for forgiveness. I hope you'll confess this."

I don't answer, but I go to my room and close the door to think this one over. Kathleen has definitely been ruined since she went into the convent. She's not the same person any more. They have turned her brain into mush, and made her into a prissy holy roller—a goody-goody that I just can't stand anymore. Now Daddy acts like she's Saint Kathleen herself, and he takes her side whenever we have an argument. Even Mama likes her when she gets all preachy, and tells me that I ought to listen to my sister, who is learning God's wisdom, and it would do me some good if I would do the same. I think of all the things me and Kathleen used to do together—like building tree houses in other people's trees, stealing apples from Mrs. Salmoni's tree, ringing door bells and soaping windows on Halloween, going alley picking, climbing the Skeleton Building, almost drowning at Belle Isle, and building forts in Burns Woods.

Kathleen wasn't always so holy, and sometimes she was even a fighter. Like the time she saw three bigger boys pushing me around. She waded into the bunch, and started pushing the leader in the chest, saying, "leave my brother alone or I'll smash your face." Last year when she was in the seventh grade, she stuck up for Marie Theresa, who was getting bullied by Betty and Sally. After that, Betty and Sally began to follow Kathleen home every day after school, calling her names, and making threats. One day after being followed by the two girls, Kathleen stood in her tracks, put her books down, and spun around saying, "let's just have it out here right now." Betty was the one who decided to take her on, slapping and trying to pull her hair the way girls fight. But Kathleen wasn't going to girl-fight. She made a tight fist and punched Betty right in the nose, which started to bleed as Betty sobbed, holding her face in her hands. Then Kathleen said to Sally that now it was her turn. They both ran away, with Betty crying bloody murder. Later Mama got called by Betty's mother, who said that Kathleen was beating up on her poor little girl. Mama talked to Kathleen about the fight, but she refused to apologize and instead said that she would do it again if she got the chance.

Now that Kathleen is so holy, I suppose the next time she would light some candles and say a prayer for the bullies, rather than punch them in the nose when they deserve it. And instead of swinging from vines in Africa, maybe she'll start making novenas and attending evening devotions, like Mama does. There's no doubt about it. Kathleen is definitely ruined.

Mama, Kathleen (14), Pat (12) and Helen (10) at Grammy's house (≈ 1949). Kathleen wears the white dress of an "aspirant" to the Order of St. Francis

24.

A Fight

In the spring I go out for the baseball team, and this gets me into a fight with Frankie. Frankie is eager to fight if he gets mad, so I always to take care to stay away from him. But things come to a head between us one Saturday at a baseball game. It is my turn at bat, but he tells me to sit down, that he is taking my place. I completely surprise myself by standing up to him. "It's my turn," I say, "and I won't give it up." Frankie's face turns red, and he says he will get me for that.

On Monday we're back in school. With every chance he gets, whenever sister isn't looking, Frankie keeps reminding me that he is going to get me after class, and he spreads word around to all his buddies. There is just no way I can get out of this one. As soon as school lets out, Frankie, his buddies, and some of my friends swarm around me. Howard says that the fight is supposed to take place in the alley, two blocks away from school. He knows better than to have a fight near school, being as that could get you into big trouble. I have no choice but to follow the excited bunch to the appointed spot.

Howard, Frankie's buddy from our class, decides to act as referee. "You get to pick the rule to end the fight," he says to me. "Since Frankie challenged you, you get to pick: *First blood, or first one to give!*" Out of my mouth comes "*First blood*," and I don't know why I said it but it sets Frankie's crowd into gleeful shouting, and I wonder if I should have picked the other way, even though it would bring shame on me forever.

So here I am, fighting to first blood. Frankie and I are eyeing each other, fists in the boxing position, doing a slow circling dance within the ring of shouting boys, like two scorpions in a dish, each waiting for the other to try a fatal sting. Howard, Gordy, and Frankie's other friends shout encouragement to him, like *Get him, Frankie!* and *Bust his face!* My friends Joey and Raymond shout encouragement to me, but I'm not sure I like having them here, even if they will make sure this will be a fair fight. I don't want them to see me get beat up, and I'll surely get the worst of this one, being as I'm no fighter.

Don't get me wrong—I have had plenty of fights, but they were always wrestling matches where no one actually got hurt. In a wrestling match, you might get the other guy into a head lock, and squeeze till he says *I give,* and that's the end of that fight. I have always been good at wrestling, and my arms are strong. But I don't know how to fist fight. Maybe if I can somehow get Frankie on the ground, I can make this a wrestling match, rather than a fist fight.

My mouth is dry, and my heart is pounding. How much blood do I have to shed to make it count? And Frankie can surely draw blood. He's tough, and he's a fighter—not afraid of anything, not even death. You can tell that by the games he plays with his boys. He does this trick where he breathes hard while squatting down, and then suddenly stands up, takes a deep breath, and holds it while his buddy who stands behind him grabs him around the chest and squeezes so hard that Frankie's feet come off the floor, making him pass out like a rag doll. After he comes to, they trade places. Frankie and his buddies even do this inside the school when the nuns aren't looking. I told Mama about it, and she said never to try that trick, that you can pass out and never come to, but Frankie and his boys don't worry about that.

Frankie doesn't worry about anything, not even getting slapped by Sister Alma more than anyone in our seventh grade class. Sister Alma is the champion slapper of all the nuns in the school. She hits mostly the boys, sometimes with a single slap across the face, and other times first with the palm, then the back of her hand from one cheek to the other. Once, after an especially long and hard slapping session on Frankie in front of the class, he went back to his seat, his face all red, but he was laughing and looking at his buddies. The first chance that Sister Alma turned her back on him, he stood up and made this motion where he hit his right arm in the crook of the elbow with his left fist, and jerked up his right hand, sticking up the middle finger, making his buddies giggle with delight. I don't know what it means, but I don't think it's nice.

Frankie does other things that take a lot of nerve. Like the time a visiting priest came to our school to conduct a three-day retreat. He did fascinating magic tricks to teach us how to be holy and to stay away from sin. One evening I came back to school after supper for a special session for boys only. Father had the shades pulled, and a film projector set up. We saw a film about a boy who got himself into a lot of trouble by doing foolish things. While the film was going on, the smell of cigarette smoke came drifting around the room, and behind me, where Frankie and his crowd were sitting, was the red glow of a cigarette being passed from one guy to another. Just then, Father saw it too, and he began to shouting angrily, and turned on the lights. But by then the cigarette was nowhere in sight, and Frankie and his boys were snickering and carrying on. This got Father even angrier, and he sent the whole class home without showing the rest of the movie. Only a really tough guy like Frankie would do something like that right there in school.

Frankie feigns a series of jabs at me, and I find that I can easily dodge these by just backing up or stepping to the side. Apparently I am faster on my feet than he is. He tries a few more jabs, but they don't connect either. Finally he lunges at me with a series of wild swings. I spin around to avoid these, and while doing this, I feel something connect with the back of my right hand. I stare in amazement at a red trail of blood oozing from Frankie's nose as he backs up. Howard runs up to him, and puts one arm around him while waving the other, like a referee calling a time out.

"First blood!" he says, "Reilly's got first blood. Fight's over. Come over and shake hands." I go over to Frankie, and grab his hand for a ritual shake.

"Good fight, Frankie," I say, thinking that this is what I'm supposed to say.

"Good fight," replies Frankie.

When I get home Mama asks about my day.

"Nothin' special," I reply. I don't tell her about my fight with Frankie. That could upset her and bring on an attack.

The next morning as I go into school, I see Howard, and I wonder if he's going to get revenge on me. "How're ya doing," Pat, he says, like he's my best friend. And as I go into my seventh grade class, a strange feeling comes over me. I realize that I'm not afraid of Frankie any more, and I'm not afraid of Howard either, or any one else in Annunciation school.

The 7th grade class at Annunciation School. Pat is in the front seat, 2nd row from the right. Frankie is in front of the first row.

25.

Kathleen Gets Defrocked

After I finish the seventh grade, Kathleen comes home from the convent. Too bad, but it's for good. She tells me how she got defrocked—washed out of the convent.

"I had climbed on the arch of the grape arbor that lines the walkway leading from the chapel. I was throwing down clusters of branches with tiny flowers to my friends below. We had completely forgotten that this was the hour for prayer and meditation. But when I looked down to see who would catch another cluster of branches, I discovered that no one was there to receive them—my two friends had suddenly vanished. I crawled to the other side of the arbor to see where they were hiding. Just then, the arbor cracked, and I, arbor, and grape vines fell to the feet of Mother Superior."

"What is the meaning of this?" asked Mother Superior, looking in shock.

"I was just trying to get some flowers for the altar, mother," I told her, as I tried to look dignified while brushing the vines, leaves, and dirt from my dress."

"Kathleen, I want you to clean yourself up, and see me in my office in one hour," said Mother.

"I sat in the waiting room outside Mother Superior's office. She reflected on events of the past few months that had gotten me into so much trouble. There was the incident when I came to prayers soaking wet, for instance. I had tried to explain that I jumped into the pond to save a small boy who had fallen in, but

Mother didn't seem to believe me. And, when I was found in the tree during meditation, I explained that I could get closer to God that way. It seemed that I was spending so much time in punishment, kneeling in chapel with my arms straight out like a crucifix, asking God for forgiveness for an infraction that probably was just a misunderstanding anyway. As I was waiting outside her office, the door opened, and she spoke to me in a very kind voice, not at all mad like I expected."

" 'Come in, my child,' she said, and I walked into her office, with my head bowed piously, and I sat at her invitation."

" 'Kathleen, I have been praying a lot about you lately', Mother said. 'I've been thinking about how much progress you've made in school under the tutelage of Sister Michael John and Sister Francis. And I have been very pleased about your devotion to God, despite some incidents that have gotten you into trouble. But I'm just not sure that this is your vocation. I'm recommending that you go home in the spring, and enroll in your home school. I think you need to pray for God's guidance on his intentions for you.' "

"And that's how I got washed out of the convent," says Kathleen. "And I saw my visions of Africa evaporating, and now I have to reconsider my whole life plan. But I am so grateful to those nuns. Now I can go on as a student who reads at my grade level, and I know history, literature, social studies, and religion as well as any girl at Annunciation's eighth grade graduating class.

26.

Discoveries

I fiddle with an electric bell that I found among the treasures in our home on Pennsylvania Street. I'm trying to hook it to a dry cell battery that I bought for a dollar at the hardware store with my earnings from the Am Pee store. The battery, fat and heavy, surely has some great power stored inside. When I connect a thin wire across the terminals on top, the wire glows red hot, then melts. Just holding it makes me feel its power. Now, I'm going to see what the power can do to an electric bell. I have connected a pair of wires to the two terminals and poke the bare ends of the wires to various parts of the bell, wondering what will happen. Suddenly the bell rings loudly, making me drop it and the battery and jerk up straight. What in the world has happened? How did this battery make the bell do that?

I run to where Mama sits in the living room. "Mama, Mama, look what I can make the bell do!" I show her that when I connect the wires the bell starts ringing, and it keeps on going until I disconnect one of the wires. "I can make it ring, but I don't know why."

"My son, the scientist," says Mama, with her most happy smile, like she's proud of me for my discovery. "If you can't understand how it works, why don't you go the library and get some books on electricity. Maybe you can learn what makes a bell ring."

The next day I go to the library and check out a book called *A Boy and a Battery*. It has a section that explains exactly how electric bells work. Electric current goes through a coil of wire and that makes magnetism which pulls a lever with a striker attached to it, and the striker hits the bell. As the lever gets attracted to the magnet, the circuit becomes interrupted so that the magnetism goes away, and the lever springs back to the original position. That reconnects the circuit, and the magnetism comes back. In that way the magnetism goes on and off, making the bell go ding-a-ling as long as you keep it connected to the battery.

The book has all kinds of experiments and games you can play with electricity. It shows how to make electromagnets, and how to make a cork sink into a glass bottle filled with water, just like a little diver man when you connect the battery to a coil that goes around the bottle. There are experiments on making different kinds of microphones. One you make from the carbon rod from an old dry cell and a pencil lead, and the book says it is so sensitive that you can hear a fly walk across the table that the microphone sits on.

I also check out another book called *Conditioned Reflex Therapy* that I found in the adult section. It is full of the strangest stories about the patients of some head doctor. I won't tell Mama about this book, because I think I'm not supposed to be reading it. When I get home, I read more of the forbidden stories. One is about a guy who was impotent. The doctor found out it was because he had the same kind of wallpaper at home that he had in some hotel room where he was with some lady that he wasn't married to. I figure out that he was doing some really bad things in the hotel, but I'm not sure what they were, and I don't know what *impotent* means, which is the whole point of the story. So I look it up in the dictionary, which says: *1. lacking physical strength or vigor, 2. Powerless, 3. Incapable of sexual intercourse, 4. Lacking self restraint.* Bingo! I think number three is the one I'm looking for. And I know what sexual intercourse is because Mama told me about the birds and the bees when I was in the fourth grade.

The next day I make a microphone as explained in *A Boy and a Battery*. I take a carbon rod from a dead dry cell battery and hack-saw two discs from it, drill holes in the discs, and screw them to the ends of a piece of wood. With a razor I slice a pencil in half the long way to get the lead, which I sharpen on both ends and fit into little indentations that I have cut into the discs. I attach wires to the carbon discs and connect the dry cell and a pair of headphones into the circuit. When I listen in the headphones, I hear a hissing noise. If I talk at the pencil lead, I can hear my voice booming in the headphones. I pull a hair from my head, like it says in the book, and hit the hair onto the wooden base that holds the microphone, clearly hearing *Boom! Boom! Boom!* whenever I hit the base with the hair. This thing really could hear a fly if it walked on it.

That night I go to bed, thinking about my new discoveries, especially my microphone. There must be a way to use this to spy on Kathleen and Helen.

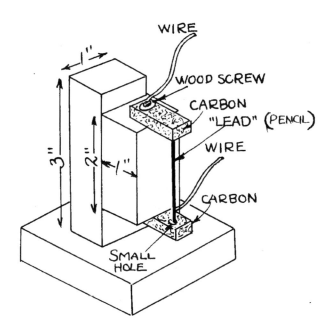

Construction of a sensitive microphone.
Source: Raymond Yates, A Boy and a Battery, Harper & Brothers, 1942/1959.

27.

A New Friend

My friend James and I walk together to school and come across Jerry. Aha! Just the chance we've been looking for to recite the poem we made up about him.

Jerry, Jerry, the big fat fairy,
Sat on top of a little strawberry.
The berry broke and down he fell,
He kept on falling till he came to Whoops!

James and I call out the verses in a sing-song way. James rolls his eyes like Eddie Cantor does in the movies. When we get to the *Whoops* part I start giggling so much that it's hard to get through the second verse, which is even more clever than the first.

The devil said you big fat head,
You better get out or I'll surely drop dead,
'Cause the sight of you just stinks PU.
So Jerry came up and he hid in his shoe.

Jerry turns and walks the other way, like he doesn't even notice. We made up this poem specially for him because he surely deserves it. He's a pudgy sissy who sticks to himself. He doesn't play handball, marbles, baseball, or any other games with my friends. He probably couldn't, even if he tried, so we don't ask him to join in. In school he shows off by trying to get the right answers to all the questions, like when we have spelling exercises. Our poem will take him down a couple of pegs, down to his own size. Only, I'm not sure if he actually heard it. What a shame to waste such a clever poem if Jerry doesn't even notice.

A few days later, I run across Jerry in the alley that goes behind the houses on Cadillac Street. Only this time James isn't with me, so I have to do the poem by myself.

Jerry, Jerry, the big fat fairy,
Sat on top of a little strawberry.

This time Jerry surely notices, because he spins around and looks straight at me, with his lips pulled back over his teeth in tight little lines. "Don't you do that to me. I don't like that," he says while charging at me, his two fists going one over the other in a circle, like the wheel on a paddle boat. His eyes are squinched down into two little slits, and I think they maybe are closed entirely. But still he comes at me, all the while saying "Stop it! You stop it!"

All I have to do is duck under the paddle wheel as Jerry comes right up to me. I poke my fist straight up and feel it connect with something, not hard like I expect, but soft and pillowy. Jerry suddenly stops the paddle wheel, and he covers his face with his hands. "Why did you do that? Why did you do that to me?" He takes his hands away from his face. I'm relieved to see that he's not crying, but there's a round red mark on one of his cheeks.

I look in disbelief at the red mark. I can't believe what I've done, and suddenly I don't know why I did it. It all seemed so right, so clever just a minute ago, but now it seems so shameful. I'm just a bully, no better than Frankie. Jerry rubs the red mark.

"I'm sorry, really I'm sorry," I say. "I didn't mean it. I was just trying to kid around. I didn't mean to hit you."

"It's okay," he says, still rubbing the red spot. "It didn't really hurt." Jerry turns and walks towards his house on Parkview.

"Wait a second. I'll walk with you," I say, hoping that I can make up with him.

As we walk slowly together towards his house, he talks about himself, seeming to completely forget about our fight. My ears really perk up when he tells me about his hobby: radio and electricity. He says he has built a crystal set that pulls radio stations right out of the air without any kind of power, not even a battery. I tell him that my hobby is electricity too, and that I also do experiments in my basement workshop.

When we get to Jerry's house he invites me in to show me his electrical workshop. We walk in the back door into the kitchen and introduces me to his mother. It seems surprising that Jerry actually has a mother, and she seems kind of friendly. He leads me across the kitchen and down the stairs to the basement, to an area with all his stuff. All the parts are arranged neatly on shelves: tubes, radios, boxes of components, and some gizmos with wires sticking out. In the middle of the workbench is a strange looking assembly of parts mounted on a wooden base.

"That's my crystal set," he says, putting on a pair of headphones and making some adjustments to some of the parts. "Here, listen to this." He offers me the headphones, and when I put them on, the most amazing thing happens. There is music, as clear as a bell coming from the crystal set, which doesn't have any power at all. What is powering the crystal set, and how does it pull stations out of the air?

He explains that you have to probe the crystal, which looks like a little silvery lump of rock, with a wire he calls a cat's whisker. He tells me about the coil of wire he wound around a toilet paper roll and the slider on the coil he uses to tune in different radio stations. He explains that the wire lead that goes from the set and disappears in a hole in the wall goes to an antenna he strung on the roof of the house, and the other wire that goes to a clamp on the water pipe overhead is called a ground. He talks about transformers that he gets from the speakers of old radios, how you can use them to step up or step down voltage depending on how you hook them up, how you can use one to generate thousands of volts from just a flashlight battery. Jerry is way more advanced than I am, and I can learn a lot from him. And I now know that I have to have a crystal set of my own.

That evening after supper I go down to my own work bench to test out some of the things I learned from Jerry. An audio transformer that I got from an old radio has four wires coming from it, which I try attaching to my dry cell battery in various combinations. With some experimentation, I can make sparks shoot between one pair of wires whenever I touch the other pair to the battery. I wonder what these sparks would feel like, as I hold a wire in each hand and experiment how to hold on to the pair of wires and at the same time to touch the other pair to the battery.

Suddenly, a jolt goes through both arms like someone has grabbed me by the wrists and has given a hard jerk that I can feel right up to my shoulders. The shock of it causes me to fall backwards onto the floor. My heart pounds as I stare in wonder at the simple little device on my workbench that has knocked me right on my butt. How could I get such a shock from a battery that carries only one and a half volts and a tiny little radio part no bigger than a golf ball? How could it make my muscles jerk so? And why does it feel like nothing I have ever experienced before?

28.

Shocking Games

Jerry and I hide behind a hedge row just off the sidewalk on Kercheval Street. We're using my special invention for giving shocks through a padlock that is placed on the sidewalk. On the back of the padlock I glued a piece of cardboard, and glued to that is a circular metal disc that I cut from a tin can. One thin wire attached to the lock and another to the metal disc go along a crack in the sidewalk and through the bushes, to an audio transformer. No kid can pass by this lock without picking it up. When a kid does try to pick it up, his fingers touch the disc on the back of the lock, and his thumb touches the top of the padlock. At that moment, we connect the other two wires of the transformer to a dry cell battery. Each time we make or break the connection, we send a few thousand volts surging through the kid's hand. That usually makes him yell and drop the lock, while we break out in laughter. We've been lucky so far and have never gotten beat up over this trick, maybe because the kid who gets shocked is afraid we have some other electrical weapons.

We have been waiting behind the bushes for a half-hour for someone to fall into our trap and pick up the lock, but business is slow today. It's my turn to operate the battery, and Jerry is the lookout. Just when we are ready to give up, an old lady with a cane hobbles up the sidewalk and stops at the lock, like she's trying to figure what's laying there.

"Oh God, she's picking it up," Jerry whispers. "Drop it, lady," he calls out, but she just holds on to it, like she thinks it's *finder's keeper's* and no snotty kid is going to deprive her of her newfound treasure. There isn't any choice but to tickle the primary wire to the battery post a few times, which makes her drop the lock onto the sidewalk, as Jerry bursts into a spasm of giggles and gets me doing the same.

"I'll call the police on you kids," she shouts, waving her cane towards the bushes. We let her hobble up the block until she's safely a half block away, and we gather up our stuff and run off.

"I just had to give it to her," I say to Jerry, who understands perfectly well the rules of etiquette in shocking pranks. "She was going to carry off my lock." Just in case she really does call the cops, we'll just have to lay low for a couple of days before playing any more shocking games.

My shocker is only one of the many things I have learned about electricity since I first discovered how to make the bell ring. I now have my own crystal set, which is connected to an antenna that goes across the top of the garage. People give me their broken radios to fix. Often I can fix them by testing the tubes at the radio fix-it store, by poking around for loose wires, or looking for a discolored part that needs to be replaced. If I can fix the radio, I just charge for the parts plus a little extra for my work. If I can't fix it, the people usually tell me to keep it. Then I take it all apart, unsoldering all the components, and drilling out the rivets from the tube sockets. My workshop is filling up with the results of my failures.

I save everything. If a transformer is bad, I take the wire out of it. If a dry cell battery wears out, I saw it open and save the carbon rod inside, as well as the zinc casing that holds in all the acid gunk, and I use these materials to experiment with. Uncle Salem gave me some neat old parts that he had when he was young. I love the variable capacitors he gave me. They look so beautiful and feel so wonderful when I turn the knob that makes their gears turn like an expensive watch.

Jerry gets great parts because he has a fantastic job at *Hank's Army Surplus* store that just opened up on Kercheval Street. They sell mostly electronic stuff left over from the war. Jerry helps out after school, and for a few hours on Saturday. Instead of money,

Hank lets him pick out one electronic gizmo each week for his pay. That way, Jerry has been getting neat-looking stuff, like a tube with four grid caps sticking out of the glass. Usually he doesn't know what to do with the parts, but he keeps them for the day when he figures out how to build a scientific machine.

My home-made hand-held transmitter is inside a small cardboard box. It has an antenna made out of thick wire that I can pull out from the box, a speaker made from a headphone, and inside is a transformer for making high voltage sparks. When I operate the transmitter, it makes static that can be heard on all the stations on a radio, and can also be heard on the little earphone speaker.

After lunch recess, as all the kids come back from home to school, Jerry and I wait outside the parish hall on Saint Paul Street for Frances to pass by on her way back to school. Next to Barbara she is the second smartest girl in our class, When she comes by, we walk along side her showing her all our inventions, like my radio transmitter. She must be very impressed, although she tries not to show it.

In school Jerry and I show off our knowledge of electricity during a spelling exercise. We are supposed to a spell the word, and use it in a sentence. I waive my hand like crazy, begging to be called on. The word is *pencil*.

"Pencil, P-E-N-C-I-L, the boy left his pencil next to the super heterodyne radio."

Another word is *magazine* and Jerry gets called on.

"Magazine, M-A-G-A-Z-I-N-E, I saw an add for an electrolytic capacitor in the magazine."

Sister Emily must realize how clever I am and will surely give me an *A* in spelling. Maybe it will stop her from being so mean to me.

29.

Daddy Leaves

Hey Mary! Over here! says the voice, in a half whisper. Mary Rogoza looks around, but she can't tell where it's coming from. Here, under the porch! Mary looks through the lattice work that encloses the space under the porch to see the crouching figure of her thirteen-year-old sister, Helen. Jesus Christ, Helen! Where have you been, and what are you doing under there? I ran away. I wanted to go to Grandma Gryniewicz in Baltimore, but I couldn't get very far. I didn't have any money. What the hell are you wearing? It's Dominik's clothes. I thought if I looked like a boy, nobody would stop me. Can you bring me some food? I'll bring you food, but you better get your stupid ass in the house. You've been gone all night, and Ma's ready to kill you. Come in and get your beating now. If you wait any more, It'll just be worse. Mary hurries into the kitchen, tears off a piece of bread, cuts a hunk of cheese, runs out the door and goes down the steps. She sticks the food through a hole in the lattice work. Thanks Mary, says Helen, as she considers her options.

*   *   *   *

The arguments between Mama and Daddy have been getting louder and more frequent. On a Saturday night angry shouting awakens me, pulling me into the dining room where Mama and Daddy are having a screaming fit. Helen stands at her bedroom door, with tears in her eyes.

"Choose," demands Mama, looking at Helen. "You choose between Daddy and me, right now."

Helen runs to Mama, and grabs her by the leg, deeply sobbing.

"Damn you Julie. You've got no right to do that. Damn you to hell."

"You brute! You blasphemer! The Lord will punish you for that!"

Now Kathleen appears at the bedroom door. "Stop it you two! Stop all this arguing," she shouts.

Now we have a sorry mess, with Daddy cursing, Mama calling on God, Helen sobbing, and Kathleen shouting, and me thinking this is some kind of nut house.

Daddy turns, and leaves the nut house.

"Go to bed now children," Mama says. "And pray for Daddy and me."

On Sunday afternoon, I work on a model airplane on the dining room table, cutting out parts, pinning them to the wax paper that covers the plans underneath, and dabbing glue where the parts join. But my thoughts aren't really on my model airplane. I think things are coming to a head between Mama and Daddy, because Daddy has his suitcase in his hand and says he is leaving for good. Mama says "let me get the door for you," and she opens the front door, and stands at it like she's a doorman. All the while I whistle a happy tune to show Daddy that I think he's the cause of all the problems around here, that he's mean to Mama, he's a lazy drunk, and I don't care if he ever comes back.

Daddy goes out the front door, slamming it behind him. A minute later I hear his new Chevy start up and drive away. Mama has that mad look on her face as I leave my models and rush up to her.

"Mama! Mama! I whistled the whole time to let him know I don't care if he leaves."

Mama's face changes from mad to sad. "Yes son, he's gone, and I think we'll be better off this way." She goes into the bedroom and shuts the door. I can hear crying behind the door. But I wouldn't cry for Daddy, not in a million years, not even if he died. I'm glad he's gone. Now it will be peaceful around here, and we don't need him anyhow, because he never does anything around the house, and he never takes us places, he doesn't care about my experiments, and he is mean to Mama. There won't be any more fights, and we all will be much happier with Daddy gone. I'm thirteen, and I can get along just fine without him.

30.

Three Rosaries

Daddy is gone, and I don't miss him, and I especially don't miss the fights between him and Mama. She doesn't talk about Daddy, and in a few days it seems to me like he never lived here at all. Kathleen pitches in more than usual with the meals after school because I think she wants to make everything seem okay. But Helen misses Daddy—a lot.

"I want Daddy back," she says to Mama, with tears in her eyes. "When is he coming home?"

"Your father moved out because he was unhappy here," answers Mama. "I just don't know if and when he will come back."

After he is gone for three weeks, a miracle happens—Daddy comes back. Mama tells us he promised her he would go on the wagon and be a better husband and father. On the first Saturday after he came back, he takes us all to Belle Isle where we have a picnic. And that evening, when we all go to Aunt Rose's house for their poker game, Daddy drinks Vernor's ginger ale, which is what he has been drinking ever since he went on the wagon.

Today is Tuesday. It has been one month since Daddy came back home. He is still at work, and Mama is out with Aunt Mary. Mama says we don't need a baby sitter any longer, because we are old enough to be trusted. Kathleen and I, standing about six feet apart, play *Helen Ball,* as we sometimes do when we are left home alone by ourselves. First I push Helen to Kathleen, and then she pushes her back to me, and so on, back and forth. According to the rules, if Helen falls on the floor, the one who pushed her gets one point, so the other guy has to keep her from falling on the floor. As usual, Helen screams bloody murder while Kathleen and I shout with glee whenever one of us scores another point. Sometimes when we play this game Helen acts like we are killing her, and she runs over to the heat register and screams loudly into it: *Stop beating me*! I wonder what the Bartons upstairs think, since her screams probably come out of their registers. Sometimes when she carries on like that, we roll her up in a rug and throw her into the closet for violating the rules of *Helen Ball,* which say you should not scream into the heat register.

Just when I am ahead in points, the phone rings in the dining room. Kathleen runs over and picks up the receiver. She suddenly goes quiet, but Helen and I keep on yelling, and poking each other. Helen goes up to Kathleen and starts pinching her on the nose and grabbing her ear, while Kathleen tries to turn her head to get away from Helen, who keeps on poking and grabbing. She puts the receiver against her stomach, like she wants to muffle the noise, and slaps Helen right across the face, saying "Shut up! This is serious." That stops Helen cold. Kathleen's face is white, and I can see she is not kidding. She tells the person on the phone that Mama is at Aunt Mary's, and she looks up her phone number and gives it. Then she hangs up the receiver. Her eyes are opened wide as saucers. At first she looks down at the floor, then at me, her eyes watering.

"Someone called from Daddy's work," she says. "They took him to the hospital. They're trying to work on him, to revive him, but he might be dead." Her message sends a sudden jolt of fear through my body, like the feeling I had when I looked down from the top floor of the Skeleton Building. Helen and I start crying while Kathleen dabs the water that collects beneath her eyes and tells us more about the phone call. "Daddy fell down at work, and didn't seem to be breathing. They think it's a heart attack. Somebody called an ambulance, and they took him to the hospital."

"What are we gonna do?" I ask.

"Come on," she says. "We have to pray."

We kneel before the statue of the Sacred Heart in the dining room, where we usually pray the rosary with Mama, who always says: *The family that prays together, stays together.* Kathleen leads a rosary, calling out the first part of each Hail Mary, while Helen and I recite the second half in response. We go through the entire rosary, all five decades, ten Hail Marys on each decade. In between decades we say an *Our Father* and a *Glory Be,* and Kathleen announces a station of the cross that we are supposed to think about for the next rosary decade. But I can't think about Jesus. I can only think that Daddy might be dead, and we have to make this rosary work to bring him back. I lead the next rosary, and then Helen leads one after that. Three rosaries—if anything could bring Daddy back, this could do it. My thoughts pray more than just the rosary words: *Please God, don't let Daddy die, and I will never complain about him again.*

After the rosaries, we sit in the living room, talking about Daddy's condition, about how they can revive people who have heart attacks, how people can go on to lead a long life afterwards, how good doctors and hospitals are nowadays. We talk for hours, not thinking about dinner.

At ten o'clock the front door knob rattles. I jump up from the couch, and run to the door. Mama walks in with Aunt Mary, Aunt Stella, and Auntie Anna behind her. It's all written on Mama's face without her needing to say a single word. I start crying, sobbing deeply, and I hear the wails of Kathleen and Helen. Mama is crying too, and Aunt Mary has her arm around her, trying to console her, but she is crying too. Auntie Anna puts her arm around me, while Aunt Stella covers her face with a handkerchief, her head bobbing up and down and her shoulders shaking. Kathleen and Helen huddle around Mama and Aunt Mary, locking arms and bodies. I join in the huddle too. Now everyone is hugging and crying. No one has to say anything, because we all know. Daddy is dead.

31.

The Funeral

Saturday morning, the fourth day after Daddy died, is the day they are supposed to take him to the cemetery. Me, Kathleen, and Helen spent the past three days at the funeral home where he has been laid out.

The place looks like a jungle with all the flowers. Some are in huge displays, held up on special holders, with banners or signs saying *From Your Loving Mother*, or *Your Loving Sisters and Brother*. Others are in pots that are placed on little tables around the edges of the room, or lined up on the sides of the casket. Daddy lies in a casket, with a raised lid so you can see all the satin and silk inside. He wears a fancy suit and tie like he is ready for work, and his hands are folded on his chest. Everyone says he looks so good, like he's sleeping. But I think he looks dead. A picture of the Sacred Heart is above the casket, with Jesus pointing his finger to his burning heart. I have seen this picture a million times, but now I try to figure out its meaning—what is Jesus trying to tell me, and why is his heart burning?

For the past three days we have been here at the funeral home every day, all day long. We even stayed here for lunch, when somebody brought us sandwiches. At night we had dinner in a restaurant down the street and went home after dark—usually in Aunt Mary and Uncle Bill's car. When I went to bed, it was hard to sleep, because when I closed my eyes, all I could see was the casket, with Daddy's dead body in it.

On the first day, everybody was going up to the casket, kneeling on a little kneeler placed along side so that you could look right into his face. Some of the people, like Mama and Grammy, would kiss his face or his hand. In the beginning I went up to the casket, knelt down, and said a prayer. When I touched his hand it felt cold and rubbery, not like a real person's hand at all. After that I tried staying away from the casket, in the back of the room where I wouldn't have to look at his face. But the casket only kept pulling me back, making me look at his face again. Yesterday I thought I could see mold growing on his lips. But still the ladies, and even Mama, wanted to kiss his face and hands.

During the days, we tried to keep busy. Me and Helen played *Hangman* a lot. Or we pretended that we were detectives, trying to hide behind the curtains or following people out to the parking lot and taking down their license plate numbers. Sometimes we played *hide and seek* outside with cousins Butch and Diane. There are two other rooms here, a lot like the one Daddy is in, each with a casket, one with a dead man, and one with a dead woman. I tried to go into the other rooms, to get away from Daddy's casket, but all the strangers there made me feel nervous, like I didn't belong there, like I should go away.

Our room in the funeral home has been filling up with people since we got here early this morning. There are so many people here, you can hardly move. On Daddy's side is Grammy, wearing a black polka dot dress and a black mesh veil over her face, and there is Baby Helen, and even Lala, who looks so odd outside of her home on Coplin street. Uncle Eddie couldn't be here because his muscles are wasting and he can't go anywhere. There's Cousin Nell and Uncle Salem. Sister Magdelan and Sister Laura are here, each with a traveling companion, because nuns are never supposed go out by themselves. The men are here from the Saint Vincent de Paul Society and from the Holy Name Society. A bunch of other men are here from Daddy's work. But mostly the place is filled up with everybody on Mama's side. There's Aunt Mary and Uncle Bill, who looks so strange dressed up in a blue suit and a tie, with cousins Donnie, Jerry, and Little Iodine—that's cousin Joyce who's only four. Aunt Stella and Uncle Stanley are here with cousin Richey, and there's Auntie Anna and Uncle Stanley with cousins Butch and Diane. There's

Uncle Joe and Aunt Rose wearing a fur coat like a movie star, Uncle Lefty and Aunt Violet, Aunt Lilly and Uncle Archie, Aunt Jenny and Uncle Stanley with their little kids Bennie, Phil, and little baby Stashu, Uncle Johnny, Aunt Dolores and Uncle Bob. The ladies are here from the Legion of Mary—Mrs. Wagner and Mrs. O'Brian, and the ladies from Altar Society, as well as the neighbors from Pennsylvania and Brinket—Mr. and Mrs. Smith with Tommy and his sister Ruth Ann.

I know what to expect, since I have been to many funerals as an altar boy. And just two weeks ago we had another funeral when Mama's grandma died, and she was laid out in Hamtramck. First they will close the casket, and the funeral home men will wheel it out to the hearse which is already waiting out front in the circular driveway. Then all the cars will line up behind the hearse, and the funeral men will hand each driver a little flag to put in the driver's window so other cars will know enough to stop for the slow procession that will be going to Annunciation Church. The hearse will stop in front of the church, and the funeral men will carry the casket out of the hearse. That's when the pallbearers take over, six men from the Holy Name Society, who will carry the casket up the steps to the front of the church, and place it on a little wheeled cart that will already be set up there. There will be a mass, with altar boys who won't be glad they got called in on a Saturday, since they won't get out of school that morning. I hope the altar boys won't be the kind who will be snickering and making faces to each other, thinking none of the people will see them, because I know all about those things, and I will be able to tell if they're acting that way. Father O'Hara will say the Mass, and at the end he will face the people, and give a talk about God's will, and how the soul of the departed is now in heaven. Then the pallbearers will take the casket to the hearse, and there will be a slow car procession to Mount Olivet Cemetery. They will carry the casket to where a big tent will be set up in case of rain, and place it along side a deep, deep hole cut into the ground. The hole will be set up with a contraption with straps for lowering the casket into the hole. At the cemetery, the priest will say more prayers, and sprinkle the casket once again with holy water. Finally, the funeral men will put the casket on the lowering contraption. That's usually when everybody cries. But not me. I'm not going to cry. The last time I cried for Daddy was when Mama came home after he died, and that will be the last time.

Father O'Hara stands next to the casket, faces the people, and opens his prayer book. The whole place goes silent, and everybody looks at Father O'Hara. Mama and Grammy are in front. I wanted to stay in back, where I wouldn't have to look at it all, but Mama said I had to stay in front with Kathleen and Helen. Father O'Hara faces the casket and says some prayers in Latin. He turns to the people and leads everybody in the *Our Father*, and a *Hail Mary*. Then he says some more prayers that sound far off, like in a dream. All the time, I try to look away, but I can't seem to really get away. Then someone starts to lower the lid of the casket, very slowly. That's when the whole place breaks into bedlam, with everyone crying, screaming sobbing, and calling out. Uncle Bill and Uncle Stanley grab Mama around the arms, because she looks like she is going to fall down. And I can't stop crying. The tears just keep coming and coming, and they won't stop. I'm crying because Daddy didn't take us places, because he never fixed things around the house, because he was mean to Mama, because he was a lazy drunk, because of his stinky feet, because of his puking in the mornings. I'm crying because he never cared about my experiments or my cartoons, because he didn't want to talk to me. I'm crying because he's dead now, and it will always be that way.

Part II

Man of the House

♫♫♫♫

32.

Man of the House

Everybody says that I'm the man of the house now, and that I have to take Daddy's place. I don't know what that means. Am I supposed to boss around Mama, Kathleen, and Helen? I don't think they would like that. But I can get a job, and help Mama pay the bills, because now that Daddy is gone, we won't have any more money coming in. Mama says that Daddy left us with eight thousand five hundred dollars in insurance, but it's not enough to last forever. Mama has a conference with us kids on what to do with the money.

"Aunt Mary and Aunt Stella tell me that a business is for sale in Hamtramck. It's a short-order grill, you know, a place that makes hamburgers, grilled sandwiches, and meals like that. There's an apartment above it, and that's where we would live. I could handle the business by myself in the morning and afternoon, and you three would have to help out after you got home from school. We're going to need some sort of income, and this is one possibility. What do you think?"

And that's when us kids put up a holy fit. "That stinks!" and "Oh, great! I would look so great in my cute little apron after school," and "how are we supposed to do our homework?", and "I don't want to spend my life flipping hamburgers!" and "I wouldn't want my dog to live in Hamtramck!"

"I didn't think you would like the idea," Mama replies. "We're going to stay right here, and I'll find some kind of job."

I like living here, and I don't want to leave my friends. And I don't want to be living above a crummy hamburger joint. Maybe if I can earn money, we can stay here.

I try the businesses up an down Kercheval Street—Joe's hamburger place, MacIntyre's Hardware, Hank's Army Surplus, Kresgee's Five and Dime—always with the same question: "Would you like to hire me to work after school?" The answer is always "No," until I try at Weinstein's Cleaner's.

"Do you want to hire me to help out in your store after school? I'm a good worker, and I need the job."

Mr. Weinstein looks at me through glasses so thick that his eyes look enormous, like he's looking through a magnifying glass. The top of his head is bald, with white wisps of hair sprouting here and there. He has a bushy white mustache that wiggles and jiggles when he talks. There are brown spots on his forehead, as well as a mole with a couple of white hairs growing out of it. Silky hairs grow out of his ears, and a thicket of bristly hairs stick out of his nose. He speaks in a thick foreign accent.

"You appear on my doorstep, asking for a job. I don't give out jobs like candy on Halloween. How old are you?"

"Thirteen, sir."

" Why do you want a job?"

" My father died, and they buried him last week. Now I'm the man of the house, and I have to earn money to support our family."

"And what is your experience?"

"I've been delivering groceries at the Am-Pee on Saturdays. And I do my jobs at home, like vacuuming and dusting, and I take my turn at washing the dishes, and sometimes I deliver stuff for MacIntyre Hardware."

"You call that experience. That means nothing to me. Maybe I could use some help around the shop. But I don't want some lazy boy who will come in here and expect to be paid for doing nothing. I don't want to spend all my time training somebody, only to have him quit, with him getting all the knowledge of the cleaning business and me getting nothing in return."

He goes on about the facts of business where he once lived somewhere across the ocean. How a boy would start off as an apprentice to a master and would work for only his room and board. If the boy worked very hard and paid attention to all the things the master said, he would eventually learn the business.

Then, when the master was ready to retire, he would give the whole business to his apprentice, who by this time would be an expert himself.

He says he'll hire me, but only under some conditions. I have to come two hours after school every day, and six hours on Saturday. My job at first will be ironing the tags he pins to the clothes, sweeping the floors, sorting buttons, and various other chores around the shop. For this he'll pay me twenty five cents per hour, but will hold back my pay for three months. If I stay three months, I get paid for the whole time; if I quit before three months, I get nothing. He says I would be lucky anyway, because I would learn so much about the cleaning business from a real master. I can start next Monday after school. I agree to his conditions.

As I walk home from the cleaners, I do the arithmetic in my head. Fifty cents for each school day, that's two-fifty by Friday. And then another dollar-fifty on Saturday, that makes four dollars for the week. That's way more than I could possibly make at the Am-Pee Store. After three months, I'm going to come home with a big bundle of money, and Mama will be surprised. I'm going to be the man of the house now.

First I have to resign from the Annunciation grade school football team where I am playing *right-end*. I wish I didn't have to give up my uniform, pads, helmet, and especially my cleated shoes that, when I walk on hard surfaces, make clicking sounds that say: *look here, this is not some sissy boy, this is a football player*. I don't want to give up my shoulder pads that make me look so big and strong, that surely must impress all the girls who come to watch our games, and especially Barbara, the smartest girl in our eighth grade class—Barbara, who I dreamed about going out with some day, if only I could work up the nerve to ask her. It was Barbara who came up to me after one game saying: *I didn't know you were on the team. Oh yes*, I had replied, trying to act nonchalant, like this is the sort of thing I did every day.

We had practiced and worked out all summer. So far, our team has never won a game. In fact, we have not yet made a touchdown. In all the games we have played this year, our team has completed only one pass, and it was one that I caught. It was in a game with Saint Charles, our arch rival. We were in the huddle, and everyone was frustrated because none of our plays were working out. So our quarterback, John, decided to make up a new play out of his head. He would fake a hand-off to Ed, our full back. Then I would run down-field for about five yards and cut to the left, behind the back-field of the opposing team. Then John would throw me a short pass. He clapped his hands, and we all took position at the line of scrimmage. John took his position behind the center, and started the count. *One, two three, four, five, six, ...* The whole team sprang to action on the count of four, the count he had called in the huddle. I ran down-field, and cut to the left. Then I looked over my left shoulder and saw John, his head sticking above all the churning bodies trying to get at him, and he threw a bullet pass to me. The ball shot into my hands, but I couldn't hang on to it. I kept running cross-field, all the time juggling the ball, trying to keep it from falling to the ground. Someone hit my legs, and then about a thousand pounds hit me at my hips on the right side, and as I was falling to the left, another thousand pounds hit me in the waist on the left, making me feel like I was being cut in half. I got smashed to the ground, with a whole pileup of Annunciation and Saint Charles guys. When they peeled me off the ground, it felt like every bone in my body was broken. But I was still holding on to the ball, our team's first completed pass. I wonder if Barbara noticed.

After school on the next day I turn in my pads, helmet, uniform and cleats to coach Doherty.

"I can't play on the team any more. Now that my father is dead, I have to go to work to earn money for our family. I got a job and I start work on Monday." He takes the stuff, and just looks at me without speaking at first. "Good luck," he says, as he turns and walks away. I feel so ashamed. I know I have let down Coach Doherty, let down the whole football team, let down Annunciation School. But I won't let down my family because I'm the man of the house now.

33.

A Letter to Grammy

Mary escaped from Ma when she married Bill Smartz, her handsome, fun-loving boy friend. But she can't stop thinking about her sister Helen, only fifteen, who she had always tried to protect, who was too young to leave home by herself. So she had asked the officials from the Tuscola County Child Welfare Administration to Ma's home. She confronts Ma with the abuses that Helen suffered. Mary stands her ground as Ma rants and swears in response. As the Welfare officials lead Helen away to be placed in a foster home, Helen can hear the angry Polish words from Ma—an unbroken series of curses, damnations, and oaths that defy English translation.

*   *   *   *

"I won't be going with you to Grammy's anymore," Mama says to me, Kathleen, and Helen. She's got those angry lines on her forehead and her mouth has that mad look, like she gets when she talks about the smut peddlers on Kercheval Street. "If you want to visit her, you'll have to get there yourself on the streetcar."

"What happened?" Helen asks, with a worried look. Mama tells what Grammy said to her after they lowered Daddy's casket into the hole: "Now I won't have to see you any more. You never were any good for my Jackie." She talks about the letter she wrote to Grammy. About how she told off Grammy for insulting her all those years she was married to Daddy, for ruining Daddy's life and making a Mama's boy out of him, for her meanness and stinginess. As she continues, she gets madder and madder, her jaw stiffening, and her eyes flashing.

I didn't see the letter, but I can guess what's in it. She was probably in one of her bad moods when she wrote it. When she's angry, Mama doesn't mince words and can wither a person like a blow torch on a dandelion. I'm sure she told off Grammy in a way she had never before been told off. I don't mind not seeing Grammy, or even Lala. But I want to see Uncle Eddie, to tell him about all my electricity experiments, to show him the cartoon strips I made with the artist's pen set he got me for my birthday, to have him teach me more about leather craft and electricity.

In two weeks, on a Sunday afternoon, me, Kathleen, and Helen take the Jefferson street car to Coplin Street and walk from there to Grammy's house. Grammy gives us a little peck on the cheek as she holds her yapping little poodle, Jerry. We get sloppy beer kisses from Lala, and then we have a great time playing card games with Uncle Eddie. Nobody speaks about Mama's letter, and nobody speaks about Daddy.

Grammy. The little tree on the table beside her was the only decoration she ever put up for Christmas in all the years we visited her.

34.

Eviction

Charley Earl sits on the living room couch while in the kitchen Mama pours coffee from the pot that is always on the stove, from morning to night. All serious business in our house is done over coffee, and from the way Charley is dressed in his dark suit and tie, and from his leather briefcase, this must be more than a friendly chit-chat visit. Mama brings two cups of coffee, places one in front of Charley, lights up a cigarette, and sits next to him on the couch. I'm in the dining room, minding my own business, working on a stick model airplane. I can see Charley, and hear everything he and Mama are saying.

"How are things going, Julie?" he asks, looking stiff and uncomfortable.

"It's only been three weeks since Jack died, Charley," Mama says, "and we're adjusting as well as can be expected. I'm thinking about getting a job, but I don't know how to go about it, or what I can do to earn a living."

Charley gives Mama some advice about jobs, telling her that she should learn typing, and look for a job as a secretary. He talks awhile about the weather, then asks how the kids are doing in school. It's plain that he's beating around the bush. Finally he gets to the point.

"As an attorney for the Hall estate, I have to advise you about a decision concerning your lease," he says, making a little tent by pressing his fingertips together. "As you know, you are operating on a month-to-month basis—that was in the lease you and Jack signed. It was felt that your present circumstances, without a head of household now, well, it presents certain difficulties, some element of financial risk, some degree of uncertainty that the estate would like to avoid. So the estate has decided that it would be advisable if you looked for other living arrangements."

Charley shuffles through his briefcase, and pulls out some papers. Mama doesn't speak. He hands her the papers. "You have six weeks. It could be thirty days, according to the terms of the lease. But in consideration of the difficulties befallen the family, the estate decided to grant you an extra two weeks. That would give you until the middle of December. I hope that doesn't present you with too much inconvenience."

Charley rises, picks up his briefcase, and inches backwards towards the door. "I'm sorry I have to bear the news. If there is anything I can do for you, just let me know." That was the same offer he had made at the funeral home.

After Charlie leaves, Mama calls for me, Kathleen, and Helen to come into the living room. "There's something I need to talk to you about," she says with the worried look on her face. She explains that we're being evicted. I don't know what this all means, but I don't think it's good. We will have to move, but where to? Do I have to leave my friends? Mama says, "We will just put our trust in God and the Holy Mother."

I'm at the cleaners telling Mr. Weinstein the news. "I'm sorry, but it looks like I have to quit before the middle of December. We're getting evicted, and we have to move soon. I don't know where we're going to go. I could keep working for a while, but I might not be able to keep it up for three whole months."

He studies me for a moment through his thick glasses. "That's just what I was afraid of, that you would quit on me. I've invested a lot in you these past weeks. Teaching you business habits, teaching you how to operate the iron, how to prepare the clothes for cleaning, how to clean the shop. Three months. That was our agreement," he says, pointing his crooked finger at me in a jabbing motion, "Isn't that right?" I nod in agreement; that was the agreement. "And so, you forfeit your pay. You don't have to bother to come back."

As I walk back home, I find a perfect kicking stone which I keep on a track in front of me. We have to move now, to give up our beautiful house and we haven't finished sorting through all the treasures in the basement. I don't have a job anymore, just when my pay was starting to add up to something big. But I didn't want this stinking job anyway, with all the hot steam, and the smelly chemicals, doing stupid things like sorting buttons, ironing labels, sweeping the floor. The last thing I would ever want to do is to work in a crummy cleaners. I have better plans. Some day I'm going work with electricity.

35.

Pinewood

Just when it looks like we're going to be on the street with all our furniture, Mama uses the insurance money to buy a house on Pinewood Street. We take two busses and one street car to see for the first time a brick house with steeply peaked roof sections going in different directions, like a picture from Hansel and Gretel. Just inside the front door is a small foyer with stairs going up on the right; on the left is a door full of little windows that Mama calls a *French door* leading to the living room.

Me, Kathleen, and Helen rush all excited into the living room, while Mama stands in the foyer with her arms folded and a proud smile on her face, like she's saying: *see what happens when you trust in the Holy Mother.* There's a fire place like in the movies, and it has a wooden mantel and above it a huge mirror. The walls and ceiling are textured like someone went over the plaster when it was still wet with a big palm leaf. All the while Helen says things like, "Oh my God, look at this!" and Kathleen says "Oh! Mama, this is great!" We go through a big arched entrance way to the dining room, but it is without our beautiful window seat that we had on Pennsylvania Street. Mama shows us two bedrooms: the small one will be mine, and the bigger one is for the girls, meaning Mama, Kathleen, and Helen. I guess I get my own private bedroom since I'm now the man of the house. In the hallway between the two bedrooms is a bathroom—not as big as the one on Pennsylvania Street, but still it has everything a bathroom needs.

Off the dining room is the kitchen; over the sink is a window overlooking the back yard. Off the kitchen is a stairway that goes down to a basement where everything looks bright and clean. The floor is tiled, the walls are painted, and there is a mural of a dancing woman on one wall. At the far end of the basement is a furnace that burns oil from a metal tank along side. And next to that is a big fruit cellar. On the other side of the furnace is a space that Mama says I can have for my electricity workshop.

We go back upstairs to find on the dining room wall a thermostat that lets you set the temperature so the furnace will come on and off automatically. Now we can say good-bye to shoveling coal into the furnace, cold mornings, and ashes and clinkers. On the second floor is an apartment, with one bedroom, a big living room, a kitchen, and a bathroom. Mama says that Kathleen can use this bedroom until she rents out the upstairs flat, which we will need for income. I can't believe the luxury of this place. It's like a movie palace. I think we owe our good luck to Tommy Smith's parents.

It was the Smith's who found us this place in St. Raymond's parish on the Northeast side of Detroit, not too far from their own house on Fairmont Street where they had moved last year. Mama had just plunked down most of the insurance money and bought the place for cash, much to the disapproval of Aunt Mary and Aunt Stella, who both thought we should have bought the hamburger joint in Hamtramck. Mama said there was a little money left over, and she would put that in the bank for a rainy day. "And so how are you going to eat, Miss Smarty Pants, now that you blew all your money on a house?" Aunt Mary had asked. "God will provide," Mama had replied, jutting out her chin and sniffing as if to say *Don't boss me around*.

Mama says we have to finish out the year at Annunciation school. That means we will have to take two buses and a street car just the reverse way we got here: first, the Schoenherr bus that turns on Seven Mile Road, then goes to Gratiot, which people pronounce like *Gra-shit*. Then we will take the Gratiot street car to McClellan, and then the McClellan bus to Kercheval. From there it is only a few blocks walk to Annunciation School.

Me and Tommy like to pretend we're stuttering, and we say *Gra-Gra-Gra shit-shit-shit*, which sets us both into fits of giggles and snickers. I don't mind taking the busses to Annunciation school. It only takes about forty-five minutes each way, counting the walking. The fare is a nickel for students.

In only two weeks it's Christmas eve. A giant Christmas tree is set up in the living room for our first Christmas at Pinewood— bigger than anything we ever had before—so big we can barely fit a star on top. We decorate the French door to the foyer with holiday scenes that we paint on the window panes using paint that Mama made from Bon Ami Cleaning Powder and food coloring. We divided up the window panes and each of us painted different scene—a Christmas tree, a snow man, a house with a smoking chimney, a face of Saint Nick, a *Merry Christmas* message, a snow flake. We also paint winter scenes on the big mirror over the mantel. We make a fire in the fire place, and sit around and sing carols. We've already had lots of visitors -- like the Smiths, Aunt Mary and Uncle Bill, and Aunt Stella. Everybody brought some gift for our house, and also for us kids.

We get a ton of Christmas cards that were forwarded by the Post Office from our address on Pennsylvania Street. One of the cards comes from a woman named Joan, who sends Mama a card every year with the same message: *Dear Julie, I thank God for putting you on the train with me to Rochester. I will always keep you in my prayers. God bless you and your family.* The card comes from the woman Mama saved from suicide on the train to Rochester, New York after she ran away from our home, when I was in the fifth grade.

Our Second Christmas on Pinewood Street (1951)
Mama, Helen, Aunt Dolores, Pat, Kathleen.

36.

Sister Emily

One thing that is definitely not a blessing in my life is Sister Emily, my eighth grade teacher. Like all the other nuns at Annunciation School, she wears a long black gown full of folds and tons of material that go clear to the floor. A giant rosary that dangles in a loop at her side makes a clicking sound when she rushes from place to place. Her chest and forehead are covered by stiff white material, and there's a fat crucifix hanging from a chain in the middle of her chest. On her head is a veil that goes down to the middle of her back. But it's not just a plain veil, like the babushkas the girls wear in the winter. The veil is on top of something stiff and white that covers her ears and the side of her face, acting like horse blinders that keep her from seeing off to the side. And that's the crucial part to know. You can act up and make all kinds of goofy gestures at her side and stay just out of her view. It's a great sport that us boys like to play, to see how far we can go without getting caught.

One of the sports we play is passing notes around the room by *Emily Express*. I write a note to Raymond saying *Your face looks like the hind end of a baboon*, fold it in half, put his name on the outside, and pin it to the back of her habit. As she makes her rounds up and down the aisle, she eventually gets to Raymond's desk, who has to take the note, read it, and then make a reply to send back to me.

Raymond pins his note towards the end of class, but Sister doesn't come by my desk for me to take it off. As class breaks up, the note is still stuck there. Raymond distracts Sister by asking her about something, while I sneak up behind and unpin the note. We came close to having her go back to the convent with a note saying *If I had a face like yours, I would cut off my head.* That could definitely have gotten somebody into trouble.

I don't know why I play these tricks in her class and face the danger of getting caught. Maybe I try to get even with her because she puts her meanness deep into you, like a knife. It's not just because of her slapping. Lots of the nuns like to slap the boys around.

Take Sister Alma, for example. I had her last year in the seventh grade. She was the all-time champion slapper in Annunciation School. She must have slapped some boy at least twenty times a day, and I mean every day. She was so used to slapping that she hit you even if you didn't do anything bad. But I didn't hate sister Alma; I felt sorry for her. She was like a nervous chicken, afraid of the class, afraid that they would find out that she's not very smart. I didn't hate Sister John Marie either, although she did her share of slapping and hitting with rulers. But I could see how sick she was, and the sickness drove her to be mean.

But now I'm in the eighth grade, and it is the worst time of my entire life because of Sister Emily. She gets right in front of your face and tells you you're sinful, insolent, delinquent, and on a path to ruin and hell. When she does this to me, I can't help staring at the little accordion lines that form around her lips as she yaks away, her lips only inches away from my eyes. It makes her look like the Wicked Witch of the West. She likes to lecture us boys about being impure, going on and on about our dirty thoughts that will send us right to hell, how we are temples of the holy spirit, and how our impure thoughts defile the temple. *An idle mind is the devil's workshop*, she likes to say. Every time an impure thought starts up, we are supposed to say a short prayer, like *Jesus, Mary, and Joseph, pray for me.* That will buy you a little time until you can get to confession.

She sometimes gets after Joey, who is a big time giggler. Almost anything sets him off. When we're in line and supposed to be quiet, his giggles will start up, and then he can't stop himself. That makes Sister Emily extra mad, as she takes him by the ear and bangs his head against the blackboard.

It's not just the boys that she's mean to, although we get the worst of it. She gets on the girls sometimes too. One time Louise came to school wearing lipstick, just enough that Sister Emily could spot it. "You dirty little girl," she said, as she slapped Louise over and over across the face. All the while Louise was crying. When she was done, she sent Louise to the bathroom to scrub her face. Although that sort of thing happens to the boys all the time, I never saw a girl get beat up like that before, and I will never forget it.

I have my ways to fight back, to get even with her. One way is to whistle softly through my teeth. I learned I could whistle even while rubbing my lips with my hands. She can hear it, but she can't tell who is doing it. How could it possibly be me if I'm rubbing my mouth while it's going on?

Brrroooiiinnggggg!!! Brrroooiiinnggggg!!! I'm playing the bobbie pin trick. A bent-open hair pin is stuck in a crack at the edge of my desk, and when I tweak it, it makes a *broinging* sound that Sister Emily can just barely hear. She shifts her eyes around the room and sniffs the air, trying to tell where the sound is coming from, like maybe she can smell it. I do this just often enough to drive her crazy, but not enough that she can get a fix on me. I've been pulling this trick for the past few days, and she still hasn't figured out who's doing it.

She makes her way around the room, going up and down the aisles, calling on kids. She gets right to my desk and calls on me. As I stand up to answer she passes by my desk. Just then, her habit catches the pin that sticks out into the aisle, and then it lets go. As I recite my answer, I hear *Brrroooiiinnnggg!!!* She must think somebody else is guilty. How could it be me if I am innocently standing up and reciting something?

She continues to walk past my desk, and I continue to recite, and I think she is pretending she didn't hear the noise, but doesn't say anything because she's not sure who is doing it.

The next day I try by bobbie pin trick while Sister Emily sits at her desk. This time she looks straight at me, and says in her meanest voice: "I know what you're doing, and you just better stop it. You might think you can get away with that, but you better not ever do that again." She doesn't use my name, and maybe she isn't really sure that I'm the guilty one, but her stare puts a shiver into my soul, and I know I have to stop the bobby pin trick forever.

The next day, Sister Emily catches me passing a note to Joey. I'm standing beside my desk, waiting for her tongue lashing. This time she doesn't holler at me like I expect. She just waits, letting the silence settle on the class like a heavy blanket. A slight smile is just barely visible on her face. She looks over the class, then to me. No one makes a peep.

"Let's all feel sorry for Patrick," she finally says, then pauses to let the heavy blanket settle down some more. "He's insane. His mother told me that, just last week. Ever since his father died, he went insane. So let's all pray for Patrick, asking God to heal his sick mind."

She leads a Hail Mary, and the class joins in on the response. Every word feels like a knife going into my stomach. I want to cry, but that would only give her satisfaction, so I hold it back. After the prayer, I sit down, feeling ashamed, feeling alone, feeling dirty.

After school, I tell Mama what happened.

"Did you really tell Sister Emily I was insane?"

"Of course not. We had a conference last week because she thought you were acting up. I told her that you were under a lot of strain from your father's death."

"But Mama, how can I face her? What will my friends think? How can I go back to class?

Mama just looks sad. "I'm sorry son. Just try to stick it out till the end of school. God willing, next September you'll have a new school, and all new teachers."

The next day at class, I feel like everyone's eyes are on me. I am too ashamed to talk to anyone. I don't have the heart to fight Sister Emily anymore. She's beaten me.

I hate Sister Emily, and I hate the eighth grade. I hate having to come all this way to Annunciation school where my life is miserable. I hate the way Mama digs into her little change purse like a poor widow lady to dole out our nickels for carfare so we can come to this horrible place, me knowing all the while that we are nearly at the end of Daddy's insurance money, and there won't be any more coming in. *Money doesn't grow on trees,* she reminds us a thousand times.

On April 21, 1950, a miracle happens and I don't have to ask for nickels for carfare. Detroit transit workers go on strike and us kids hitch-hike to school; Helen and I go together to Annunciation, and Kathleen goes separately to Saint Charles.

Helen and I walk up to Gratiot, stick out our thumbs, and wait for a car to come, and one pulls up with three rough looking men inside, and we have to make a quick decision: should we get in and maybe get abducted, or should we pass up this car and wait for one driven by some old lady? But we get in, as we usually do, and we don't get abducted, like we never get, and we get a ride to Gratiot and Harper, where we get off and stick out our thumbs for the next leg of our trip to Jefferson Street. We go back and forth like this every day. I figure we save

Mama ten cents per kid every day—that's thirty cents for three of us, a dollar-fifty for one week, and twelve dollars after eight weeks of hitch-hiking, when the transit strike is finally settled.

Sister Laura of the Immaculate Heart of Mary (IHM) order—the same order as were the nuns at Annunciation Church. This lady is Daddy's aunt on his father's side. She taught music and played the church organ.

37.

Charity

Mama decides to earn money using the Royal typewriter the men from Daddy's office gave her after he died. Mama said it was the Holy Mother who sent it to her. She practices from a self-teaching book, and soon she gets good enough that her fingers can make fast clikety-clack rhythms, like a snare drum. There is always a fat ashtray with a pile of cigarette butts and a glowing cigarette on one side of the typewriter, and on the other side there is always a cup of coffee, which she keeps filled from the pot that is always kept hot in the kitchen.

She finds a job addressing envelopes, which turns out to be a family enterprise. Kathleen, Helen, and I sit around the dining room table folding fliers and stuffing them into envelopes, while Mama addresses the envelopes on the typewriter. She works from the Detroit phone book, going line by line over the portion of the alphabet she was assigned.

I can't resist going over the lessons from Mama's typing book, which start off with exercises like:

asdfghjkl;

qwertyuiop

When my fingers get strong enough, I graduate to typing whole paragraphs using all my fingers. Soon I can help typing the envelopes when Mama isn't doing it. And Kathleen takes her turn at the typewriter too, using the skills she learned at Saint Charles High School.

After hours of working together, we produce boxes of stuffed envelopes which Mama delivers to some office. The check that shows up in the mail for all this work is worth peanuts. No matter how hard we all work on those stupid envelopes, the pay we get hardly amounts to anything.

Then the worst calamity of all befalls our family. The Saint Vincent de Paul Society of Saint Raymond's Church decides we need charity food baskets.

I sit in the living room, reading *Boy's Life* magazine when the door bell rings. Before anyone can answer it, a man from the society walks in carrying a big basket full of food. He walks straight past me without saying a word or even looking at me, goes into the kitchen, and plunks the basket on the kitchen table. Then he turns quickly, walks past me again, and disappears out the front door as I hold the magazine in front of my face, hoping that he won't see who I am. My face burns like it's on fire. Mama and Helen come up from the basement and start oohing and aahing over the things in the basket. Mama makes a fuss over the canned chicken, and Helen acts like the cans of fruit cocktail are gifts from heaven. I wish they wouldn't make such a fuss over something so shameful. And I wish the do-gooder who turned us in would just mind his own business, because we don't need any stupid charity.

Mama wants to learn to how to drive so she can get around to find a job. She enrolls in the *EZ Method Driving School*. Before long, they give her a diploma, and she takes a test from the Detroit Police Driver's Test Station near the city airport. I don't think the test was very rigorous because she is always in a big fluster when she drives, can't make turns, constantly stalls the engine when the light turns green, and can't park to save her soul. She especially had trouble getting into our garage. It's tricky because the driveway takes a jog at the point where there is the corner of our house on one side and a fence post on the other. Whenever Mama wants to get the car into the garage, us kids have to work as a team, one person in front of the car, one on the right side and one on the left shouting directions. But that doesn't help much, because the car has dents and scratches where she hit the house or the fence post. She finally takes to parking out front on the street.

Then she decides to be her own boss as an Avon lady. She goes out on her rounds, her face all made up with lipstick, rouge, and powder, wearing high heels and her best dress. She carries a case filled with cosmetic samples, like tiny tubes of lipstick in all different shades. *Avon calling*, she says as she knocks on the doors of the neighborhood. She had to pay twenty bucks for the kit of samples after answering an ad in the *Detroit News* saying: *Be your own boss. Great business opportunity for ambitious young woman. Set your own hours. Good pay*. But I don't think she makes very much money at that either, and what little she does make, she spends on samples and some nice clothes to make a good impression as she goes from door to door in the neighborhood. She gets all her sisters to sign up for beauty products, but her commissions just don't seem to amount to anything. And food baskets keep coming from the Saint Vincent de Paul.

Why do we need this charity? How did we come to this? I'm supposed to be the man of the house, and it's my responsibility to see that we have what we need. I'm almost fourteen years old, plenty old to hold a job, but no one wants to hire me. *We are in God's hands,* Mama says, not once, not twice, but a hundred thousand times.

38.

Paper Boy

It's my fourteenth birthday and I should be the man of the house, and I shouldn't have to ask Mama for nickels for carfare or fifty cents for the movies, and I should be able to pay for my school books and buy my own clothes, and I should have my own money so I can take my bike to White Castle and buy a bag of hamburgers. Kathleen brings in money from her new job at Awrey's Bakery, and Helen is too young to work because she's only eleven going on twelve. I'm old enough, but I don't have a job.

And then another miracle happens. In the Spring Mama calls the Detroit News and finds out that a paper route will soon be available in our neighborhood. She contacts the boy who is planning to give up his route and pays him the twenty dollars he asks for selling it. The route is on Goulburn Street, from State Fair to Eight Mile Road; sixty-two customers in all. Now I'm a paper boy.

On my first day as a paper boy I get home at three-thirty after school, change into my Levi's, and bike over to Alcoy Street to pick up my papers at a converted garage next to the back yard of a house. About twenty-five boys come here to get their papers. A truck is already there, delivering big bundles of papers tied up with wire. Inside there is a long high bench with a lady behind it. I file in the line waiting at the bench. My turn comes up.

"I'm Pat Reilly. I have a new route on Goulburn Street."

"Well, I'm glad to meet you. I'm Mrs. Elliot—everybody calls me *Mrs. El.* I live in the house right next to the station. I have your name right here in the ledger, and it says you get sixty-two papers. You can take them over there, and fold them," she says, nodding to one of the benches along the wall.

I take a place next to Gene Klein who I already know from the Explorer Scouts. He's fifteen years old—one year older than me. But he looks like he couldn't be a day over twelve. He's short, has a thin, bony face and wispy brown hair. Mama says he looks so angelic, but little does she know. He makes up for his shortness by acting tough, and he likes to pick fights with much bigger guys who generally don't take his bait, being as a bigger guy would look bad fighting someone half his size. So Klein gets to act tough without actually having to fight. "Let me show you how to fold these," he says, folding a paper that stays together in a tight cylinder. "You have to stick these in your bag, like this. Then I'll show you how to attach the bag to your handle bars."

That day I ride down Goulburn Street, and I try to throw the papers on my customer's porches from my bike, but most of the papers miss the porch or fly open after I throw them, and I have to stop each time, pick up the paper, carry it to the porch, and ride on to the next customer.

On the second day at the paper station, I park my bike on its kick-stand outside paper station, but it falls and knocks over the bike next to it. With that, a guy walks up to me. He has a huge ugly scar on his neck and his ear looks like it has been half burnt off. It's Larry Byrnes, someone Gene Klein warned me about. "Stay away from that guy," Klein had said. "He's one mean sucker. He once threw a cat in a can of burning trash. Don't get twisted up with Larry Byrnes."

"What the hell do you think you're doing, Reilly. You knocked over my bike."

"Sorry, Larry. I'll pick it up for you."

"That's going to cost you fifty cents."

"I'm not paying you anything. I didn't even scratch your bike."

"You don't pay me, Reilly, and you're gonna get depantsed. We'll take off your pants and throw them up on the electric wires in back of the station. Make sure you have my money tomorrow."

That night I go to bed in a sweat, worrying about Larry Byrnes, worrying about getting depantsed, worrying about getting picked on by the other boys.

On my third day as a paper boy, Byrnes demands his money but I refuse to pay.

"I'm giving you one more day, Reilly."

After I finish with my route that day, I meet Klein at the end of his route on Westphalia and State Fair.

"What am I going to do about Larry Byrnes? He's trying to make me pay him money."

"You better not pay, Reilly. You do that, and your name will be shit. You have to act tough. Here, take one of these cigarettes. Make sure you smoke it when you get to the station tomorrow. And it doesn't hurt to cuss and spit a lot."

On the third day I park my bike outside the paper station, and Larry Byrnes is already outside, attaching his bag of papers to the handle bars of his bike. I have a lit cigarette dangling from the corner of my mouth. "Shit! This is nothin' but goddam shit! I say to no one in particular. And I spit a gob onto the ground, and walk into the station past Larry Byrnes, who doesn't say a word.

While I'm folding my papers, I try inhaling the smoke, but it makes me dizzy, and I feel like I'm going to puke. Still, I act like smoking is something I do every day.

It still seems next to impossible to ride my bike with a its heavy load of papers balanced on the handle bars, let alone to throw the papers up on the porches when I get to my route. But as the days go by, I learn to go up and down curbs with my load, to ride on the sidewalk in front of my customers' houses, and to throw the papers accurately.

It takes a lot of skill to throw the papers while zipping along on the sidewalk. If I throw the paper too high, it hits the aluminum storm door everyone has on his front door; if it's too low, it hits a concrete step where it splits and tears. If I throw too hard, the front page rips as it slides on the concrete porch; if I throw too soft the paper doesn't make it to the porch, and I have to stop my bike and run up to get it. The trick is to lob it just exactly right so it plops down on the porch in perfect condition. One of my customers has a big elm tree right smack in front of the house. To reach that customer, I have to first pass up the tree, and then throw while I'm looking backwards. I have learned to throw like a pro, and almost never miss any of my porches, including the one with the elm tree in front.

I've been delivering papers for one month now. It's six-thirty on Sunday morning and pouring rain. Mama and the girls are still asleep. I'm sitting in the kitchen with my cold feet propped on the handle of the oven, reading Al Capp's *Lil' Abner* in the Sunday comics. I came home after delivering part of my paper route because I got soaked from head to foot, including my stupid wing-tip support shoes, which are now drying in the oven. I've been wearing this type of shoe ever since Aunt Helen Maloney in Grand Rapids took me to a doctor who said that I had fallen arches and needed support shoes. After that Mama insisted that I wear these torturing things. They cost twenty-five dollars instead of eight bucks like regular shoes and only come in an ugly style that looks like the ones Daddy used to wear— old man wing-tip shoes with little round dents on the toes. They have steel arch supports that dig into the sides of my feet and are so painful until they get broken in. When I dry out, maybe the rain will have slowed down, and then I can finish the rest of my route.

Al Capp is running the story in his comic strip, *Lil' Abner*, about the people in Lower Slobobia, where it is perpetually cold and where the snow is always several feet deep. The Slobobians are so poor that they are nearly naked except for furry short pants and tall fur hats. There's always some polar bear in the village, munching on one of the poor guys. One Lil' Abner story was about how the United States ambassador came to the capital of Lower Slobobia, and the whole town came out to meet him. A little Slobobian kid, named *Little Noodnik*, gave the welcoming poem, which ended with the lines:

And so, Mister Ambassador,
we think you're really swell.
But if you don't like this place,
you can go to .....

and just then, his mother clasps her hand over his mouth and says, "That's enough Little Noodnik." Ever since they ran that strip, Mama has been calling me *Little Noodnik*, which I just hate. If I do something she thinks is clever or else really dumb, she will say, "That's my Little Noodnik." Like the time I mixed chemicals on the kitchen table that were supposed to change color with temperature, but the mixture blew up and made a splot on the ceiling that turned blue or pink, depending on how hot it was. After that Mama told half the world about that splot, acting like she was so proud of my accomplishment, and she would point to the ceiling and say: "That's my Little Noodnik.".

By the time I finish Lil' Abner and get to the Dick Tracy strip, an odd smell like burning tires reminds me of my shoes in the oven. I yank the oven door open and pull out two shriveled shoes that are bubbling and sizzling around the soles. Oh my God! Mama's going to kill me. These aren't just ordinary shoes, they're the special arch support shoes that we have to go down town to buy, and they're only one week old!

I try to put my foot into one shoe, thinking that it might stretch back to the right size. But I can only get my toes inside. I try putting my hand in, but it's so hot that I have to pull it out.

These shoes are a lost cause, ruined forever. I find my old worn-out shoes and change into dry clothes. I hop on my bike and ride off to Goulburn Street. The rain has slowed, and I can finish my route now without trouble.

At home, I meet Mama in the kitchen, and she's holding the ugliest pair of shoes you have ever seen.

"And so, John Patrick Reilly, what in the world is this?"

I tell Mama about how I got soaked in the rain, how I tried to dry out my shoes, how I forgot because of Lil' Abner. "I hate these shoes. They hurt my feet. They're ugly. I don't ever want to wear these stupid things again."

That's my little Noodnik," says Mama, looking half exasperated, and half like she wants to burst into laughter. "From now on, you can wear whatever kind of shoes you want."

The next day I buy a pair of Keds tennis shoes, right in style with all the other guys.

The days and weeks go by, and I continue to deliver my papers. With tips and my earnings, I make big money—eight dollars a week—enough to pay my own way in school and still have enough left over for my own shoes, clothes and other things I need when I start at Nativity High School in September. At the end of August I plunk down a wad of bills for Mama—forty dollars from my paper route earnings to pay for books and tuition. "God Bless you, son," she says. "You are truly the man of the house."

39.

An Attack

Hurry! Hurry! Hurry! says the circus barker, working the crowd. The side show is about to start! See the bearded lady! See the human pin cushion! See the ape woman! Get your tickets now! A knot of men form around the small stage beside the barker to watch the shapely hoochy coochy girls swing their hips. One of them is Helen Rogoza, seventeen years old. She flashes a smile and gives a wink to the men, like the barker wants her to do.

*　　　　*　　　　*　　　　*

We're supposed to be happy in our new home. Daddy's not here to make Mama and us kids miserable. I'm bringing in money from my paper route, Kathleen earns money after school working at Awrey's Bakery, Helen started in the seventh grade at Saint Raymond's, I started school at Nativity High School, Mama just got a new job as a sales lady at Winkelmann's, and the charity food baskets with their cans of fruit cocktail keep rolling in from Saint Vincent de Paul. And now that Daddy's gone, Mama's attacks are supposed to stop. Wasn't he the one who pushed her into them with his arguments and meanness to her? And they did stop after he died—for nearly six months.

"Wake up Pat, wake up." Helen gently shakes me by the shoulder. "Its Mama. She's having an attack. She wants you to come sit with her."

Helen sees that I'm awake, and she turns and leaves my bedroom. I rub my eyes, and swing my feet off the bed, sitting there for a few moments. The clock on my dresser, lit by the hallway light, says eleven o'clock. It's set to wake me up for school tomorrow at six thirty. I know what I'm in for. Ever since Daddy died, it's us kids that have to sit up with her during her attack.

I wish I could get out of this, just pull the covers over my head and go back to sleep. But I hitch up my pajamas and shuffle over to the girls' bedroom. Helen and Kathleen are sitting at Mama's bedside. The room is dimly lit by the hallway light that filters through the half-closed door, keeping the room in shadows, the way Mama wants it when she has an attack. Helen and Kathleen sit at her bedside. There is an empty chair for me.

"Oh, my dearest son. Come sit by me," Mama says, extending her hand. "Take my hand." I don't want to touch her. I just want to get away. I don't know if she'll get through one more night like she always has before. I don't want to be with her, knowing that she may be just on the verge of death, watched by her rotten son who only wanted to get away from her at her final hour.

I put my hand in hers, feeling her warm, sweaty palm. Her fingers tightly grasp my hand, like she's afraid I'll get away. I sit down, feeling trapped and guilty. She's stretched out on the bed, wearing her ragged blue night gown with the little white cotton ball designs, beads of sweat forming on her forehead. Her mouth gapes open, and her breath comes in short gasps. Mercifully, she's wearing her dentures.

"Do you love me, son? Tell me you love me," she says, the words coming out with short huffs of breath.

"Yes, Mama, you know I love you."

"How can you love me? I'm just a worthless person. I'm no good, just filthy rotten trash. I'm such a failure to you children. Aren't I a failure?"

"No Mama, you're not a failure. You do the best you can".

"Oh yes, the best I can. That's all I can do, isn't it. But my best isn't good enough. Everything I do is a failure. I pray for only one thing. That God will give me the strength to live until my youngest daughter, Helen Therese, gets to be eighteen. Lovely Helen Therese, the promise of the Little Flower—my only son Patrick—my dear, beautiful first-born, Kathleen. I just want to see you children to the point that you can take care of yourselves. Then He can take me. Would you be better off if I died right now?"

"No, Mama. We don't want you to die," Helen says. I chime in too, mumbling something under my breath, but I don't really mean it. I just want to go to my bed, to go back to sleep.

I could see this attack coming a week ago, when she went into a rage, throwing the radio down the basement stairs. It was the radio Daddy got her as a present just the day before Christmas two years ago. After that she got bills for the radio because Daddy had charged it on credit, and Mama pays all the bills. I picked up the pieces of the radio where Mama had smashed it, and I patched it back together, replacing a couple of tubes and soldering the antenna wire back in place. Although the plastic case was cracked, the radio worked just fine after my repairs. But Mama didn't seem to appreciate the favor I did for her.

The radio reminds me of the expensive rhinestone necklace that Daddy got her a couple of years before. Just like the radio, he bought the necklace the day before Christmas, and she started to get the bills soon after. The necklace always seemed to make her mad, and she never wore it.

A couple of days ago, Mama started to slam-bang everything around and snap at us kids for stepping out of line, like on Saturday when I didn't get to the vacuuming and dusting of the dining room fast enough, which was my chore for the week. It was then I could see her attack brewing. When that happens, you have to watch out for the strap, which Mama keeps hung up in the kitchen, right where she can reach it from the table. It's a leather purse strap, round and tough, like a whip. She mostly uses it nowadays on me and Helen for bickering, which is what we do half of the time. When the bickering gets on her nerves, out comes the strap. Mama goes for skin, aiming for anything pink, like your legs as you roll around on the floor, or your bare arms, and she doesn't miss like Daddy used to. That strap will leave red welts for several days. When Mama goes on the war path, I just try to stay out of her way.

Nowadays Kathleen doesn't get the strap so much as me and Helen, maybe because she's getting too big. And Kathleen doesn't lie down when Mama goes into a fit. She and Mama stand toe-to-toe, screaming at each other. That happens so much that I just try to stay out of the house whenever I can.

I'm always afraid that Mama might die at any minute, even when she isn't having an attack. She always says, "Just because I don't carry a sign on my back announcing how I feel, it doesn't mean that I'm not in pain." In the evenings, she props her legs up on a stool, and you can see the fat varicose veins sticking out like blue ropes beside her shin bone. She says that if she ever were to cut one of those veins, the blood would spurt all over and would even reach the ceiling. Sometimes when Mama goes into a fit, stamping her feet and screaming out in Polish, I'm afraid that she will slice one of those veins, and then it will be a bloody mess. I have read my Boy Scout manual over and over on where the pressure points are to stop the blood from spurting out, so I'm prepared for the day when it finally happens.

Mama sits up. "Get me the bed pan, quick." Kathleen jumps up, and goes to the closet, pulling out the bed pan. "Here it is, Mama." She sets the bed pan on the side of the bed, where Mama leans over it, making coughing and gagging noises, like she's going to throw up. But the only thing that comes out of her mouth is a string of drool. She plops back down on the pillow, crying out "Water! Water! Please, get me water!" Helen runs to the bathroom and comes back with a glass of water, handing it to Mama, who props herself up on one elbow, takes a sip, hands the glass to Helen, and falls back on to the pillow.

"Son, please, get me a hot water bottle." I rush to the bathroom and pull the red rubber bottle from the hook on the wall. I know just how Mama likes her hot water bottle, since she showed me long ago. First, I have to get the water temperature just right, not too hot or not too cold. Then I fill it just about half full. Then, and this is the really important part, I push out the air before screwing the cap back in. After that I wrap it in a hand towel, bring it to Mama, and hand it to her. She puts it on her stomach, and adjusts it over and over, like she can't find the right spot.

She starts to arch her back, as if writhing in pain. "Holy Mother in heaven, take me. Please take me."

"Please, Mama, don't die," Helen sobs.

"I'll call the doctor," Kathleen says, running to the dresser beside Mama's bed, where we keep the phone. She flips through the address book, looking for the number of Doctor Johnson. "I'll get him to come right out."

"No," Mama says, gasping for breath. "I don't want the doctor, not yet. I'll tell you when it's time for that. Please, just wait."

Kathleen goes back to her chair, sits down, and stares vacantly ahead. Mama starts talking about things she thinks are happening to her but they're really not, about things in her imagination, in her memory. Some of the things are from when she was a little girl. She talks about getting beaten by her mother. About how her mother threw things at her, dishes and bowls smashing onto the wall. About how she had to clean up all the mess afterwards. About how she wanted to go to school, but her mother wouldn't let her. She talks about how she's failed us kids, how she wants our forgiveness. Mama talks and talks, and we just sit there listening, knowing that we're not supposed to say anything.

Finally, Mama seems to be tiring, slowing down. She lets out a long groan, like she's exhausted. "Please, son" she says, breathing in deep, slow breaths. "Light me a cigarette." I pull out one of her Camels from the pack on the dresser, and light it with a match, taking a few drags to get it going well and hand it to her. She takes deep drags, and blows the smoke up to the ceiling. This is the stage of Mama's attack where I know the worst is over, and that she will pull through it. She talks more, taking a long drag from her cigarette every once in awhile. Finally, the cigarette is finished, and she smashes the butt in the little bean-bag ashtray beside her, circling it round and around with a feeble motion of her hand.

"I'm ready to sleep now," she says. "You children go to bed. And pray for me."

I shuffle back to my bedroom. The clock says a quarter to two. I know that six-thirty is going to roll around quickly, when I'll have to take the buses and street car to Nativity High School. And I know what will be in store for me for the next few days. Tomorrow, when I get home from school, Mama will be up and around, in a mad cleaning mode, vacuuming every corner of the house, washing floors and windows. She will keep that up for maybe another day or two. During that time, I'll have to keep out of her way, because she'll be on a hair trigger. Then she'll be all back to normal.

This time we got through one more attack, and Mama didn't die. How much longer will she keep having them? Why can't the doctors cure her? They took out half of her insides, and they gave her all kinds of pills, but still the attacks keep coming. Will the next one will kill her? Will it kill me?

Mama smashes the radio several more times during screaming fits in the weeks following this attack. I don't know why it angers her so, and I patch it up each time. In a final rage against the radio, she hurls it against the floor, again and again, stomps on the pieces, all the while shouting with rage in Polish. She grasps the radio's cord, swinging the broken chassis in a wide arc which connects with her varicose-veined leg, causing a shockingly monstrous and ugly bruise. I think this may be the time when I have to use my boy scout first aid skills, but the bruise holds, and blood doesn't spurt. This time the radio is destroyed beyond even my powers to resurrect it.

40.

Nativity

Sister Michael Linda patiently listens to me read my English composition as I stand beside my desk. Half way through, I crouch down to tie my shoe, and that signals everybody else in the ninth-grade class of Nativity High School to do the same thing, just the way we planned it. Then I stand up and continue with my composition as everyone else sits up, acting like nothing has happened.

Sister has a big smile on her face. "Well, John, I see that you and the rest of the class are having trouble with your shoes today. I can fix that. I want each person to remove their right shoe." We do as she says. "Now pass your shoe to the person in back of you, and the last one in the row has to bring that shoe up to the front." Laughter and giggles fill the room as we carry out her orders. "Now put on your friends shoe." By now our English class has fallen to pieces, and there is general pandemonium as we try on shoes that won't fit. Eventually, after a lot of confusion, everyone gets his shoe back, and we take a stab at the rest of the English lesson. These shenanigans aren't unusual in Sister Michael Linda's class at Nativity High School, where I entered the ninth grade. She jokes with the kids, and, to boost class spirit, sometimes encourages us to sing popular songs in class.

They call me *John* here, and this leads to embarrassing situations when someone calls out: "John," and I don't even realize that I'm the one being spoken to. This *John* business started on the first day of school when I reported to my ninth-grade class. There were little cards on each desk with each student's name, telling where you were supposed to sit. Mine said *John Reilly*. I was too shy to tell Sister Michael Linda, my new home-room and English teacher, that John was my father's name, not mine. I would look like a fool if I tried to explain that my real name is *Pat*, and *John* is just a legal name on a piece of paper. So now I'm *John* to everybody, a name I really hate. I'll just have to get used to it, because it's too late to change now.

Sister Michael Linda is out of the room for a potty break, Chris leads a discussion about what song to sing when she comes back. She is one of the smartest and most popular girls in class. She has a quick smile, is friendly to everybody, even the class drips, and she's a natural leader in the class. We decide to sing Johnny Ray's new hit *Walking My Baby Back Home*, but there is a troublesome part that goes:

> *We started to pet, and that's when I get,*
> *Her powder all over my vest.*

To clean up the verse, Chris suggests that we substitute *We started to talk*. Although it won't rhyme, it won't scandalize Sister Michael Linda, who probably doesn't understand boy and girl things.

"Well, what did you decide to sing?" asks Sister Michael Linda as she returns to the classroom. Chris stands, and leads the class in song.

> *Gee but it's great after staying out late,*
> *Walking my baby back home.*
> *Arm in arm over meadow and farm,*
> *Walking my baby back home.*

The whole school is now assembled in the gym where they are playing records. Some of the kids are dancing, and the others are gathered in groups of all-boys or all-girls. All the popular boys and girls are going on dates, but I could never work up the nerve to even talk to one of the girls. When I tried, my tongue got all twisted up, and my face went red. And when it comes to dancing, my feet never knew what to do. But I've been practicing dancing at home with my sister Kathleen, who taught me a new step.

I notice Chris standing in a group with her girl friends. She is not only smart, pretty, and popular, she is one of the nicest girls in class, and I think I can work up my courage to ask her for a dance. I saunter over to her circle.

"Hi, Chris. Would you like to dance with me?"

"I'd be glad to, John," and she gives me a big warm smile that puts me right into heaven.

I start the dance step that Kathleen taught me, but it must be something new to her, because the two of us keep stumbling over each other's feet, with her almost falling to the floor. The whole school must be watching. Chris regains her composure, and whispers in my ear "Just do the two-step," and we switch to the simple step I learned at a seventh-grade party. It seems like the dance piece will never end, and my embarrassment only grows with each passing minute. Finally, the tune is finished.

"Thank you for the dance, Chris," I say, but I'm thinking: *Oh God! I've made such a fool out of myself.*

"My pleasure, John," she says, and she turns and walks to her circle of friends, probably to talk about how mortified she is.

At my circle of friends, all the guys are laughing and mimicking me, saying things like "Here's Reilly," and they pretend to be dancing like Frankenstein. I don't know if I'll ever again be able to work up my nerve again to ask a girl to dance, let alone to ask her out, because from now on I will have the reputation as the *toe crusher*.

Even though I have trouble socializing with the girls, and I have to get used to all new kids, Nativity High School is like heaven compared with Annunciation. For one thing, the Nativity nuns are much nicer, and they never slap anybody around. In the Dominican order they wear cheerful-looking white habits with a black veil rather than the dark outfits that the IHM nuns at Annunciation wore. The best thing I like about Nativity is that we keep switching classes, and we have different nuns for each class, like English, history, religion, algebra, and general science. So you don't have to worry about getting one mean nun on your back all day, every day, like at Annunciation.

To get to Nativity, I take two buses and then the Gratiot Street Car. The trip here is a lot faster than going to Annunciation last semester.

Just like at Annunciation, we begin every school day by going to Mass. But all is not perfect at Nativity. Our morning Mass is always said by the pastor, Father Geller. Although the nuns here aren't mean, Father Geller has enough meanness to go around for everybody. This guy is so disagreeable that he makes Father Carol, the crabby pastor at Annunciation, look like your best friend.

You never know when Father Geller is going to get a bug up his ass, and rail at the whole school. This usually happens right after Mass, when, instead of walking off the altar, he sets down the chalice on the altar and walks out of the sanctuary to the big center aisle of the church. Then he begins his harangue, starting slowly at first, then working himself up into a frenzy, with his strong baritone voice thundering and echoing in the church while he makes his way up and down the center aisle. Usually he goes on about the evils of teen-agers.

On one Saturday he spotted a convertible parked alongside the school, with four kids in it, laughing and smoking cigarettes. Father Geller has a strict rule against smoking within two blocks of the school or church, even if it is on a Saturday and on the public streets. And it was especially bad that it happened in a convertible, which he thinks is the very symbol of decadence in teenagers. That incident got him to work up a forty-five minute tirade on the following Monday after Mass.

I learned my lesson: never go to confession to Father Geller. One time I tried him because all the other confession lines were longer. I confessed a sin of impurity, using a small voice that I hoped he wouldn't notice. But that only made him give me a loud, angry lecture that made my sins the business of the whole church.

It's hard to make friends at a new school, and I must have looked like a jerk on the first day because of my haircut, with the sideburns shaved off, just like I had been getting it cut all my life. After a few days of class, Marty, one of the popular guys in our class, whispered in my ear "Your hair cut makes you look like a jerk. Why don't you let your sideburns grow out?" At first I thought he was trying to tease me, but I could see that he was dead serious. I didn't say anything to him, but now my sideburns look like all the other guys'. I think Marty saved me from becoming the class dork.

Joe is in my class, and he knows a lot about electricity. His brother owns an electronics store where they sell the newest things in radios, TVs, and audio equipment. Its hard to impress Joe with my electrical inventions, which are pretty simple compared the fancy stuff he brings from his brother's store. I don't tell him about my electric shocker and the tricks I play with it—Joe is too sophisticated and serious for the likes of that!

Joe and I often work together on school projects. Around Christmas time we write a play and perform it for the whole class. I play the blind beggar, and Joe is the narrator. In the play, the beggar stumbles around in the snow looking for the new Christ child while running into snow drifts and walls and tripping over fences because he can't see. All he has in life are his ragged clothes and a penny, and he wants to give that to Jesus. Finally, after trudging through three-foot snow drifts, nearly freezing to death because his clothes are ragged and his shoes are full of holes, he finds the manger, and he gives the penny to baby Jesus. Just then his blindness is cured. After we finish performing, the whole class is dead silent, kind of looking straight ahead. I think maybe they are overcome by the emotion of the whole thing.

I write another story called *Jungle Terror*, which I read aloud in class. It is about these two guys who go off to Africa to hunt for diamonds, and they get stuck in some stinking hut in the jungle. Then these monstrous ants come in a swarm across the jungle, and the guys barricade themselves in the diamond mine, but the ants can smell them in there and keep trying to eat through the mine entrance for days. Just as their food is running out and the ants are making it through the door, the Congo birds save them by killing the ants. While they were in the mine, they discovered a vein of diamonds, which means that they will be rich. I like my stories to have happy endings.

Sister Michael Linda says she really likes my story, and that I should submit it to a literature contest for high school kids sponsored by the *Detroit News*. So for two weeks I stay every day after class while Sister goes over the story with me, word by word, line by line. On every sentence she says something like "Wouldn't it be better if you said it this way?" and she writes something over my sentence, or "Let's try this other wording," or "I think you need to add a couple of sentences here," as she writes in something.

She gets me to look up stuff about diamonds in the encyclopedia, and I work in a part where, just as the guys are thinking about killing themselves, one of them says: "What's this? Look! Jack, see this bluish-green rock! It's serpentinous rock. This rock contains diamonds!" Sister is very impressed, especially with *serpentinous*, which makes me feel really smart. When we are finished, my story is a hundred times better than the one I started with. Mama types it up, and I submit it to the *Detroit News Scholastic Writing Contest*.

After a couple of months I get an award for *Jungle Terror*. It is a dictionary with a page that reads:

This Book is Presented
by the Detroit News
To John Reilly,
Winner of an Achievement Key
in the Southeastern Michigan Regional
Scholastic Writing Awards Program,
May 1, 1952.

Mama is ecstatic and she brags about me to everyone in sight. I don't tell her that Sister Michael Linda really deserves the award.

41.

Gene

"God damn you, Klein! You say one more word, and I'll bash your head in!" Mr. El holds a piece of a two-by-two as a club above his head, while he straddles the cowering figure of Gene Klein lying on his back on the cold cement floor of our paper folding station. He tightly grips the club, like he's ready to swing it in a crushing blow. The sides of the garage are lined with us paper boys, standing at the benches along the walls where we had been folding and stuffing papers into our delivery bags. Just moments ago Klein was needling Mr. El without let-up, and Mr. El had warned him with polite little hints like "Shut your damn mouth Klein, or I'll shut it for you." But that only egged on Klein all the more. Then I heard Mr. El cursing, and he grappled with Klein and threw him to the floor.

Every one silently stares at the scene in the middle of the station. Nobody speaks or even moves, like a movie frozen on one frame, with Mr. El standing there poised like the statue of liberty, only he holds a club instead of a torch. Gene looks up at him from his position on the floor, and he's breathing hard. I know he's weighing the possibilities. *Should I push the old fart a little further, or does he really mean to smash me with that club?* I say a silent prayer for Gene because I think he's really going to need God's help this time. *Please God, keep Klein's mouth shut.* I hear my own breathing, and can see the steamy puffs of my breath in the cold winter air. Klein stays silent, not moving a muscle.

It seems like an eternity, but finally Mr. El throws the club against the side of the garage where it bounces and clatters to the floor. He goes behind the long wooden counter where he hands out our papers. Klein gets up and goes to his place on the long bench lining one wall where he was setting up his *Bulldogs*— the Saturday night supplements to the Sunday morning Detroit News. Mr. El counts out some papers from the stack for the next guy in line, but his hands are trembling. Klein resumes stuffing his papers into his delivery bag, and his hands are trembling too. For once in his life he keeps quiet. The rest of the guys resume talking and kidding, but it's much more subdued than normal, and no one says a word about what just happened. I think everyone realizes that Gene pushed Mr. El just about over the edge this time, and nobody wants to push him any further. I take my papers to my bike outside, where I wait for Klein.

This was probably a bad time for him to mouth off to Mr. El, who likes to take a few pulls on his flask on Saturday nights. And it was an especially dangerous time because Mrs. El, who hands out the papers during the week and who knows how to keep all the guys in line, doesn't usually work Saturday nights.

Mr. El is a tall guy, as skinny as a bean pole, with a bushy little mustache under his nose. His eyes are generally bloodshot, especially at six o'clock in the morning, the official time for getting our Sunday papers, when someone has to pound on the back door of his house, shouting out a wake up call like "Get your ass out here Mr. El. We need our papers." That will generally get him to stagger out, mumbling curses under his breath, his bloodshot eyes looking like he will bleed to death.

Mrs. El handles the papers on weekdays when we get them after school, and she collects the money and keeps the books Saturday afternoons when we have to pay in advance for the next week's papers from the money we collect on Friday. The guys all like and respect her, even though she likes to joke around. If Mrs. El had been here, none of this would have happened; she knows how to handle both Mr. El and Klein.

Klein finally has his Bulldogs set up in his delivery bag, and he takes them out to his bike, where he hoists up the heavy load on to the handle bar. He steps on the pedal with his left foot, scooters with the right foot, and swings his leg over the bike, riding right past me. "Let's go Reilly." I take off after him as he rides up Manning Street, and I catch up to him a block away where he has stopped. He is wedging one of the rolled-up Bulldogs in between the handle bar and the paper bag strap. I stop alongside and start doing the same. Then he takes out a stick match and lights the loose end of the roll, where it builds up to a healthy flame. I get mine going the same way. When we both have a flaming torch, we blow them out, and are left with a red glowing ember which will warm our hands in the frigid air.

Gene hands me a fat stogie, the kind we often buy on Saturday nights at two for six cents. We both bite off a piece of the stub end, spit it out, and get the business end going by sticking it against the glowing torch, and puffing a few times. With our glowing arsenal, we pedal away, first across to State Fair, and then up to Westphalia, which is the start of his route.

"Meet you later, maferdyke, after the route," he says.

"Okay, dick head, I reply," and I proceed one more block to the start of my route on Goulburn Street.

Delivering the Bulldogs is especially miserable in the winter because it is dark and can be so awfully cold. The Saturday night Bulldogs and the Sunday morning papers are always too thick to fold, so I deliver them by taking each one up to the customer's porch. On the other days the papers are thin enough that they can be folded for throwing. Though I'm not throwing papers tonight, it's hard to even get them out of the bag because my hands are so frozen. I keep my hands bare, because gloves just make them clumsier, which slows me down. They start to feel numb, so I cup them around the glowing stub end of the Bulldog wedged on my handle bar and I blow it into a hot red coal that will make my hands work for another half a block. I take a few drags on my cigar, which warms me some more.

I work the four blocks to Eight Mile Road, the end of my route, cross over, and make my way back to State Fair, delivering the papers on the other side of Goulburn. When I finish with my deliveries, I bike down to Westphalia and wait there. Usually, Klein finishes first, but tonight he seems to be off his stride, because it takes another five minutes before he gets here. We ride together down to the vacant lot on State Fair and Joann and push our bikes near a shallow pit. We scrounge for scraps of wood, piling them into the pit, and soon we have a roaring fire that will warm us to the core. We like to sit around these fires on Saturday nights, telling stories. But tonight I feel that I need to give some wise, friendly advice.

"Klein, you are a class-A ass hole. You coulda got yourself killed tonight, needling Mr. El like that. You gotta learn to keep your mouth shut when you're getting someone pissed off."

"Don't worry about it, fart-face," he replies. "I know how to handle the old geezer."

"Some day, you're going to get yourself killed," I say. I remind him of the time he got on the nerves of the guys at the station, and they made him walk the plank. They tied his hands behind his back, tied his feet together, and then tied one of the delivery bags over his head. Lilla and Nelson put him on a wooden board, carried the board with him on it out to the alley, and held the board about two feet above a muddy puddle. *Jump Klein! Jump!* they had shouted. Just when it looked like he wasn't going to play along, Byrnes came up behind him, and gave him a push. But instead of jumping off, he keeled over like a dead man and fell flat on his face into the puddle where he thrashed around for a few seconds. That's when Lilla and Nelson ran over and pulled him out of the puddle, untied his hands and feet, and removed the bag. When Gene sat up, he was soaked and covered in mud from head to foot, with blood running from his nose down his chest. The inside of his bag was covered with blood too. Klein wasn't crying or the least bit mad. He accepted the apologies of Lilla and Nelson, hopped on his bike, and rode off. After about twenty minutes he came roaring back to the station, screeched his brakes outside as he slid in the gravel and strode in wearing a fresh set of clothes, to the cheers of half the guys still in the station.

"Aw, Reilly, you worry too much," Gene says as he pokes the fire to get it flaming. Those guys were just kidding. Don't worry about me. I know how to take it."

We talk on and on. After awhile, the fire dies to glowing embers, which we put out by kicking dirt into the pit. "See you tomorrow, gorp," he says, as he shoves off on his bike. "See you, puke face," I reply.

42.

Fever

Just before her thirteenth birthday, Helen comes down with a sore throat and a fever that lingers for a week. Mama takes her to the doctor who prescribes penicillin, but she keeps running a fever. She goes back to the doctor once again, but this time Mama comes back with bad news. "Rheumatic fever," she says to Kathleen and me, out of Helen's earshot . "It can settle in different places of her body and can cause permanent damage to vital organs. They're worried about her getting a rheumatic heart, and that could weaken her heart for life. The doctor gave me the option of taking her home or to the hospital."

"What are you going to do?" asks Kathleen.

"I asked the doctor to admit her to Holy Cross. And I'm getting admitted there too, right along with Helen."

"What are you talking about?" Kathleen and I ask, almost in unison.

"It's my colitis attacks. God knows they're not getting any better. Doctor Johnson wants to do some tests, and I thought this would be a good time to do it. Helen and I will be in the hospital together, and I can visit her there. Kathleen, you're sixteen, and Patrick, you're fifteen. The two of you can take care of yourselves."

Kathleen and I fend for ourselves at home, which is strangely quiet and peaceful. After one week, Mama comes home. "Helen will have to stay in the hospital for three more weeks," she says. "But she'll recover. As for me, they are baffled about the source of my attacks. My sister, Lilly, came to visit me in the hospital, and she gave me her explanation. 'It's in your head,' she said, and Mama effects a snippy tone, mimicking her sister. 'I read where people who get colitis attacks need a head doctor.' Can you believe that? How dare she suggest to me my illness is in my head." She says this through her teeth, with her jaw hard set, and I can see that she is getting steamed because someone dared to suggest she is sick in the head. And I'm afraid that Mama can read my thoughts, because sometimes I think that too, and I have to chase those ideas away, like I have to do to the impure thoughts that sometimes come without warning and need confessing if you don't get rid of them.

Mama shuttles Helen's homework from Saint Raymond's so she can keep up with her seventh-grade class. At the end of June, after a month in the hospital, Helen comes home.

"The fever has settled in her heart," informs Mama. "She shouldn't exert herself until they are sure the fever is entirely gone. They're worried about permanent scarring of her heart."

Helen spends another six weeks lying in her bed or on the living room couch. . "No excitement for her," Mama says. "It could kick up the fever again. She has to be peaceful and quiet at all times. We put our trust in the Holy Mother to bring her through."

Mama juggles her work schedule at Winkelman's so she can care for Helen, Kathleen pitches in when she's not working at Aurey's bakery. When the weather is nice, I carry Helen out to the back yard, and place her in a reclining lawn chair, and she feels as light as a rag doll. Mama makes sure we pray the rosary together every day, with Helen joining in from the sofa, while Mama, Kathleen, and I kneel around her.

I don't know how Helen can stand it, having to lie in bed all day long. If that ever happened to me, I would surely go nuts. But the good part of all of this is that Mama seems to feel well, full of energy. She stays calm, cheerful and focused on Helen's illness—no rages, no broken dishes, and no attacks. Did her stay in the hospital finally cure her for good?

43.

The Explorers

Mr. Zindler is the Leader of Explorer Post Sixty-Six, which meets at seven o'clock every Wednesday at Saint Raymond's Church. I joined the Post as soon as I turned fourteen—the minimum age to be an explorer scout. Right off, I knew I was going to love this outfit. The boys run the meetings and Mr. Zindler acts like an advisor, keeping us from doing anything dumb or illegal. He brings in literature and information on activities from scout headquarters and he rounds up the drivers and gear if we need to go somewhere. Last year we made a three-day canoe trip of ninety miles on the Au Sable River.

I like being in scouting. It's like my own special family. I like the meetings, the way we get to plan our events, the service projects we do in the community, the merit badges and awards, the music and singing, the close friendships, the archery the guys in our Post pride ourselves on, and the precision knife throwing routines we have developed. I like learning so many things, like canoeing, horseback riding, survival skills, and first aid skills—things I want to keep doing all my life. The best part of Post Sixty-Six is that Mr. Zindler acts like a father to all of us. He has a family of his own, but he is separated from his wife and young boy, who is retarded with Down's Syndrome. So I think he considers us as his family.

Our big outdoor activity this summer is a cabin trip here at Camp Menamora. The boys are in a neat row facing Mr. Zindler in a cabin at Camp Menamora. He leads us in the scout oath.

The Scout Oath: On my honor, I will do my best, to do my duty to God and my country, to obey the scout law, to help other people at all times, to keep myself physically strong, mentally awake, and morally straight.

The Scout Law: A scout is trustworthy, loyal, helpful, friendly, courteous, kind, obedient, cheerful, thrifty, brave, clean, and reverent.

The Scout Motto: Be prepared.

"Okay, guys," says Mr. Zindler, "Free time till *lights out* at eleven o'clock." Dinner tonight was cooked by Mr. Zindler and the Lessard brothers, Danny and Denis. I had to help tonight's assigned dinner cleanup crew as extra KP duty because of the little trick I pulled yesterday on Mr. Favor, the adult advisor here at the camp. He was taking a nap in the afternoon, with his bare feet sticking out of the covers. I couldn't resist wiring up his toes to my shocker and giving him a short zap, just as a wake up call. Some people just don't have any sense of humor.

I light up a cigarette, knowing with satisfaction that the other guys will have to sneak out in the woods for their smokes. Other than the adult advisors, I'm the only guy in the post who is allowed to smoke out in the open, with the one exception of Johnny Bober, who lights up one of his green-tobacco *Asmadore Cigarettes* whenever he has an asthma attack. But nobody counts that as a real cigarette. This is how I got permission to smoke.

I started smoking soon after I turned fourteen, when I started delivering papers. I had been bumming cigarettes one or two at a time from my buddies at the paper station. When I would come home after smoking, I would usually run straight into the bathroom to brush my teeth, hoping that Mama wouldn't smell the tobacco smoke on my breath. I got away with that for a while, until one day when Mama called me aside for a little private talk. She looked straight into my eyes, and asked: "Patrick, I want you to tell me the truth, are you smoking?"

Mama has a way of telling if you're lying, by just looking into your eyes. So it doesn't do any good to even think about lying.

"Yes, Mama," I admitted, looking down at the floor, "but only a couple of times," wondering how she found out.

"Well, I thought so. Look here." She pulled up one of my shirts she had been holding, and turned the pocket inside out, like she does whenever she prepares the clothes for washing. "Look at this." There at the bottom of the pocket were little brown flecks of tobacco, the dregs from the cigarettes I keep in that pocket.

I wondered where all this was leading. Was Mama going to give me a punishment, or just forbid me to smoke again, with some threat starting with *If I ever catch you smoking, I'll ...?* Instead she said: "Well you might as well do it out in the open. I don't want my son sneaking behind my back." That night Mama and I lit up cigarettes after dinner, to the utter amazement of Kathleen and Helen who sputtered and looked at me with their eyes as wide as saucers, saying, "What are you doing? You can't do that!" But Mama just sat there, with a little smile on her face.

Now it just so happens that fourteen is also the age when you are allowed to graduate from Boy Scout Troop Sixty-Six to Explorer Scout Post Sixty-Six, both of which meet at Saint Raymond's school. When I first joined, Mr. Zindler told me the rules of conduct that included: *If you are under eighteen, no smoking at scout functions, and that includes meetings, unless you have written permission from your parents.*

Since Mama gave me permission to smoke at home, I asked her to write a note giving me permission to smoke at scout functions too. At the next meeting I presented Mr. Zindler with a note signed by Mama:

My son John Patrick Reilly has my permission to smoke at scout functions.

Mr. Zindler studied the note for a while. "Pat, just let me check this out with your mother, before you light up, okay?" "Sure, Mr. Zindler," I said, knowing full well that he would be honor-bound to let me smoke. After all, didn't we go over the Scout

Law, explaining the meaning of each and every word? Under *trustworthy*, we said that a scout always keeps his word, always lives up to his agreements. And I knew that Mama was honor bound too, by her own law.

The next week, I lit up, right there in the classroom at Saint Raymond's School, where we hold our meeting. The best part was the slack-jawed looks I got from the older smokers, like Danny and Dave, who still had to sneak their smokes.

The KP is finished, and the guys gather around the mess table. Bober pulls out his accordion, and Wallace gets out his ukulele. They strike up *Has Anybody Seen My Gal*. The music that comes out of those instruments is wonderful, like nothing I've ever heard performed live. Wallace strums a complicated string of chords, while Bober's fingers dance on the keys and buttons. Everybody joins in on the song.

> *Five foot two, eyes of blue,*
> *But oh what those five foot could do,*
> *Has any body seen my gal?*
> *Turned up nose, turned down hose,*
> *Flapper yes sir, one of those,*
> *Has anybody seen my gal?*

I've never heard music played up close like this, except for my harmonica and the bugle, and those don't count as a real instruments. It seems like I'm watching a movie, only I'm in it. I've just got to learn how to play a real musical instrument.

At ten-thirty Mr. Zindler calls us to our night time ceremony. Since we are a Catholic explorer post, we get in a prayer at every scout function. Krajewski leads in an *Our Father* and a *Hail Mary*. We ask for the blessings of Saint George, the patron of scouting, and Saint Raymond, the patron of our parish. We then make the scout sign over our hearts and recite the solemn prayer that ends every scouting function, and every scouting day.

And now, may the Great Master of all good scouts, be with us until we meet again.

We file into our bunk beds, while Krajewski goes through the cabin, turning the valves to shut down each of the six gas lamps that light up our cabin.

The next day after breakfast we make the trek from the cabin to the lake. On the way we throw rocks at the giant hornet's nest that hangs like a huge fat football high up in a tree branch above the path. Everybody makes a few tries, but no one connects. Finally, Wilson hits the nest dead center, splitting it in two, with one half falling to the ground. Everyone runs like crazy to the lake and dives straight in—they say a hornet won't follow you into the water. I swim to the platform in the middle of the lake along with the other strong swimmers who are allowed to go there—the ones who have either passed the tests for life saving, or have proven they can swim fifty yards. The weak swimmers, like Klein, are supposed to stay at the shore.

There is a wooden ladder that lets you get up on the platform. Once there, I shinny up a fat piling and stand on it, looking down at the water fifteen feet below. I decide to do a dead man dive by holding my hands against my side and just keeling over head first to the water. I call it a dead man dive, because I'm acting like I'm dead, but the dive is supposed to be perfectly safe, nothing that would actually kill you. I feel my head strike the surface of the water, and my body slides in the water with hardly a ripple—a perfect dead man dive. I decide to see how far this will carry me, so instead of putting my hands out to divert myself to the surface, I just keep them at my sides, and I'm still in a dead man dive. It feels like I have been sinking for a long time when I feel a cold layer on my face. Then, as my momentum slows, my head sharply strikes the bottom, and it surprised me. I do a quick reversal, and spring my feet against the bottom to propel myself up to the surface. Everyone is laughing and splashing. I climb up the ladder, and sit on the platform, jittery from my dive, which seems to haunt me for some strange reason. I rub my sore neck. "You okay?" asks

Denis, standing at the ladder. "Sure, I'm fine," I say, not telling him about my dive. But I wonder where I would be now if that lake had been one foot shallower. Would I be a dead man?

In September, during my ninth grade at Nativity High School, something strange happens. Mama gets all excited, and she dresses up in her best dress, puts on bright lipstick and rouge on her cheeks. "I've got a date with Vincent Zindler, your explorer Advisor. He's coming to pick me up for a date. We're going to dinner," she says with a shy grin, like a young school girl. And when Mr. Zindler rings the bell, I know it's not to see me. He's here to pick up Mama for a date. He's dressed not at all like he going to an explorer function, but he wears a white shirt and a spiffy tie. Imagine that! Mama and Mr. Zindler going out, like two school kids.

After that, Mr. Zindler comes again and again. They go dancing, they go roller skating, they go to the movies, they go to Bell Isle for walks. And Mama has never been happier. She sings around the house, jokes around, and even does a little dance while she dusts the furniture. Is Mr. Zindler is going to be my new father?

After six weeks of dating Mr. Zindler, Mama stops singing and acting like a young school girl. Her mood suddenly shifts to anger.

"If you really want to know why I'm angry, it's because of that lying Vincent. Zindler. If he wants to go to hell, he'll not drag me with him. When we first began to date, he told me the church was annulling his marriage, and that we were free to date. Now I find out that it's a divorce he's getting, not an annulment. And we're committing a sin before God and the Holy Mother by dating. I told him in no uncertain term what I thought of him."

The following week I go to our Post meeting at Saint Raymond's. I don't know if I can even look at Mr. Zindler, I feel so ashamed. It's not because of anything he did. It's because I don't know what Mama said to him, and I know she can be devastating when she's mad. But Mr. Zindler conducts the meeting as if nothing has happened. 9

The Explorer Scouts at Camp Menamora, Summer of 1952. From left to right: Mike Wilson, Don Kryewski, Denis Lessard, Pat Reilly, Mr. Favor, Dave Wallace, Danny Lessard, John Bober.

44.

Free Tuition

Kathleen is in the eleventh grade at Saint Charles, I'm in the tenth grade at Nativity, and Helen is in the eighth grade at Saint Raymond's. At the beginning of the year, Helen walks the four blocks from our house to State Fair Street, takes a bus for another four blocks, and walks the final two blocks to school. The short bus ride saves her a bit of walking, which is necessary because the doctor says she is still weak from her rheumatic fever and is left with a heart murmur, which means the valves in her heart are scarred, probably forever.

During the next few weeks, Helen becomes stronger, and she eventually walks the whole way to school and back.

In the middle of October she comes home from school in a miserable state of tears. She blurts out her story to Mama in between sobs.

"I'm so embarrassed. Sister Amelia called on me in class. I didn't know the answer to her question. So she said it to me in front of the whole class, 'I would think you would try harder, Helen, you being a charity case.' I was never so humiliated in my life. Why am I a charity case, Mama?"

"Sister had no right to embarrass you in front of the class. You're not a charity case. It's just that they are giving you free tuition at Saint Raymond's to help our family in our time of need."

"I don't want to be a charity case. I can't face Sister Amelia. I can't face my class. I don't want to go to Saint Raymond's anymore. I want to go to the public school."

"I don't think that's possible, Helen. It's my obligation to see that you get a proper Catholic education. And besides, you can't possibly switch schools in the middle of a semester."

"Then I want a job. I'm strong enough to work now. Kathleen's working at Awrey's, and Pat has his paper route, and I can work too. I want to pay my own tuition. I don't ever want to be a charity case again."

Helen gets her wish. Mama finds out that there's a family in the parish needing help after school, and Helen takes the job. After a few days, she tells me all about it.

"I'm working for the Mahoney family. Would you believe that Mr. and Mrs. Mahoney are both blind, and they have six kids. I'm supposed to go there after school on three weekdays, and half a day on Saturday. Mr. Mahoney is a State Representative, and Mrs. Mahoney works from home."

"What are your jobs?"

"I watch the kids, help clean the house, and help with preparation of dinner. I do ironing too, but Mrs. Mahoney doesn't want me to iron her husband's shirts. She says she wants to be sure they are done right. Can you believe that? She's blind, but still she irons, cooks dinner, and cares for the family. And Mr. Mahoney somehow goes downtown on public transportation. I like the family, and they treat me real nice, but what I don't like about working for them is the walk home. When I get out of school, I have to go there in the opposite direction from our house. When I come home, it's dark, and I have a long walk home. It scares me to walk alone after dark."

For her work, Helen is paid five dollars a week, which she hands over to Mama. Within a few weeks, Mama says she has used Helen's earnings to pay for her tuition for the semester. Helen is off the charity roster of Saint Raymond's School.

45.

Unsavory Adventures

Gene and I are up to nighttime adventures. We have placed a packet of my homemade gun powder with a two-minute time fuse on the window sill of a house on Fairmont Street, where we could see through the open front window the flickers of a television set. Two minutes is plenty of time to sneak out from the bushes, jump on our bikes, and ride to the end of the block. There we stop our bikes and wait for a prank to unfold just one-half block away. When it seems we have waited just over one minute, we slowly start walking our bikes back to where a little surprise is awaiting one of the Fairmont residents. Ten houses up the street an intensely bright light suddenly appears, illuminating the bushes and trees in an eerie white glow against the dark surroundings. The bright light lasts for ten seconds, just exactly as it's supposed to. We quicken our pace a bit as we see a couple of people run out of the gun powder house. We get closer to a woman and a girl about thirteen years old.

"Good evening ma'am," we both say politely.

"Did you see someone run from here?" asks the woman.

"What happened?" Gene asks, as if he didn't know.

"It was a big light. It tried to get in through the window," says the girl, puffing as if she's out of breath.

"We saw Ralph Evans ride up the street on his bike a minute ago," says Gene. We blame everything on Ralph, the imaginary fall-guy who takes the blame for our pranks. We talk with the girl for a few minutes while the woman looks up and down the street, behind the parked cars, and then in the back yard, and comes back to the girl. "Good evening ma'am," we say, as we slowly push our bikes along. At the end of the street, we hop on our bikes, and ride off.

"Man! That was so cool," I say. "Did you see the look on her face."

"Oh! It was trying to get in the window," mimics Gene in a little girl's voice. "I was so scared, I coulda peed my pants."

Walking innocently right into the heart of our own mischief is a trick we've used over and over without fail. After all, who would suspect the perpetrator to walk right into the place of trouble. And my time fuses give us perfect cover, so no one ever suspects us. Gene and I both look like little angels who would never cause any mischief. And besides, where would a fifteen year-old kid get dangerous stuff like gun powder?

I originally learned to make it from a book I found in the library on chemistry, which gave the exact ingredients and proportions. At first I bought small amounts of the chemicals from the drug store, thinking that I would tell the pharmacist it was to replace the chemicals in my chemistry set in case he was suspicious of why I wanted those particular ingredients. But when I found he really didn't care, I began to buy large quantities at a much cheaper price, which gave me the amounts I really needed for all my experiments and tricks. I also learned to make a time fuse from a string that was soaked in a chemical bath, a fuse that would slowly fizzle along after a touch of a lit cigarette and wouldn't go out no matter what, one that I could cut to a length that would give a precise fuse time. I also learned that mixing the gun powder with different substances, like copper or zinc filings, would result in bright, beautiful colors that I could use on sparklers.

Sometimes we use my time fuses on firecrackers, which we buy from the little corner convenience store on Westphalia and Eight Mile Road, where the store keeper stashes the illegal merchandise under the counter. You can get almost any kind of fireworks you want there, but our favorites are hammer heads and cherry bombs, which are powerful enough to blow a hole in a trash can, or blow off your hand if you're not careful.

One time I put a firecracker on a six-minute fuse in the room next to our lunchroom at Nativity. Just to spread the excitement, I got Tom to help me with this caper. We placed the fire cracker and fuse in a remote spot, and went to the lunch table in the next room with the other kids. But he got chicken after two minutes, and walked from our lunch table to the outer room where he snuffed out the fuse and put the firecracker in his pocket. He didn't just ruin the prank, he probably spared us from having to listen to an hour-long tirade by Father Geller the next day after Mass, or worse, getting expelled from school.

Our cigarettes and incendiary adventures require ready fire, so we are never without our Zippo lighters and a bunch of kitchen matches, the kind that have a phosphorous tip that will light when struck on anything. Gene and I pride ourselves in being able to light a stick match one-handed by flicking the head with a thumb nail. The challenge is to do it without getting a burning chunk of phosphor under your nail. This trick also lets us light matches as we ride along on our bikes. Gene perfected the technique of dropping burning matches in the leaf piles that accumulate at the edge of the streets in the fall while whizzing along on his bike. The advantage of leaf piles is that they are slow to start, and you can be long gone before there is an obvious fire going.

One of our routines that takes the most guts is to play *Ralph's meeting*. For this, we get four or five guys together, and we draw straws to see the order we have to go in. The loser, who we call the *fall guy*, goes last. The first guy goes up to some house we picked at random and rings the bell, while the others hide out of sight up the street. When the door opens, the first guy says "Hi! I'm here for Ralph's meeting." To which the resident will usually say, "I'm sorry, but Ralph doesn't live here." After apologies, guy number one leaves and goes up to where the others are waiting. Then guy number two goes to the same house and pulls the same routine. By the time guy number three comes along, the people are either getting irritated, or else they are very helpful, pulling out the phone book, and looking up the address of Ralph Evans. Finally, the fall guy goes up to the house and says, "Hello. My name is Ralph. I'm holding a meeting here tonight. Has any one has shown up yet?" Half the time, you have to run off the porch from an angry, cursing person, but half the time they laugh, and sometimes even invite you in for cookies and milk.

I've just crossed over the end of Goulburn Street to start the second leg of my paper route—from Eight Mile Road to State Fair. One of the houses—not one of my customers—has a giant leaf pile in the front yard. I pull a match out of my pocket, flick the head with my thumb nail, throw the sizzling stick into the mound, and continue along without even a hiccup, continuing to throw the papers on my customer's porches. At State Fair I look back towards Eight Mile Road to see big clouds of black smoke billowing from the front yard of a house on the side of Goulburn that I just delivered.

The next day, after crossing Goulburn at the Eight Mile Road end of my route, I see a huge black crescent shape in the lawn where there used to be a leaf pile.

On Saturday evening I'm kneeling on one side of Father Hogan's confessional booth, waiting for the person on the other side to get finished. I want to get my sins cleaned up for the nine o'clock mass tomorrow—one of the Scout Sundays when our Explorer Post goes to Mass at Saint Raymond's Church. On this occasion we will march in our uniforms up the center aisle just before Mass with two flag bearers, one with the American flag and one with the Boy Scout flag, and we will file into the first two pews on the left side of the aisle, which will be reserved for us with a bow-tied ribbon. When it comes time for communion, I don't want to have to bear the embarrassment of sitting back in the pew because there's a bad sin on my soul, and I've got a few to tell. Somehow, that burned lawn seems like something that needs confessing, although I don't know for sure which commandment it violated. I decide to camouflage that sin by squeezing it in the middle of a recitation of some of my more usual sins. I've picked Father Hogan, because he hardly pays attention to you, and he doesn't question you or give you advice on how you can avoid the near occasion of sin the next time. I hear the little confessional door slam shut on the other side and then the little door on my side slides open.

"Bless me father, for I have sinned. My last confession was two weeks ago. I disobeyed my mother three times, I committed a sin of impurity three times, I lit some leaves on someone's lawn, and I used the Lord's name in vain eight times," I blurt out, sort of mumbling the part about the leaves.

"Say five Our Fathers, and five Hail Mary's, and make a good act of contrition," says Father Hogan, sounding bored.

Oh my God, I am heartily sorry for having offended thee, and I confess all my sins because I dread the loss of heaven and the pains of Hell. But most of all because they have offended thee my God, who art all good and deserving of all my love. I firmly resolve with the help of thy grace to confess my sins, to do penance, and to amend my life, Amen.

As I recite the prayer I'm thinking that I got off easy, that I didn't have to answer any probing questions about the burned leaves and whether I should make restitution, which would greatly complicate my relationships on Goulburn Street. Tomorrow I can go to communion with a clear conscience.

But the confession doesn't ease my conscience. I just can't shake from my mind the shameful memory of a black crescent on a lawn on Goulburn Street.

46.

Chair Talk

Helen Rogoza came to the Folkman family as a nanny and housekeeper. But her new work is much more exciting. She stands watch as Mr. Folkman loads cases of booze into the back seat of his car. Then she will ride with him to the speakeasy, where her job is to knock on the front door, give the password, and help unload the delivery from the alley into the back room. She doesn't want to get caught by the G-men. The year is nineteen thirty, and alcohol has been prohibited as long as she can remember.

*   *   *   *

I come in late on a Saturday night after delivering the Bulldogs on my paper route. Kathleen and Helen are both staying overnight with their girlfriends. It's just me and Mama—a very dangerous situation, because it is too easy for her to trap me into *chair talk*. She's sitting in the living room, puffing on a Camel, drinking beer, looking angry: all bad signs. Maybe I can tip-toe past her, without triggering something.

"Hi, Mama," I say, as nonchalantly as possible as I pass her on the way to safer territory in my bedroom.

"Just one minute, young man. I want to talk to you. Sit down."

Now I'm in for God only knows how many hours of *chair talk*. Chair talk is nothing like *attack talk*, which is pathetic, sad, self-condemning, apologetic. Chair talk is angry, accusatory, spiteful. There are two rules when I'm trapped into listening to either kind of talk: shut up, and listen.

"When did you last go to confession?"

"Saturday, Mama."

"Do you keep your mind clean?"

"Yes, I do."

"You know your body is the temple of the Holy Spirit."

"Yes, Mama."

From here on, I don't need to speak anymore. She goes on about sin, about smut, about eternal damnation, about that despicable communist Charlie Chaplin, about that prostitute Lana Turner with all her husbands, about the fornicators, about the sad state of the country, about the sad state of the world.

I sit without moving, without speaking. One false move from me and I could trigger her into a rage when she will smash the nearest thing made of glass against the wall or the floor. She goes on and on. I hope some distraction will stop her. Maybe the phone will ring, but it doesn't. Maybe someone will knock at the door, but it's too late for anyone to come calling. I try to occupy my mind while the voice drones on in the background. I recite in my mind a poem by Edgar Allen Poe I memorized in school:

Once upon a midnight dreary, while I pondered, weak and weary,
Over many a quaint and curious volume of forgotten lore —
While I nodded, nearly napping, suddenly there came a tapping,
As of some one gently rapping, rapping at my chamber door.
" 'Tis some visitor," I muttered, "tapping at my chamber door —
*   Only this and nothing more."*

Mama's ashtray fills with butts as she chain-smokes one cigarette after another. The voice in the distance mimics a television commercial in a sing-songy way through clenched teeth: "Be Happy, Go Lucky! Be happy, Go Lucky Strike! That's all the young people care about, Be happy! Happy! Happy!" Each *happy* is spoken louder and more spitefully than the last.

Ah, distinctly I remember it was the bleak December;
And each separate dying ember wrought its ghost upon the floor.

Eagerly I wished the morrow; — vainly I sought to borrow
From my books surcease of sorrow -- sorrow for the lost Lenore --
For the rare and radiant maiden whom the angels name Lenore --
    Nameless here for evermore.

The voice talks about greed, about avarice, about lies, about evil, about wasting time, about all the bad television programs, about the good ones by Bishop Sheen, about sanctifying grace, about everything, about nothing.

And the silken, sad, uncertain rustling of each purple curtain
Thrilled me — filled me with fantastic terrors never felt before;
So that now, to still the beating of my heart, I stood repeating
" 'Tis some visitor entreating entrance at my chamber door —
Some late visitor entreating entrance at my chamber door; —
    This it is and nothing more."

After an eternity, the voice slows, seeming to come to a conclusion. It pauses for awhile. "Why don't you go to bed now. It's very late," it says.

After an hour and a half of chair talk, I shuffle off to bed, glad to be released from prison and torture, unhappy that the alarm will ring at five-thirty to awaken me for my Sunday morning paper delivery. I hate being here. I would give anything for an opportunity to get out of this nut house, even if I have to go to the hospital with some horrible disease.

47.

The Accident

This December Monday morning is cold, dark, and rainy. The wet streets reflect street lights and car headlights. If this bus doesn't move faster, I'm going to be late for my tenth-grade class at Nativity. I get off the bus at the intersection of Seven Mile Road and Gratiot, juggling my books and papers. The Gratiot street car is approaching Seven Mile Road. To catch it, I will have to cross Seven Mile, and then go part way across Gratiot to the street car safety zone, and I'll have to hustle if I'm going to make it. I run across Seven Mile Road, watching the street car slow down as it approaches the safety zone.

As I run across the street, a bright light suddenly appears next to the books I hold at my right side. Then there is a dull thumping sound that I hear not with my ears, but right inside my head, inside my whole body, like nothing I've ever heard before. The bright light goes out, as do the street lights, making the world almost totally black, except for little bright speckles that flash all around. The world spins, and I'm spinning too, like I'm falling from the sky. Now I'm sliding, like going down hill on my sled in the snow. The street lights come back on, and I see that I'm sliding along on my back on the wet street. The white speckles have now turned to tiny black polka dots that fill the air.

I've stopped sliding. I want to get up, but I can't move. All I can do is lift my head a bit to see that I'm lying in the street. I lay my head back down as the black polka dots continue to swirl around, making a terrible toothache everywhere in my body.

People are standing around in a circle, staring at me. Don't they realize how impolite that is, to stare at somebody who has fallen down?

Two girls break through the crowd. One of them kneels down beside me, takes off her coat and puts it under my head like a pillow. It's my sister, Kathleen.

"Don't you worry, sweety pie, everything's going to be all right," she says. "An ambulance is coming to get you."

"But I don't want an ambulance. I just want to go to school."

Kathleen holds my hand. "You can't. You've been hit by a car. You're hurt. You have to go to the hospital."

Oh God! Now I've really messed things up. I'm probably going to miss school entirely today with all this commotion.

"Kathleen, could you do something for me?"

"Sure, honey bun, what is it?"

"My books and papers, and all my homework. They fell on the street. Could you get them for me?"

Kathleen calls to the other girl, who I can now see is Lois St. Croix, Kathleen's best girlfriend. "Lois, see if you can find Pat's books and papers. He's asking for them."

"Sure Kay," she says, and she disappears through the ring of people.

Kathleen continues to hold my hand, saying everything is going to be all right, don't you worry, and let me put my coat under your head. But why can't I move, and why does every place in my body hurt so?

A man in white pants crouches beside me. "We have to straighten out that leg, son, so we can get you on the stretcher. It's going to hurt some." Its funny he calls me son, like Mama does when something bad has happened. He gently and slowly moves my right leg, which causes a horrible blinding pain. Another man comes beside me, and together they lift me gently onto a stretcher.

I'm riding in an ambulance, lying on a little table with wheels that they had put the stretcher on. The muffled wail of a siren seems to come from a distance. Then it dawns on me: this siren is for me. The man in white sits at one side, and a policeman sits on the other side. Kathleen and Lois ride up front.

The policeman asks me questions: my name, address, phone number, how did the accident happen?

"I don't know. I was just crossing the street."

"Was the light red or green?"

I think for a moment. This must be all my fault. I've made a mess out of everything. I'll bet I was running against the red light, like I did last month trying to catch the street car to come home from Nativity. That time I only bounced off the car's bumper as he screeched to a stop and I rolled in the street before darting onto the street car, hoping I wouldn't be found out and get in trouble. I'll bet I caused this driver a lot of trouble, because this time I'm in an ambulance.

"It was probably red."

"Are you sure?"

"Well, no. I'm really not sure."

"Okay. I'll just put down *doesn't know.*"

We arrive at Saratoga Hospital, which is on Gratiot, just a few blocks from Seven Mile Road. As they wheel me out on the stretcher, Kathleen and Lois walk along side.

"Kathleen, did they get my papers?"

"We got 'em, kiddo," Lois says as she waves a bunch of papers. I can see that they're a wet and dirty mess—my English composition, the play that Joe and I were writing for Christmas, and my algebra homework that's due today—it's all messed up.

With its twenty-three other beds, the big ward that I'm in looks a lot like the one Uncle Eddie used to be in at Eloise. I've been here two nights so far. A brace keeps my leg immobile. The smallest movement kicks up the most awful pain in my leg. Three nurses work together to change my bed linens. I tell them we only change my bed linens at home every two or three weeks, so just leave me with the dirty ones. But they say it's hospital policy, as two lift me above the bed and a third slides a fresh sheet underneath me, which sends lightning bolts of pain through my whole body.

Mama sits by my bed. "Your femur bone is broken just a couple inches below your hip. Dr. Maguire looked at your X-rays. He says he has to operate, but he can't do it until the swelling goes down. He says you'll be on your feet in no time."

"Did you find out who drove the car that hit me?"

"Yes. It was a Mr. Roberts. His wife called and asked if I was the mother of the boy who ran into her husband's car. I guess you must have been running pretty fast. You went completely over the top of the car and down the back side."

"What's going to happen to my paper route?"

"Gene Klein did it yesterday. And the Fouchet boy, the one that subbed for you when you had the flu, will do it from now on. I found your list of customers, and gave it to him. He says he'll give you all the Christmas tips too. So don't you worry."

"I want my route back, as soon as I get back on my feet."

"Of course. No one is going to take your route from you."

Mama stays a long time. Nobody bugs her about visiting hours.

In the bed to the left of me is an old guy named Bernie, who is about forty-five years old—even older than Daddy was when he died. A bar above his head goes from the head of the bed to the foot, and above his chest is a cross bar that he grabs onto when he wants to shift his weight around. Going right through his shin bone is a metal pin, and attached to that is a rope that goes to a pulley at the end of the bed with metal weights attached to it.

Bernie teaches me how to get along in the hospital. "The most important thing you need is a straightened-out coat hanger with a little hook on one end. You can pick up all kinds of stuff that you drop from your bed with that." He demonstrates how he can retrieve a box of Kleenex. He shows me how to use the trapeze bar, how to get yourself on the bedpan, how to shift your weight around. He tells me how to get good food out the kitchen staff, not the garbage they usually give you on the trays, by sending little love notes back on the tray after you finish your meal. He tells me which nurses you have to watch out for, and which ones are nice.

Bernie has been in here for a whole month after falling off a scaffold while painting a building. He says his leg doesn't want to heal. "I'm running up one hellava big bill, and I don't have insurance or a red cent to my name."

"How are you going to pay for all this?"

"I'll just have to paint the hospital for the rest of my life."

Most of the time during the day I don't even think about the pain, because of all the action in the big ward. There is constant joking and bantering. A couple guys are half dead, but most are alert and friendly. There's another kid my age with his leg in traction, but he just whines all the time. I hate whiners, and it's something I refuse to do. It's the others that I like, the ones that can walk or get around in wheel chairs and do stuff for those who can't get out of bed.

The guys like to play tricks on the nurses. Bernie showed me how to make your pulse disappear by putting a rolled-up handkerchief in your armpit, and squeezing. When the nurse takes your pulse, which they do every day, you let her get a few counts and then squeeze your arm. Then she fishes around on your wrist, looking for the lost pulse, and then you let up, and she starts to count again. It drives them crazy. With all the fun and games going on here, I usually don't even think about my pain.

But when night comes, the hospital isn't so friendly anymore. The sounds of snoring come from somewhere in the darkness. Little red lights glow here and there. Nurses come by with their flashlights. The air smells of rubbing alcohol. That's when the pain wants to settle down on me. That's when I start thinking. What am I doing here? Are they going to fix my leg? When can I go back to school? What's going to happen to my paper route? Can Mama make ends meet without my paper route money? Just as I'm about to fall asleep, I hear a thump, not with my ears, but with my whole body, and it jolts me awake.

After they take away the dinner trays, Nurse Riley comes to my bed, carrying a tray full of hospital things. She looks like a movie star, with her gorgeous face, long wavy dark hair, and large brown eyes that seem to pierce through you when you look straight at her. Miss Riley is gentle and kind to all the guys. Nobody plays tricks on her, not just because she is beautiful, but because she has this dignified air that says *I'll be considerate and professional, but I won't stand for foolishness*. I don't have to play the pulse trick on her. When she takes my pulse, my heart starts to race all on its own. I wonder if she can tell just by feeling my pulse how she affects me .

She puts the tray down on the little table beside me, and starts to draw the curtains to encircle my bed. This is not a good sign. They only do that when something bad is going to happen. I try not to stare at her beautiful face, but instead look at the tray. There is a little silver basin, a cup, a brush, a razor. She finishes drawing the curtains.

"I'm going to shave you for your surgery tomorrow morning."

What does this mean? I don't shave. I'm only fifteen, and I just have peach fuzz under my nose. I don't like the looks of this.

"Wha-what do you mean you are going to shave me? Why do you have to do that?" I ask suspiciously.

"It's so there won't be any germs when they operate on you. We want everything perfectly clean. It's something we routinely do before any operation," she says as she works up a lather by stirring the brush in the cup. "I'm going to shave you from your navel down to your knee."

She gently pulls up my hospital gown and then pulls the covers dangerously far down, but she stops right at a crucial place, saving me a tiny bit of dignity.

With one hand, her beautiful fingers gently touch my stomach below my navel as she aims to apply the brush with the other hand. But I feel electricity from her finger tips, and my stomach makes a sudden jerk, and she pulls her hand away, like she's surprised. She tries again, but again the electricity makes my stomach jerk again, like it has a mind of its own. A third try ends up the same way.

I keep trying to think about other things, like my school play. But it doesn't work. I just know something is going to happen that I can't help, and this is going to be the most embarrassing day of my entire life. My face is burning.

Miss Riley pulls the covers back up to my neck. "I'll be back in a few minutes," she says, as she disappears through the curtain.

A few minutes later, Fritz shows up. He's a short, ancient guy who speaks half German and half English, and, according to Bernie, is the only male orderly in the hospital. He pulls the covers down and lathers me up. He takes the razor, but his hand shakes, like he has the palsy. Scritch! scritch! goes the razor as he mows through the lather. Only his hand shakes so much that every once in a while he makes a slice through the skin, staining the lather red. Each time that happens he applies alcohol with a cotton pad, but his hand shakes so that it makes the cuts sting even more. After about fifteen minutes he finishes all the way down to my right knee, with numerous slices along the way. He gathers up the stuff onto the tray.

"Sher gut. Das ist alles. Zie ist a gut boy" he says as he gently pats me on the head with his shaky hand.

"Thank you Fritz, I really appreciate your work," I say, greatly relieved that it was he, and not Miss Riley who did it.

48.

Hospital Life

Sleep comes and goes. In my dreams I am lying in a hospital bed, with a plastic tent around me, a steady hiss coming into the tent from an oxygen bottle along side. On each side of the bed is a hanging bottle with a tube going to each arm: one bottle drips clear liquid into a little glass holder for the tube that goes to my arm; the other bottle drips blood. Drip! Drip! Drip! I watch the drops, one by one. I'm more thirsty than I've ever been in my life. But they only give me a wet washcloth to suck on every once in a while. A silver pitcher sits on the little table beside my bed. I reach through the slit in the tent and just barely reach the bottle, heavy with liquid. I get the bottle up to my lips, tip it a bit, anticipating the cool water. Just then, a hand reaches into the tent and pulls the bottle away. "Oh my God!" someone says. "He's trying to drink out of the urinal."

The oxygen tent is gone now, and I get all the water I want. I'm no longer in the big ward, but in a semi-private room. Mama comes into the room and sits beside the bed, where she sets her purse, sending a surge of pain through every part of my body. Every vibration causes excruciating pain, even if someone just shuts the door of the room or walks too hard alongside the bed.

"Please Mama, don't shake the bed. It hurts so much. Why can't I move my left arm? It's completely dead. And why does everything hurt so much?"

"You were in surgery for six hours," Mama says. "Your leg was smashed up pretty bad, just below the hip. Doctor Maguire had to put a plate in your leg to hold the bone together. He says you must have hurt your arm in the accident. That's why you can't move it."

"But my arm was fine before the surgery. I think it was messed up by the stuff they pumped in that arm during the surgery. Or somehow they screwed up during the operation."

I can ask for a pain shot anytime I want, but I try to wait until I just can't stand it anymore. I'll get addicted if I get too much morphine and will have to spend my life after I get out of here being a crazed addict looking for the next fix. So I wait until night time to ask for a fix, when that hospital gets quiet and my room is full of shadows and the pain becomes unbearable.

Shortly after they take away the oxygen tent, my roommate gets out of his bed to go to the bathroom, when he stumbles and breaks the window beside his bed with his elbow. The room soon gets very cold and they pile blankets on me. Some workmen come to board up the window, but too late to prevent the freezing cold of Detroit winter taking over the room. Two days later I have pneumonia and pleurisy, and back comes the oxygen tent and the I-V tubes.

Days pass. Little by little the pain abates, and I can get by without any morphine at all. Eventually I can raise myself onto a bed pan without needing two nurses to help lift me, and without pain electrifying my body. Little by little my left arm recovers; first I can lift an empty glass, then an ash tray, then a book. Going entirely through my shin bone is a silver pin, and attached to that is a rope that disappears over a pulley at the end of the bed, just like Bernie had. Strangely, it doesn't hurt at all, although it looks like it ought to. I keep it covered with a towel so it won't upset my visitors.

My roommate is Ivan Panarovitch, a big burly Russian guy who is a professional wrestler. His hands and face are covered with bandages from the burns he got when he threw gasoline into a burning trash can. It's really gruesome when they do the treatments on his face and hands. He tells me a story of the missing forefinger on his right hand in his thickly accented, broken English.

"I vas vorkink in bootcher shop during var ven I geet letter from Army. I geet draft into var. I haf three children for feedink. I look at dees letter, an den look at chop block. I poot my finger on dees block, an I chopink it off. I no go into var."

Ivan's wife comes every day during visiting hours, and sometimes his two daughters come too. Mama comes most every evening, and Kathleen and Helen usually visit after school, as well as lots of my friends from scouting and school. I get lots of other visitors too. Aunt Stella visits, usually bringing some sort of game or a book for me to keep busy. I can't read the comic books she brings because the pictures upset me so. Whenever I see a cartoon character get hit with an anvil or fall off a cliff, I relive the whole accident— the bright light by my side and the polka dots that hurt so, and worst of all, the thumping noise that filled my body. That noise comes back to me again and again, even in my sleep.

I like being here in Saratoga Hospital. I like all the company and friends who come to see me. I love to hear Ivan's tales from the wrestling ring where he is known as *Ivan the Terrible*. I love the nurses who fuss over me. I love being away from the nut house.

Just before Christmas the nurses decorate a little tree in my room. Mama brings me the tips from my paper route—over 25 dollars. "I think you'll have to let your paper route go to the Fouchet boy," she says. "Dr. Maguire says it will be a good while before you can deliver papers again. I'm so sorry, I know how much you had your heart set on getting back to your route."

This news is so distressing, and I don't know what I'm going to do. Am I going to be stuck in bed for a long time? Can I get another paper route later on? If I don't, how am I going to earn money, and how is Mama going to make ends meet?

A group of kids come in and sing carols. I get a million cards from all the kids at school, from the explorer post, and from all the uncles and aunties. On Christmas eve, Mama, Kathleen, and Helen come for a visit and give me a stack of gifts—a crossword puzzle book and the book *Treasure Island*. Mama gives me a rental TV set with a little earphone so I won't disturb any of the other patients.

Mr. Siefert comes to visit a couple of days after Christmas. He lives on my route on Goulburn Street, although he wasn't one of my customers. He's the scout master at Saint Raymond's boy scout troop.

"Sit down Mr. Siefert," I say, pointing to the chair beside my bed."

"No thanks, I can't stay long." He's silent for a minute, like he's thinking about what he wants to say. "I just want you to know that I forgive you for what you did before your accident."

He's talking about the snowball incident that happened the week before my accident, when I was delivering my paper route. I was crossing Bringard Street, just beyond the Siefert's corner house, when I heard Indian war whoops. As I looked back towards their house, a bunch of kids came running from the back yard, throwing snowballs. Splat! Splat! Splat! I was getting hit everywhere. When I took two hits in the face, I lost control of my bike and fell. The papers that were balanced in the bag on my handlebars spilled into the slush at the curb, ruining them. I saw six or seven kids, about twelve years old, running back into the Siefert yard. I grabbed up a handful of snow. Someone is going to get a face washing over this, I thought.

I caught up with the Petrus boy and grabbed him by the hat, but the chin strap just tore off. Then I tackled the Walters boy, held him down, and began rubbing the snow into his face.

That's when Mrs. Siefert grabbed me by the collar with one hand, waving a rolling pin in the other. "Get out of here, you dirty bully," she shouted. "Now you just get, or I'll give it to you!" I stopped what I was doing and looked straight into the fury of Mrs. Siefert's face. I wanted to tell her what happened. But I'm not one to argue with a hysterical lady, especially if she is holding a rolling pin. So, without saying a word, I got up, picked up my papers, rode off, and delivered the rest of the route. Half my remaining customers got a wet paper that day.

Mr. Siefert goes on with his forgiveness speech. "We're terribly sorry about your accident. You being in the hospital, it wouldn't be good for you to feel guilty. You're still a young boy, and you have a lot to learn. Some day you'll look back on this incident and realize how serious your behavior was. I want you to know I don't hold any grudges. And I know Mrs. Petrus forgives you for ruining her son's hat."

But I don't feel like a forgiven sinner. I feel angry, and my face is getting hot. I want to say: *I don't want your crummy forgiveness, Mr. Siefert, and I don't want your stupid pity. I didn't do anything wrong. Those kids got what they deserved, and if I had another chance, I would do it again, only the next time I would get the rest of them as well. And besides, I told Mrs. Petrus that she could deduct the cost of a new hat from what she owed me for the newspapers.*

"Thank you, Mister Siefert," I say, swallowing my anger. "I appreciate your visit." I shake his extended hand.

"I wish you a Happy New Year," he says. Then he turns and disappears through the door.

It's been a month since my accident. Tomorrow they're going to kick me out of the hospital. Mama says that our insurance will only pay for one month in the hospital at a time. She rented a wheel chair for me at home, and says that all my friends worked together to scrape off the ugly dark paper from my bedroom walls at home and paint them a light aqua color. She organized a work party consisting of all my buddies: Gene Klein, Mike Wilson, Johnny Dreer, Johnny Bober, Dick Tomak, Tim Allord, and Bob Perham. She said there was so many layers of old paper and paint that they had to use a blow torch on it.

I really hate to leave this place. I've become friends with so many of the nurses and aides, and I like all the men who come around to talk to me. That night, in my prayers, I thank God for sending me this accident, for giving me a new family in Saratoga Hospital for stopping dead my progress on a troubled path—the fires, the petty vandalism, mouthing off to my teachers, pulling pranks that were bound to get me into trouble.

At home I can easily slide into my wheel chair from my bed. I think of Uncle Eddie. He has to use contraptions just to get to his wheel chair and, unlike me, will never walk again because his muscles are wasting and his legs are frozen forever.

After one month, the ambulance men come to take me back to the hospital. When Doctor Maguire sees the new X-rays, he shakes his head from side to side while tisk-tisking and says I had to go back for more surgery. The plate in my leg is bent like a pretzel, and the bone is misaligned. I don't know how that happened, since I never tried to walk and got around in the house in my wheel chair like I was supposed to. I don't think the wrestling I did on the floor with Tomak or Klein had anything to do with it, because I was always careful not to put pressure on my bad leg. I had hardly noticed the hard lump just below my hip, right where the plate was and where the bone became separated.

A week later I'm back in the hospital, with Fritz once again doing the shaving routine. Only this time, he shaves me all the way down the left leg, rather than the right. He has to come back a second time to do the other leg, which at least gives me a matched set. They wheel me down to surgery the next morning with my pubic area and two legs looking like minced meat. The doctors and nurses assembled in a little group are already wearing their masks. "Aha! conspiring against me," I say. I can see Doctor Maguire laugh through his mask. They shift me from the gurney to an operating table. A nurse wheels a thing that looks like a coat rack with a bottle hanging from it—sodium pentothal, the anesthetic that will drip in my arm throughout the operation—and connected to the bottle is a hose with a needle on the end. She sticks the needle into my left arm—the same arm that ended up paralyzed the last time I had surgery. I decide to see how far I can count backwards from one hundred, ninety-nine, ninety-eight, ninety-seven, ninety-six ninety-five...

I'm coming out of a dream, and my body feels so heavy. The lights slowly come on. I'm in a hospital bed, and Mama is sitting next to me. This time there's no oxygen tent.

"I'm thirsty, Mama. Can I have something to drink?'

"Just a little sip," she says. "You're not supposed to drink anything until the anesthetic wears off."

Mama pours a little bit of water from a pitcher into a glass, and brings it toward my mouth. I lean against my elbows, trying to sit up, but my body feels heavy and I can't move. I try again, but it feels like I'm in a vice from head to foot. I try to feel my tummy, but only feel something hard, like a rock. I test my stomach with my fist, making a rapping sound. What's this? My stomach feels like concrete. With my hand I try to feel my side and my back, but it too feels like concrete. I try to wiggle my right foot, but it won't respond. "Am I paralyzed, Mama? I can't move. I can't feel anything."

"No, Pat. You're not paralyzed. You're in a body cast. It goes from just below your ribs to the tip of your right foot."

"I want to see it, Mama. Help me sit up."

Mama pulls the cover from my leg, and stuffs a pillow behind my back. I can barely sit up enough to see a long expanse of white, from my stomach to the tip of my foot, with only five toes sticking out, and it gives me a shock that I can feel in the pit of my stomach.

"A body cast! Doctor Maguire had no right to do that. I didn't give him my permission. I want this thing off, right now!"

"I'm sorry, Pat. Doctor Maguire said it had to be done. You weren't healing. It was the only way."

"But I can't even be in a wheel chair this way. How am I going to move around? How am I going to live?"

"I'm so sorry. Just give it some time."

That night, after the lights are shut off, I think about the movie: *The Man in the Iron Mask*. They clamped an iron mask on the hero, and threw him into prison, while the villain laughed: "You'll be strangled by your own beard." Am I going to be strangled by this thing? I'm a growing boy, and there's no spare room in this thing. I'm trapped in the worst prison on earth.

The next afternoon Doctor Maguire stops by my bedside to check on me.

"How's it going, John?"

"Doctor Maguire, I'm pissed at you."

"What are you talking about?"

"I want you to take this thing off. This body cast. Take it off!"

"I can't do that, John. You need it so the bone won't move around."

"I didn't give you permission to put this on me. It's not your leg, it's mine. You have to take it off."

"We'll do that, John, just as soon as the bone shows healing. You'll be just fine. Just try to be patient." And with that, Doctor Maguire turns and walks away toward the door."

"Wait, Doctor Maguire!" I call in my meanest voice. "I've something else to tell you!"

"What's that, John?"

"Stop calling me John! That's not my name! My name is Pat!"

That evening, Mama comes for a visit. I'm still feeling depressed.

"I don't like this room, Mama. If I have to be in a body cast, I don't want to be in this room."

"What's wrong with it?"

"There's only one other guy here, and he's half dead. I want to be in the big ward. I'll have more friends there. It's where all the action is. Please get me transferred."

The next day they wheel my bed to position number sixteen in the big ward. And later that day, Miss Woods and Mrs. Houseworth bring in a younger kid into position seventeen. He's in traction, like I was the first time.

"We brought you a friend," whispers Miss Woods. His name is Gary, and he's thirteen years old." The nurses leave, and I can see Gary looks scared.

"Hi. I'm Pat. What happened to you?"

"I fell out of a tree and busted my leg. The put in a pin that goes right through my shin bone."

"That's for the traction; there's a weight attached to that at the end of your bed. I had one of those a couple of months ago. It doesn't hurt. I'm an old pro here. I can tell you a couple of things that will make your life easier."

With that, I show Gary how to make a hook with a coat hanger, how to fool the nurses when they take your pulse, how to use the trapeze bar to shift your self around, which nurses are nice, and which are mean, how to get special treats on your food trays, and on and on.

In the days that follow, I slowly get accustomed to the body cast and learn how to deal with it. I can lean up part way, since the cast ends just below my ribs. My friends want to know how I can go to the bathroom wearing this thing. I just give them a little smile and say "that's my secret."

I'm friends now with most of the guys in the big ward. We joke around and play tricks on each other and on the nurses. Some guys come around in their wheel chairs to talk to me, and some can walk over under their own power. The nurses still make a big fuss over me. I put notes on my meal trays, and get special treats from the kitchen crew. Somehow, I feel like I've come home.

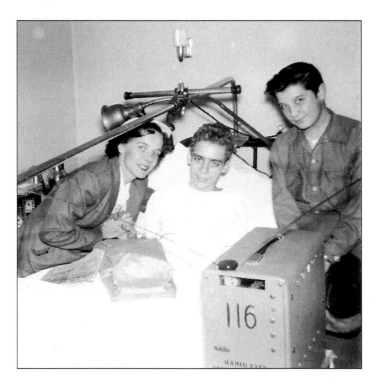

Mama and Explorer Scout Don Kryewski visit me at Saratoga Hospital a couple of weeks after my first surgery. December, 1951.

49.

Mike

The clock beside my bed says ten past eleven in the evening. Mike Wilson sits at my bedside in the big hospital ward. At the edge of the bed is a chess board, and there my king is surrounded by half of Mike's power pieces. In a minute, there's going to be a slaughter of my defenses, and my king will surely be check-mated. Ever since Mike taught me how to play chess, I've been trying to beat him. Looks like I'm going down again.

While I study the board, we munch on the last of the ten White Castle hamburgers that Mike bought at five for a quarter with a coupon in the *Detroit News*. They're made with little scrawny patties of meat of suspicious origin stuck in a pathetic little bun. But they have a taste that I get a real craving for, and that only a whole bag of them will satisfy. I like to say that White Castle hamburgers make me feel so joyful that I want to whinny and gallop around after eating one. Occasionally Mike sneaks in a pop bottle filled with home-brewed wine, which he gets from a stash in his basement—wine payments his father had taken from a poor Italian immigrant he had defended against deportation. The stuff tastes pretty awful, but it's a thrill to know that you're getting away with something.

Visiting hours are supposed to be over at eight-thirty, when they ring a bell in the hallway. Usually the nurses go to the rooms soon after that, reminding the stragglers it's time to go. But they let Mike stay as long as he wants, which is often past midnight, as long as we are quiet. So after ten o'clock, we turn the conversation volume down to whispers. Even if we're up yakking past midnight, some nurse will still wake me up at six-thirty in the morning.

I think the nurses let Mike stay because he can charm them like he's a movie star. He's a tall, skinny guy, with a quick smile, sandy blond hair that comes to a little V-shaped peak on his forehead, blue eyes, and crooked teeth. To me, he doesn't look the least bit handsome. But my sister Helen says that when he bats his extra long eyelashes, it makes a girl's heart go pitter-pat. He's smart, I mean real smart—smart enough to be a lawyer like his father was before he died. Even so, he never brags about himself or takes center stage, and he always listens to the other guy. Maybe everyone likes him because of that, along with his corny sayings. When someone asks him "Got a match?" his usual answer is "Not since Superman died," or he'll say "That's a very deep subject," when someone says "... well..."

I knew Mike from our Explorer post, but we were never really friends then. It was soon after my accident that he started to show up at the hospital. Shortly after Christmas Mike's father died of a heart attack—like Daddy. After that Mike's visits became daily, first at the hospital, then at home when I got discharged.

Mike comes to the hospital with his older sister Judy, who brings a rolled up paper tape from an adding machine. She has a smile like an little leprechaun from the Irish forest and eyes that sparkle like she's thinking of the punch line of a cosmic joke. As I unroll the tape, I see it is filled with notes from all the girls in Judy's class at Dominican, the all-girls Catholic high school in Detroit. There are jokes, poems, sayings, riddles, and cheery little notes and cartoons, probably a hundred feet of them if you unrolled the whole tape. Some of the notes are signed XOXOXO, which means *hugs and kisses*. In the following nights, I dream of the beautiful girls who wrote me those notes.

They usually rotate the nurses, and I seldom get the same one two days in a row. Your morning nurse wakes you at six-thirty by throwing a wet washcloth in your face and pulls the curtains around your bed for privacy. Then she gives you soap, a basin of water, a bedpan, and other clean-up stuff. Later you get your breakfast tray. After that, she changes your bed gives you fresh water, and takes care an your needs. At three o'clock, the afternoon shift shows up, with a whole set of new nurses. The last thing the night nurse does for you is to give you an alcohol back rub. The guys like to ask for a good night kiss, but the nurses usually answer with something like, "sorry, but it's not in my contract."

The trays that come up from the kitchen are marked with someone's name, because some of the guys are on special diets. I get special things on my personal food tray because I send little notes back with my tray to the kitchen help like: "I'll bet you are as beautiful as Marilyn Monroe. How about bacon, scrambled eggs and an extra carton of milk on my breakfast tray." Pretty soon my trays were coming back with whatever I asked for. One day, a couple of women who looked like they could be lady wrestlers came up from the kitchen just to see who was writing all those notes. We laughed and joked together. After that, I got extra desserts on my lunch trays.

Miss Woods is my favorite day nurse, and we like to talk and joke around as she does her jobs, like changing my bed. After getting her for three days in a row, I ask her how come she isn't rotating.

"I requested this end of the ward so I could make sure you keep out of trouble."

At the end of her shift, I teach her how to play poker. I play cards with everybody in sight. I even taught poker to Sister Michael Linda, who comes around every once in awhile. At first she said she couldn't, because nuns aren't allowed to gamble. But I convinced her that it wasn't gambling, since we were using chips rather than real money.

Mike checks my king with his knight. I take his knight with my white bishop, which he takes with his queen, saying with a chuckle "Check mate!" He's beat me again. But the day will come when I'll wipe that smirk off his face. Nurse Georgina comes by to chat.

"Why aren't you in school?" she asks him.

"It's the feast of Saint Michael—a holy day. No school today," he lies with a broad smile, leaving Georgina shaking her head and looking unconvinced.

"Mike, you're going to screw yourself up, skipping school all the time like that." I say after Georgina leaves.

"Let me tell you a story from the Bible, Pat." he replies. "Jesus met a man who was in despair. I can't believe in a just God, the man says. How could he desert me in my time of trouble? But Jesus says: Look at the birds of the air. Doesn't my Father take care of them? And don't you think that you are infinitely more important to my Father than the birds. Keep your faith in God the Father, and he will provide for you, too. And that's how I feel, Pat. God will take care of me, too."

"God helps those who help themselves," is the best reply that I can think of. It's one of Mama's favorite sayings. But I know it won't sink into his thick head.

In a couple of weeks Mama helps me pack my stuff to go back home. Mike is also here to help, saying he skipped school just for me. The guys from the ambulance service are ready to lift me and my body cast onto the stretcher for the trip home. But I feel like this is my home. I'm going to miss all the guys in the big ward, and especially the hospital staff—Miss Woods, who stays after her shift to play card games and talk to me; Inga, the nurse's aid, who tells me about her home in Sweden; Mrs. Houseworth, the big matronly nurse who smoothers me with hugs when she is assigned to my bed; beautiful Miss Riley, who always knows exactly what to do when I need something; Georgina, the squat little Italian nurse, whom we call *Mama Mia*—I told her I was sorry that I accused her of not watching carefully enough over Old Man Hawkins, who died in the ward during her shift; Miss Powell, who likes to embarrass me with her stories of her exploits with soldiers when she worked in the hospital outside of Fort Sill; the lady wrestlers from the kitchen downstairs; Mrs. Smith, the nurse's aid whom I told to go to hell—I did apologize to her later; and even Miss Bateman, the tall, nervous afternoon nurse who slapped me for defying her by listening to my radio, and then requested never again to be reassigned to the big ward; and kindly old Fritz, the butcher of Saratoga Hospital.

Mike Wilson at his home on Fairmont Street.

50.

A Birthday Disappointment

Today is my sixteenth birthday—March nineteenth, nineteen fifty-three. I'm sure that I'm going to get a snare drum. I have been practicing ever since I got home from the hospital, using the drum sticks and lesson books that Johnny Bober got for me. Although I don't have a drum, I bang away on everything in sight—on my body cast, which is always right within easy reach, and on books, pots, pans, and pot lids. I keep time with the music on the radio, and I've taken to drumming with my fingers if my sticks aren't handy. I can keep that up even when holding a conversation, which seems to drive Mama nuts. I've learned how to read drum music, and how to do all the basic strokes, like the *roll, flam, flamadiddle, paradiddle, and ratamaque*. The only thing I need is a real drum, which I've been hinting for like crazy.

Mama comes into the bedroom with a cake and lit candles, followed by the birthday revelers who cram into my tiny bedroom, and some of them overflow into the hall. Besides Mama, Kathleen and Helen, there's Mike Wilson, Johnny Dreer, Johnny Bober, Tom Smith, Tim Allord, Gene Klein, Bob Perham, Dick Tomak, and Lois St. Croix. Mama starts up Happy Birthday and everybody joins in. I work in a drum beat on the bottom of a pot that has been serving as my latest drum. After the birthday song, I blow out the candles on the cake, which gets everybody to break into applause. Then the gifts start coming: a carton of Luckies, a Zippo lighter, a Hardy Boys book, a subscription to *Popular Science*, but no snare drum.

Just as I'm about to despair of getting a drum, Mama makes a sly little smile, like she has some great surprise for me "And now for something special," she says. I know exactly what it's is going to be, but I'll have to act surprised, so I won't spoil it for her. She works her way out of the crowded room, and a minute later comes back with a giant gift all wrapped in paper, which she plunks on the bed. It's sort of big enough to hold a snare drum, but what an odd shape! As I tear off the paper, I see that it's not a drum, but a guitar—painted black, with a red color worked around the sound hole. Across the top, above the tuning pegs, it says *Stella*. A Stella guitar! What kind of gift is this? Why would Mama get me this, when she knows full well that I want to play the drums?

"Oh! It's a guitar. Thank you," I say, forcing a smile, trying not to show my disappointment. "I'll have to learn how to play it."

"It's a good one," says Johnny Bober. "Look here." He takes the guitar from me, and shows off a few chords, which ring out loud and clear. "I tuned it for you."

"Johnny helped me pick it out. We got it from a pawn shop," Mama says, with a proud look. "And here's a book, too!" and she places on my lap *The Nick Manaloff Guitar Method*.

"Oh thank you, Mama. I'll always remember this birthday."

That night, after I turn off the light to go to sleep, I can't help thinking about the drum I should have had. As soon as I get out of this bed, I'm going to get a job, and buy a drum set. Meanwhile, what am I going to do with this stupid guitar?

The next morning I grudgingly pick up my Stella guitar and try our a few chords that I already learned on the ukulele. I'm surprised how good they sound on the guitar, even if I'm only using four of the six strings. In the days that follow, I work my way through the Nick Manoloff book, eventually using all six strings. By the middle of May I can alternate bass notes with chords. At the end of May, six weeks after my sixteenth birthday, we have a song fest in my bedroom—Mama, Kathleen, Helen, Klein, Bober, Wilson, Dreer and Perham—with me accompanying the songs on the guitar, and I know that I'm hooked for life on this wonderful instrument.

Some of the gang at a typical song fest at our home. Back row: Kathleen, Artie & Bruce & Baby (upstairs tenants), Florence (Artie's sister), Bob Perham, Tim Allord, Mike Wilson. Middle: Dick Tomak, Mama, Johnny Bober. Foreground: John Andrews (St. Raymond's music director and constant family friend). Picture taken ≈ 1951

51.

Lure of the Au Sable

Ninety Miles on the Au Sable River in Three Days was the name of one of my ninth-grade English themes. In it I told of our Explorer Post's Adventure from Grayling Michigan to Mio Dam, with two nights of camping and ninety river miles of paddling. I was awestruck by the swift-running water, so clean that we drank it, so clear that I could see speckled trout swimming beneath the canoe. It was the greatest adventures of my life.

Canoeing got into my blood from the first time two Boy Scout counselors took me for a canoe ride while on a camp-out. It seemed like we were floating in space, without effort, without sound. In the Explorers, we began canoeing at Belle Isle, with its miles of canoe trails. It was there that I practiced the strokes that I would need on the swift Au Sable River: the bow stroke, the J-stroke, back paddling, bow- and stern-rudder, draw strokes, cross-bow strokes, and up- and down-stream ferrying. I soon felt that the paddle was part of my own body. Now I have a chance to relive an even greater adventure on the Au Sable. There's only one small problem that I have to deal with: my body cast.

Even though I've been stuck in my body cast for two months, I've been actively planning the next trip on the Au Sable River for our Explorer post this coming August, writing away for maps and information, corresponding with canoe liveries, and eventually negotiating a far better rate from Mead's Canoe Landing on the South Branch of the Au Sable than we got last year from Ray's in Grayling. This trip is going to be a smashing adventure of over two-hundred river miles, with seven portages, the first one over the Mio Dam, where we stopped last year. The thought of doing all this planning and then being left behind eats at me. Mike and I have a long conversation about the possibilities.

"I negotiated a much cheaper rate than we got last year," I tell Mike. "They'll provide canoes, paddles, and pickup at the end. You guys are going to have the greatest adventure. Oh, how I wish I could go with you."

"Why can't you go?"

"Well, I've got this little detail—my body cast."

" Why should that stop you? There is a solution to any problem. And we can solve this one."

In a couple of days, Mike calls a meeting with the guys behind a closed door in my bedroom: Mike, Johnny Dreer, Gene Klein, Bob Perham. No sense in alarming Mama until we get the details worked out.

"We've got it all figured out," says Mike. You can ride like cargo stretched out in one of the canoes. We'll make a back rest so you can sit up enough to handle a paddle. Your canoe will have three paddlers: one in the bow, one in the stern, and you."

"We're going to tie life preservers to your chest, your body cast, and to your other leg so you won't sink in case the canoe tips over," explains Dreer.

"We've even got the portages figured out," advances Perham. The longest one is half a mile. We'll carry you along with all the other gear."

"We're going to make a stretcher on two poles that are to be carried by us four guys, and you'll be in the stretcher," says Klein.

I can see in an instant that this plan is simple, yet effective and foolproof! My first hurdle is Mama. I speak with her about our plans.

"Mama, I want to go on the AuSable River trip. We've got it all figured out."

"What? You can't be serious. You're in a body cast."

"No Mama. I'm serious. I can ride in the middle of the canoe. I'll have life preservers tied to me. The guys are going to make a stretcher to take me over the portages. I'm not going to strain my leg at all."

"No! Absolutely not."

"But Mama, you don't understand anything about canoes, about our solutions to all the problems, about how capable my buddies are, about how badly I want to go."

So I beg and plead. But the best I can get out of her is that she agrees to ask Doctor Maguire for his okay. She will explain our solutions to all the hurdles and problems. If he agrees, then I'm off to the Au Sable River. Doctor Maguire, being a man, will surely understand the logic of our solutions and won't be taken in by Mama's hysterical worries. Mama has made a deal with me, one that she is honor-bound to keep.

"Well, did you see Doctor Maguire?" I ask, remembering that Mama said she was to go to his office today to discuss my progress, and that she would ask him about my canoe trip. "And did you ask him?"

"Yes, I saw him, and I asked him," she says, hesitantly.

"Well, what did he say," I ask, wondering if the look on Mama's face means bad news for me, or does it mean he said okay, and Mama is worried that she will have to keep her word.

"He said: 'Woman, are you some kind of fool?' And I felt like a fool. He says you have to stay in that body cast until the X-ray shows healing, and any kind of physical activity is out— especially canoeing. Period! Mother in heaven, what I don't do for my son."

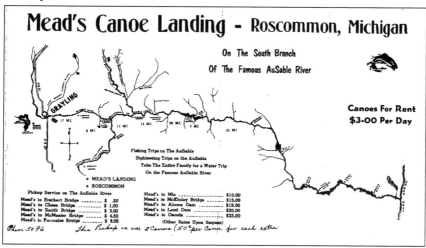

52.

A Radio Hoax

"CQ! CQ! This is W8JPR calling CQ!" I say, dangling the bait with the lingo that an amateur radio operator uses when he's trying to connect with anyone who happens to tune onto his signal.

I flip the toggle switch from transmit to receive, while Lois puts her hand to her lips, pretending to stifle a laugh, but lets snorts and snickers leak out between her fingertips to let me know she's thinking: *Who's he trying to fool?* Well, the answer is: *Lois St. Croix, my sister Kathleen's best friend,* that's who. And in just a minute, I'll have hooked her, just like I did Mike Wilson.

You see, it's all a scam. The call letters are fake, and the transmitter is nothing more than a regular radio that I rigged up to amplify the microphone that I wired to it. Unless I point them out, nobody notices the thin wires leading from the back of the radio, down the little table beside my bed, along the toe molding on the floor, taking a turn in the hallway, disappearing into a hole in the floor to the basement, then going across the basement ceiling to the fruit cellar, where Dick Tomak is hidden, ready to play his role in this hoax.

I wait a respectable length of time through the radio silence to make the dangling bait more tempting, then throw the switch to transmit.

"CQ! CQ! This is W8JPR calling CQ! Is anyone there?"

Lois breaks into a broad crooked smile—half her face is frozen from the dental treatment she had just before coming here. Mama and Kathleen, who are standing nearby in the room, are in on the hoax too.

"I converted my radio to a transmitter, and now I can talk to the Hams," I tell Lois.

"Get out of here! I'm not as dumb as I look," she replies. "You don't know how to do that. Besides, you need a license to go on the air."

So much for the bait. Now for the hooking.

Dick and I have been working on this hoax for the past two weeks—right after he got off school for the summer. We listened to the amateur radio operators they call *Hams*, and caught on to their lingo. I showed him how to hook up the wires in the fruit cellar—I can't do it myself since I'm still stuck in my bedroom in a body cast. We first tested our hoax on Mike Wilson, who has been coming over every day. Dick has to get here even earlier so he can run down the basement stairs the minute Mike shows up. He uses different voices when he plays the part of several Hams—his own voice for one, he puts the microphone in a mayonnaise jar for another, and he uses a handkerchief over the microphone for yet another. Mike has been so impressed by my conversations with all these Hams, that he now practices Morse Code with me—one of the prerequisites for getting an Amateur Radio Operator's license.

Tonight, it just so happened that Dick was still here when Lois came to sleep over with Kathleen. Either she stays here, or Kathleen sleeps over at her house; those two are inseparable. So long as Dick was handy, we decided to play the hoax on Lois. He greeted her when she first arrived, said his good-by, went through the kitchen and down the little landing to the side door, which he slammed before tip-toeing down the basement stairs to the fruit cellar, where he has been practically living these past two weeks.

"CQ! CQ! W8JPR calling CQ!"

I know this will be the final call, since this is the way we rehearsed it. I throw the switch to *Receive*, and wait, letting Lois continue with her snickering and carrying on.

"W8JPR, this is W8RJT, your old radio buddy Ralph Evans," comes the voice from the radio speaker in deep resonant tones that belie Dick's sixteen years. Lois's face goes from snickering to wide-eyed surprise, her jaw dropping. She stares at the radio, missing my smug look.

Dick plays his part like the seasoned actor he has become. He makes up a story about the FCC looking for an unlicensed operator that is rumored to be on the air. He talks about the plane he pilots, and how he is studying to be a doctor at the University of Michigan.

"Can I talk?" asks Lois.

"Sure," I say. "Ralph, I'm going to let you talk to one of the most beautiful girls in Detroit. Her name is Lois St. Croix," I say, handing her the microphone.

Lois starts the conversation tentatively, warms up to the mike, then to Ralph, the con man downstairs.

"Tell me about yourself," she says.

"Well, I'm six foot two, I have blond hair and blue eyes, and I weigh a hundred eighty pounds. I'm twenty-one years old. I've got a bit of a sore leg right now from a football injury I got last week playing on my college team at University of Michigan. But that doesn't keep me from dancing or piloting my plane. Would you like to go for a flight sometime?" I can imagine how all this is sitting with seventeen-year-old Lois.

"Oh, I'd love to," she says, looking like she's going to melt in ecstasy over the prospect of meeting this handsome pilot. *What do I do now?* she whispers to me, cupping her hand over the microphone.

"Here, give that to me," I say, reaching for the microphone. "Come to our house sometime, Ralph. Lois is here all the time. Write down this address: 13641 Pinewood Street."

"I'll be sure to do that," says Ralph. "I have to sign off now. This is Ralph Evans, W8RJT, signing off for the evening."

Now the hook is fully set. We only have to reel in the big catch.

"Let's get our jammies on," says Kathleen, not even hinting at her role in this hoax, as she leads Lois out of the room. "We can watch TV and have some snacks before going to bed." Mama leaves too, only to sneak a glass of Vernors' downstairs. Dick waits patiently for another half hour, sneaks out the side door and goes to the front door, where he rings the bell.

"It's almost ten o'clock," says Kathleen, who jumps up from the living room couch where she and Lois have been sitting. "Who would be calling at this hour?" She puts on her bathrobe, opens the door, and admits a young man into the foyer, just out of sight of Lois in the living room.

"Hello. My name is Ralph Evans," says Dick, in a loud booming voice. "I'm here to see Lois St. Croix."

"Oh, what a surprise. I'm sure Lois will be very glad to see you," says Kathleen, as Lois bounds from the couch, crosses the living room and dashes into the bedroom.

"Here, come in and have a seat on the couch," she says in a loud voice. "I'll get Lois. She's right in the next room." She proceeds to the bedroom where Lois wears a shocked expression.

"Is he really here?"

"I'm afraid so, Lois. He's the same guy you've been flirting with on the radio."

"Oh, my God, Kay! I didn't think he'd actually come. What does he look like?"

"Lois, he's as ugly as sin. I've never seen such a vile looking guy."

"Kay, you go out, tell him you're me. I can't face him."

"I can't do that, Lois. He already knows who I am."

"What'll I do now?"

"You've got no choice. You're the one who invited him over. You just have to get dressed and face the music."

Lois changes out of her jammies and into the dress she was wearing when she came over. She goes to the bathroom to put on her lipstick, while Kathleen watches in amusement. Lois has a problem applying lipstick from her shaking hand onto her frozen face, which just won't cooperate, causing her to smear the red color in an odd pattern around her mouth.

"You look great," says Kathleen, surveying her shaking friend. Come on into the living room," she says, holding Lois's hand to make sure she doesn't bolt for the bedroom again.

"Lois, I'd like to introduce you to Ralph Evans. Ralph, this is Lois St. Croix," Kathleen says, motioning towards Dick Tomak sitting on the couch.

"Hello, I'm Ralph Evans, W8RJT. Glad to make your acquaintance," says Dick, displaying a wide grin as he stands and extends his hand."

Mama, Kathleen and Dick break into hilarious laughter, while Lois buries her face in her hands. "You bums! You got me on that one."

My next view of Lois is her poking her head into my bedroom door and shaking her fist in my direction. The sight of her crooked smile and smeared lipstick makes me break into laughter.

"Okay, mister funny guy. You zinged me that time. But one of these day—one of these days, just you wait. When you're least expecting it. Pow! Right in the kisser."

Lois St Croix (lower) & Kathleen (upper); both at age 16.

53.

Mama's Treatment

She has a new name and a new life. First she was Helen Julia Rogoza—the name given to her at baptism. Helen was the name Ma, Pa and her brothers and sisters called her. But when she sent away for her birth certificate to apply for a job, they couldn't find anyone under that exact name. They sent her a photo copy instead that said just "Julia Rogoza"—daughter of Dominik Rogoza and Stella Gryniewicz, both born in Poland. So Julia is her new name. All those terrible things happened to Helen—not Julia. But still the memories come back to her, again and again.

*   *   *   *

I hate being stuck in bed at home with a body cast. I depend on others for everything: food, drink, incoming and outgoing bed pans and urinals, wash up stuff in the mornings, books from the library, games to play, pencils and paper. I pull the curtain behind my bed, and watch the kid next door playing ball in his yard, and I want to be outside too. I want to be out with the explorer scouts. I want to canoe the AuSable River. But, in time, I grow to accept my life as a new routine.

My homework and assignments from Nativity get shuttled back and forth every few days. I do homework; I do Indian beadwork; I draw; I read books of adventure by Jules Verne and Robert Louis Stevenson, books on electricity, books on science, books on magic; I practice card tricks; I start working on the first draft of the constitution of Post 66, one of the ways I can still be active in the Explorer Scouts. My buddies find our front door always open and they no longer even bother to knock. Not a single day goes by when some friends don't come to call. We play cards, we tell jokes, we sing songs, and Mike sneaks in bottles of home-made wine from time to time.

At the end of June, after three months at home, just when my life is becoming routine and organized, Mama decides to go on a treatment Dr. Johnson prescribed for her, a treatment that is supposed to stop her attacks, a treatment that is bound to turn our lives upside down.

Doctor Johnson told Mama she needed to rest for an entire month to cure her of her attacks. So he gave her a bottle of pills, from which Kathleen doles out her dose every day. When she's not sleeping, which is half the time, the pills keep her in a stupor, like she's drunk. When she talks, she sounds like a drunk four-year old little girl. She even raises her voice to a little girl pitch when she talks.

I hate the routine of Mama's treatment. Now my sisters empty my bedpan and urinal, bring me wash-up stuff in the morning and a food tray three times a day. It's embarrassing enough to have to be an invalid, but its positively humiliating to have your sisters care for you. And to make matters worse, Kathleen and Helen have to get a baby sitter to watch over Mama and me when they're gone. When someone outside the family watches us, I do everything possible to avoid having to ask to have my urinal emptied. Sometimes Ardie or her sister Florence, who both live in the flat upstairs, serve as a baby sitter. Once Lois, Kathleen's best girl friend, baby-sat me—a humiliation beyond all of them. And occasionally, when one of my buddies come to visit, Kathleen or Helen asks him to watch Mama and me while she goes out to shop or to do some other chore.

My body cast makes it impossible for me to get away from all this craziness. Maybe I should be thankful that I can't really do anything for her, that Mama's not my problem, that it's Kathleen and Helen who have to do the shopping, house cleaning, cooking, caring for Mama and for me too.

"I don't want to eat this, I want dessert," I hear Mama say, "I don't have to eat vegetables," she says, her voice pitched high like a little girl.

"You need to eat it Mama," comes Kathleen's voice. "It's good for you. Here, let me spoon it for you. Open wide!" I can imagine Kathleen making an airplane out of the spoon, like you do for little babies when they won't eat their dinner.

"No! No! No! I-want-de-sert! I-want-de-sert!" Mama calls out in a sing-songy way. Then I hear Mama make airplane noises, like she's flapping her tongue against her lips. "Brrrrrrrrrr...!" God! I wonder if she's got her teeth in. I can't stand the thought of her burbling like that without her teeth.

I turn up the radio beside my bed to drown out her babbling. Helen comes in with a tray, and lays it on the side of my bed.

"I guess Kathleen's got the Mama duty tonight," I say.

"Oh, don't worry. I get my turn tomorrow. I'm so happy, I can hardly wait," Helen replies, rolling her eyes. We hear Mama's little girl voice from her bedroom, which puts Helen and me into a giggling fit. One compensation of all this craziness is that we laugh a lot about the silly things Mama says. Another compensation is that Mama hasn't had a mean mood or an attack since she started the treatment, and her treatment is supposed to make that permanent.

After I finish my dinner, I wait for someone to pick up my tray. I can hear Kathleen and Helen helping Mama to the bathroom—the usual custom after dinner. Mama's baby noises, along with thumping and clunking noises, make me imagine her staggering and falling against the wall as my sisters try to steady their unstable burden. Someone lifts the toilet lid, and more noises tell me that they're trying to shift her onto the toilet. God, I hope she can wipe her own ass. If she can't, I don't want to know about it.

Mike comes into my room to visit and pulls up a chair beside my bed. Mama calls out to him in her drunken voice. "Mike. My dearest Mike. Come talk to me."

"Don't bother with her," I say. "Mama's just sick and she can't talk straight. Don't pay any attention to her. Let's just play some chess." Right now my thoughts aren't really on chess. I'm thinking about how embarrassing it will be if Mike or any one of my friends finds out about Mama.

"It doesn't bother me, Pat. I'll just see what she wants."

Mike leaves my room, and I hear his footsteps go down the hall toward Mama's room. He's there for a long time. I can imagine Mama talking to him like a baby. Or going on with attack talk. I feel so ashamed. After an hour, Mike comes back into my bedroom. He sits beside my bed and starts to set up the chess board.

"What did she say, Mike?" I ask, feeling the shame burn in my face like a hot coal.

"I'm sorry, Pat. She just wanted to talk. It's just between me and her," he says, as he holds out two closed fists, inviting me to pick the one which holds the chess color I will use to start the game.

Father O'Hara sits in the chair beside my bed. It's the first time I've seen him since I left Annunciation Parish. He said his mother lives not far away, and he heard that I was laid up from an accident, so he came to visit me. But I wonder if he really came to visit Mama. She calls out in drunken, slurred speech from her bedroom.

"Father O'Hara! It's Julie. Come see me."

I think of all the eternities that Mama knelt in his confessional booth while I waited in the pew, of the many visits she made to see him at the rectory. I just know they've got a special relationship, and he's sure to go in there, and I'll be embarrassed to death when he sees what she's come to.

"She's on a medical treatment," I say. "It keeps her dopey."

"I'll come in later, Julie," Father O'Hara calls back to Mama. "When I'm done talking with Pat." He asks me about my schooling.

"Last semester I took Latin and English from Nativity—the kids brought me assignments, and shuttled my homework back and forth—and I took Biology and History from Mr. Rubin, a guy from the Public Schools." After saying this, I feel suddenly embarrassed. What will he think of me getting schooling from the Protestants? But he doesn't seem to be shocked at all. "That's good," he says, "Just keep plugging away."

While we talk, Mama calls out every once in a while for Father to come see her, but he ignores her. After a while, he gets up to leave. I ask for his blessing.

"In nomine Patris, et Fílii, et Spíritus Sancti, Amen," he says, as he traces a little cross on my forehead with his thumb. "Take care of yourself, Pat. I'll keep you in my prayers."

Father O'Hara turns from my bedroom and walks out the door. His footsteps turn into the dining room, not Mama's bedroom. Kathleen says a few words from the distant room, and then the front door closes. *Thank God he skipped Mama*, I think.

Mama's treatment continues for one month. It takes her three whole days to get the medicine out of her system. When she regains her senses, she seems in a good mood, but she says she can't remember much about the past month. So we tell her a bunch of stories about all the silly things she said, how she would stumble as Kathleen and Helen took her to the bathroom. Each of us tries to recall some amusing thing Mama said, like we were the parents laughing at the antics of a four-year-old child. At first Mama seems to be amused too, but as the stories go on, I can see that it is a big mistake to tell her all this stuff, because she stops laughing, and starts to look grim, then outright angry.

The following day Mama goes on a cleaning rampage, with her hair-trigger anger, like when she's working up to an attack. Luckily, I don't have to worry about crossing her since she vents all her anger on Kathleen and Helen. I suppose that I escape her anger since I am the invalid around here. And if she does have an attack, I won't have to sit up with her. God! How I long for Saratoga Hospital, where I had my own family, where they knew what to do, where everything was orderly—not like this nut house.

54.

Crutches

At the end of September, when I am in the eleventh grade, the ambulance men strap me into a stretcher, maneuver me through the bedroom door, down the landing to the side door outside, and into a waiting ambulance for a ride to Saratoga Hospital, where I get X-rays taken. It has been seven months that I've been in my prison of a body cast.

"I've got great news for you, John," says Doctor Maguire. "I see definite signs of healing. We're going to take off the body cast, and let you go on crutches."

Dr. Maguire uses an electric cutting tool to cut the cast from my ribs to the bottom of my foot. The tool has what looks like a rotating cutting blade that slices through the plaster, and every once in a while it goes right through, and I'm sure that he's going to slice my skin, and it scares me half to death. He continues to work without the slightest hesitancy, finally slicing the plaster cast from my ribs to the tip of my toes. Then he uses a prying bar to further separate the cast and lifts off the upper half.

For some strange reason, I'm surprised to see a leg appear, covered by a long stocking. He gently lifts the leg out, pulls off the stocking, and a greater surprise awaits me. The inside of the cast has a pool of blood in the area that was below my knee, and the back of my leg has a gaping wound. The underside of the stocking is a bloody mess.

The sight of all that blood frightens me, but I hide my fear. "I'll bet that's why I had all that fierce itching these past months."

"A cast ulcer," he pronounces, calmly, like he sees this every day. "We'll fix that," and with a cotton swab he dabs something into the wound that burns like fury. "Congratulations, John," he says. "You are graduating to a pair of crutches. No weight on that leg, though. And no wrestling with your buddies." He hands me a pair of crutches. "Let's help you off this table."

With Doctor Maguire holding me under one arm, and Mama the other, I slide off the table, and put both feet on the floor. It's a dizzying sensation, like being in the clouds. It has been nine months since I have stood up. How strange the world seems from this great height!

"Good mother in heaven!" exclaims Mama, with a glowing smile. "I'll bet you've grown two inches since you last stood."

Doctor Maguire instructs me how to use the crutches. As he leaves, I call out to him: "One more thing, Doctor Maguire."

"What's that?"

"My name is Pat, not John."

Mr. Rubin from the public school system comes twice a week to tutor me. The kids from Nativity continue to bring me assignments, and shuttle my homework and tests back and forth. Kathleen and Helen are relieved from baby-sitting duty. It is a luxury beyond description to be able to take a bath without needing others to shuttle the bath water in a pan.

It is not so easy to learn to use crutches. At first they hurt terribly in my armpits where I rest my weight when I want to relieve my tired arms. But soon my arms become powerfully strong, and I can get around with ease, even being able to scamper up and down stairs by holding both crutches in one hand while holding the railing with the other. I'm seventeen now, and my buddies are old enough to borrow their family cars and take me out of the nut house. Mike Wilson, Johnny Dreer and I often go to shoot snooker at Pat's Pool Hall on Eight Mile Road where I put my crutches under the table and lean on it when I walk around it, trying to look normal.

My buddies are protective of me, although I don't ask for it. Dick Tomak and I are out late in his car. Although he isn't doing anything wrong, a cop pulls him over—guilty of being a teenage driver. After looking at Dick's driver's license, he aims his flashlight around the car and stops when he spots my crutches on the back seat.

"What are these crutches all about?" the cop asks, suspiciously.

"Why don't you mind your own damned business. They're his," snaps Dick, nodding towards me in the front seat along side him. "Just back off and leave him alone."

Amazingly, the cop does just that, saying, "Just watch yourselves, and drive safely."

In October Mike picks me up to go to our Explorer Post meeting. It's time for election of officers, and I am voted as Deputy Senior Crew Leader, the number two position held by the boys. Mr. Zindler gives a congratulation speech.

"Pat, all of us in the Post want to thank you for all your contributions while you were laid up. We thank you for helping to plan our wonderful trip on the AuSable this past August, and we hope you'll get off those crutches and will be dancing soon." With that the guys give me a round of applause, and I feel like I'm glowing.

Although I feel right at home with my buddies, the part that's difficult for me is when it comes to dating girls. Judy Wilson fixes me up with Barbara, a friend of hers. I go out with her on double or triple dates, when someone else has a car to drive. I like her all right, but I feel so ashamed that I'm a cripple. Even though we've been out several times, I can't work up the nerve to kiss her after a date because I feel like such a freak.

Still, my crutches give me a tremendous sense of freedom compared to the body-cast days. The best part is that I can get out of the nut house, that I can get away from Mama and not have to worry if she's going over the edge.

55.

Mama Gets Courted

Julia Rogoza hides her bandaged hands behind her back, hoping that the handsome floor sweeper with curly hair and brown eyes won't see them and think her a freak. Eight finger tips were lanced to let out the infection she got from handling the sharp metal parts at Detroit Machine Works. When the doctor had sliced those X-shaped cuts she wondered if her fingers would be scarred forever, and would her children some day ask about those scars. Better find a new job, the doctor had advised. But it's nineteen thirty-four, and jobs don't just grow on trees. Twenty-two skidoo, and how are you, she says to the cute guy with the broom. She flutters her eyelashes in imitation of a vamp from the movies. I'm Julie. What's your name? Jack — Jack Reilly, replies the shy young man. Why, you're kinda cute, she says, flashing a broad smile. Want to go out for coffee after work? Ah, ah, okay, I guess, he stammers, feeling a blush rush to his face. Sometime a girl has to take matters into her own hands, thinks Julia.

*　　　*　　　*　　　*

Tonight is a special occasion for both me and Mama. It's going to be my first time to eat pizza, and Mama has a date.

Thanks to Mama's open-door policy, the living room is packed with teenagers: Mike Wilson, Johnny Dreer, Dick Tomak, Johnny Bober, and Bob Perham. My sisters are here too: Kathleen with her friend Lois St. Croix, and Helen with her friend Gertie Rail.

Kathleen and Lois are planning to go from here to a USO dance to act as hostesses to servicemen on leave, Helen is going to stay overnight at her girlfriend's, and I'm going with my friends to Singing Sam's, a pizza joint on Eight Mile Road. We kids get ready to leave, but Mama asks us to stay so we can meet her new friend who is soon to arrive—an actual date, someone she has never seen before—a blind date arranged by Mrs. Smith. Mama is dressed up in her fancy blue dress and high heels, and she wears lipstick and rouge that makes her look young and pretty. The whole gang is in high spirits with the prospect of some romance in Mama's life. And Mama too is in an especially good mood, and she requests that we all sing her favorite song— a number from our many song fests. I strum the guitar chords to *Your Cheatin' Heart*, as Mama belts out the melody, along with the rest of the gang.

> *(The first part we sing soft and gentle)*
> *Your cheatin' heart, will tell on you.*
> *You'll cry and cry the whole night through*
> *You'll walk the floor, the way I do.*
> *Your cheatin' heart, will tell on you.*

> *(The next part we sing fortissimo, in a revival style)*
> *When tears come down, like fallin' rain,*
> *You'll walk around, and call my name...*
> *(ZELDA! shouts Bob, at the top of his lungs.*
> *(Then we sing soft and gentle again)*
> *But sleep won't come, the whole night through.*
> *Your cheatin' heart, will tell on you.*

I hope this date works out better than the last one Mama had. That was when she went with Melba, her friend from work, to a bar where they were supposed to meet men. Both Mama and Melba did meet guys that night, and one of them offered to drive Mama home, and she accepted. When they got in front of the house, the man tried to kiss Mama and take indecent liberties with her. Mama slapped his face, slid out of the car, slammed the door and went into the house in shock and anger. Kathleen said what did she expect, meeting men in a pick-up bar.

But this time it seems different. This one is an upstanding widower friend of Mrs. Smith, who arranged this blind date.

The doorbell rings, and Mama runs to answer it.

"Hello! I'm Richard Mansfield," says the voice in the foyer.

"Oh hello! I'm Julie Reilly. I'm so pleased to meet you," gushes Mama. "Come in and meet the gang."

She leads in a man, not so tall and handsome as I think Mama probably expected. But still he looks nice for an old guy of about forty-five years. He wears a spiffy suit and tie, like he expects to take Mama to a fancy restaurant. But he looks nervous, shifting his gaze from one side of the room to another.

Mama stands by, looking triumphant, like she's proud of her big family.

"I want you to meet my children. This is my daughter Kathleen, my son, Patrick and my daughter, Helen Therese."

"Pleased to meet you," I say when Mama points to me, and I grasp his extended hand. It feels warm and sweaty, and his grip is weak and shaky. Mama wears a big smile as she points one-by-one to the other kids.

"And this is Dick Tomak, and Mike Wilson, and Johnny Dreer, and Johnny Bober, here's Bob Perham, that's my adopted daughter, Lois St. Croix, and last but not least, Gertie Rail."

As each kid's name is called, he or she jumps up and grabs the shaky hand of Richard Mansfield, giving a big hearty *hello*, or *glad to meet you*, or *how do you do*. But Mr. Mansfield doesn't seem to be as perky as the kids in the room. In fact, he looks downright queasy, like maybe he wants to throw up or something.

When all the introductions are finished, Mr. Mansfield speaks in a nervous, quavery voice.

"I - I'm pleased to meet you all. Now if you will just excuse me for one minute, I have to get something out of my car. You just wait here, Julie. I'll be right back."

"So long, Mr. Mansfield," shouts the gang, as he turns and exits through the front door.

Soon after Mr. Mansfield leaves, I follow the kids out the front door, which Mama holds open for the gang's exit.

"Have a good time Mama," I say, working my way down the front steps with my crutches.

"Don't do anything I wouldn't do," says Lois.

"Be good, Mrs. Reilly," says Mike, "and if you can't be good, be careful."

"And if you can't be careful, name him after me," adds Bob.

"I want you home by eleven o'clock," says Johnny Dreer, shaking a finger at Mama.

A bunch of us head for the Willys parked at the curb—the car that belongs to Mike's mother, and that he seems to be able to get any time he wants. Johnny Dreer sits in front, and Bob Perham slides in back along side of me. Kathleen, Lois, Helen, and Gertie walk down the street.

At Singing Sam's, we all manage to squeeze into two booths. Everyone dumps their pockets, making a big pile of pennies, nickels, dimes, and quarters. I add in my share of fifty-five cents. It all adds up to six dollars and fifty cents—enough for two large pepperoni pizzas and cokes for everyone.

I first learned about pizza from Kathleen when I was still laid up with my body cast. It sounded so good from her description, that I couldn't stand it just thinking about how it would taste. When I got on my crutches, Singing Sam's was one of the first places I wanted to go.

If you've never had pizza, you've just got to try it. Its a new dish that comes from Italy, but it's not like anything you've ever had in an Italian restaurant. It comes on a big round pan. The base of it is a type of bread that gets crispy on the bottom after baking. On top they put tomato sauce with spices, cheese, and spicy slices of a type of sausage they call *pepperoni*. It's then baked in a special oven, until the bread rises, the cheese melts, and the pepperoni becomes hot and sizzly. The cheese is a special type that blends with the tomato sauce. The part that gets to you first is the aroma of the hot pizza when they put it on the table, so wonderful that you can taste it just from the smell. It comes cut into pieces like a pie—that's why its called a pizza pie. The white cheese they use becomes melted and stringy, so when you bite off a piece, some of the cheese stays connected from your mouth to the piece, like a long piece of spaghetti that you have to cut off with a fork. Once you've had one piece, you're hooked for life.

When the pizza finally comes, it is everything I expected. The only problem is two pieces just don't seem like enough. We sit around laughing, nursing our Cokes, joking and smoking cigarettes, which most everybody in our gang does.

At ten-thirty Mike drops me off at my house. As always, the front door is unlocked. In fact, I never carry a key with me. As I walk into the living room, I see Mama sprawled out on the couch, wearing her tattered blue night gown with the little white cotton dots. Her legs stick out from the gown, showing fat varicose veins that look like they're ready to burst. There's a bottle of Goebel's beer on the coffee table, and a half-filled glass alongside. She takes a long drag from her cigarette, making the end glow bright red, inhales deeply, and blows a giant cloud of smoke to the ceiling. She looks old and tired.

"How was your date, Mama?" I ask, looking into her watery eyes. It's then that I can see that she's drunk—something that happens a lot nowadays.

"That no good stinking rat. He never came back," she says, slurring the words like she does when she's drunk. "He went out to his car and never came back."

"I'm sorry Mama. I really am," I say, thinking that somehow I must be responsible. Maybe it was something in the way I greeted him. Or maybe it was one of my friends.

"I'll never have anything to do with that rotten, stinking, stupid man again."

"I'm sorry Mama," I say as I make my way to my bedroom. But I'm not thinking of how sorry I am. I'm hoping that Mama won't corner me with one of her drunken chair talk sessions. But she doesn't call me back for drunken chair talk. She's muttering something unintelligible to herself. It sounds like Polish.

56.

Kathleen Escapes

When Kathleen graduates from Saint Charles High School in June, she tells Mama she plans to take the Grey Hound bus to Biloxi Mississippi for a couple of weeks vacation. But she tells me something else privately.

"I have a boyfriend in Biloxi who I met at a USO dance downtown. He's the cutest guy you've ever seen. He is on duty at the Air Base there. But my biggest reason is Mama. I just can't stand it here any longer. I'm hoping to get out of this nut house for good."

I don't know if this is a good deal for me, or not. Although Kathleen will leave Helen and me to deal with Mama by ourselves, she won't be here to stir her up either.

In two weeks, what comes back is not Kathleen, but a letter from Kathleen to Mama.

Dear Mama,

I just love it here. I've made a lot of friends, and I'm having a great time. But I've made a little change in my plans. I've found a job as a playground director and will be staying here for a while. I've also found a place to live with a wonderful retired school teacher, Louise Mallard. And don't you worry. Louise acts like a mother to me. I'll be in good hands.

With my love to you, Pat, and Helen,
Kathleen.

I think that Mama ought to be delighted to get the news that she will now be rid of Kathleen, who was constantly doing battle with her when they were together. But Mama is furious.

"That little snip. She should be here to help with the household. She should be helping to pay the bills. Who does she think she is to just cast me aside and let someone else take my place. Isn't that just like your sister—selfish and ungrateful!"

Mama writes to the pastor of Saint Martin's, the Catholic Church in the parish where Kathleen will be staying in Biloxi. What kind of woman is this Louise Mallard? she demands to know. The letter that comes back does little to mollify Mama.

Dear Mrs. Reilly,

I received your letter inquiring about the character of Mrs. Louise Mallard. It is an inspiration to know of a loving mother's concern for her daughter.

I can assure you that Mrs. Mallard is a fine upstanding Catholic. She is old enough to be a mother to your daughter. She taught high school here in Biloxi, and she is a loyal member of Saint Martin's Church. I am sure that Mrs. Mallard will be a fine guardian of your daughter's virtue.

Faithfully yours in Christ,

Father Lebec
Pastor
Saint Martin's Catholic Church
Biloxi, Mississippi

Rather than reassuring her, the letter only seems to get Mama more anxious. "Her soul is at stake," she says. She buys a bus ticket to Biloxi and is gone on a life-saving mission for two weeks.

When Mama returns she is in a black mood. She doesn't want to talk about her mission in Biloxi, and I don't want to ask, fearing that I might stir up the hornet's nest that is buzzing in Mama's head.

57.

Return to Saratoga

At the end of the summer, Dr. Maguire decides that I can go to school on crutches. It's my Senior year at Nativity High School and I'm given a front seat in the row nearest the door in each class. Just before the bell rings, the nun teaching that class is supposed to give me the word that change of classes is about to begin. Then I get a head start out the door and make my way to the next class while the halls are still empty. The word was sent out to the whole school not to bump into the guy on crutches. The kids try to be nice to me, saying things like "Good to see you, John," or "Welcome back, John." But it all seems so strange. Can't they understand that my name is *Pat*, not *John*, and that all this fuss makes me feel like a freak?

I go to school on my crutches for two weeks, and still don't get used to all the attention they're giving me. I feel especially awkward when I change classes, when the whole school can get a good look at the cripple of Nativity High School. I hate going on the bus and streetcar on my crutches, where everyone stares at me, and especially when some old lady jumps up and offers me her seat. I don't know why I have to come here for school. I was doing just fine, taking four courses each semester at home. But Dr. Maguire had to ruin it all by saying I could start the school year on crutches. Tomorrow I go in for an X-ray. Maybe then I can throw away these crutches and act like a normal person.

Mama and I sit in a little room in Saratoga Hospital. Dr. Maguire puts some X-rays on a box on the wall with a lit up window. He points to the femur at a point just below the hip socket.

"I don't like the looks of this," he says. "It's not healing the way it should. We've given it plenty of time, but there's little evidence of new growth."

"What do you recommend?" asks Mama.

"I would like to do a bone graft. Its really a very simple procedure. I just take some bone out of the hip, and pack some splinters around the area of the fracture. This has a very good success rate in cases of non-union fracture like John's. What do you say Mrs. Reilly? And you, John, are you willing to try it?"

"It's all right with me," I say, wishing he would call me *Pat*. "When do we do it?"

"Yes. God willing, it sounds like the best thing to do," says Mama.

"Good. I can schedule you for surgery in two weeks."

I sit in the front seat, while Mama drives home from Saratoga.

"I've been thinking," she says. "There is another possibility of a cure for you, something we haven't tried yet. I've been talking with Mrs. Wagner. You remember her from Annunciation. Well, we were talking about all the cures at Fatima. You know, the place in France where the little girls saw the vision of the Blessed Mother. People come there from all over the world, bringing sick and hopelessly crippled people. All kinds of miracles happen there."

I see images from the books I read on Fatima: crowds of people transporting sick people on stretchers, piles of crutches, blind people beseeching the Virgin for a cure, images of the Virgin with rays coming out of her hands, touching the blind and crippled. I imagine myself in this crowd, a hopeless cripple in a crowd of religious fanatics like Mama. The images make words of anger spill out of my mouth.

"I'm not a hopeless cripple, and I'm not going to Fatima. I don't want to talk to you about that ever again."

Mama is silent as we finish our drive home.

I'm in the big ward at Saratoga. This time the stitches go along the side of my thigh, starting at a few inches above the knee, and going clear above my hip, where they took some bone for the graft. I thank God that there's no body cast this time. Everybody fusses over me. I get a big hug from Mrs. Houseworth; Georgina seems happy to see me; Miss Woods says me she needs more poker lessons because she's getting rusty; Miss Smith says I look like a grown man now; and Miss Riley looks as beautiful as ever. There are some new nurses and aides here now, but I'm getting to be friends with them too. As usual, Mike comes to visit every day, sometimes bringing White Castle hamburgers, sometimes staying late into the night. I feel like I'm home now.

After four weeks they send me home on crutches and back to my home schooling with Mr. Rubin, who is supposed to tutor me in biology and algebra, although, like before, we spend most of the time slinging the bull. I also take English and history from Nativity High School, with the kids shuttling my homework and assignments back and forth. By keeping up this way, I am able to get enough credits to graduate with my class, the Nativity High School graduating class of 1955.

I attend my high school graduation ceremony on crutches. I can't refuse to go to that, although I feel embarrassed about hobbling down the aisle to get my diploma, with a thousand people watching. Ken, one of the guys from school, takes me around to some parties. He is really great about it, especially considering that I hardly even know him and haven't had any contact with him since the beginning of my sophomore year when I had the accident. We start out at his house, where I get a little tipsy drinking two gin and tonics—a drink I never even heard of before. After that I am feeling pretty good, and we go to a string of other parties. I have no trouble showing off how I can dance on my crutches, with both feet off the floor.

I have another X-ray in early July. Dr. Maguire says that the bone graft is taking nicely, and that the bone is almost healed. He schedules me back into Saratoga Hospital for my last operation to take out the rod that runs throughout the center of the thigh bone. Only this time the operation is very simple. I wake up in the big ward once again, but I seem to recover in one day. I stay there for only ten days, and they send me home on crutches for what we think will be the final time. On the first of August Dr. Maguire looks at another X-ray and says I can throw away my crutches, forever.

I hand my crutches to Mama. "Hold these for me, Mama."

With that I take a tentative step, putting my full weight on my right leg. Nothing breaks, and I don't fall down. I take a few more steps, and turn around, looking at Doctor Maquire, and then at Mama. She has tears in her eyes.

It has been almost three years since my accident. I've been in a wheel chair, a body cast, then crutches. I've had four surgeries Now I can finally put it all behind me, and I have the whole world to look forward to. I'm free at last!

58.

Used Crutches for Sale

I've been walking for one week now. My right leg is weak, and the right foot gets pretty sore, but I can walk under my own power. Mike Wilson and his girl friend Jill pick me up in his mom's car to go to a party. He says he first wants to swing by his house so he can dress for the occasion. I wait in the car, while he and Jill run into his house. After fifteen minutes, he comes back out, looking little different from when he went in.

This is going to be my first party since I got off crutches—my debut as a regular person. I feel good about going to this party. Only I'm not sure whose party this is. As usual Mike is being cryptic about where we're actually going, but he assures me there will be some cute girls there.

"Whose party?" I ask.

"You'll see. We have to stop back at your house to pick up something," Mike says.

"What are you talking about? I don't need anything."

"Yeah, but I do. I forgot something there."

"What is it?"

"That's for me to know, and you to find out."

So Mike is up to his games again, playing *Mr. Mysterious*. I'll just have to play along, because he won't tell me until he is good and ready anyhow.

We pull up in front of my house on Pinewood Street. Mike goes upstairs and holds the door open for Jill and me, and he swings his hand as if he's the doorman of the Ritz inviting us to come in.

"After you Madam. After you Sir."

I go in first, as Jill hangs back. When I pass through the little foyer, I'm startled to see the living room filled with people. Mama is in front. She starts singing *For He's a Jolly Good Fellow*, and the rest of the gang joins in. Behind her is my sister Helen, and there's Lois St. Croix, John Andrews, Johnny Bober pumping on his accordion, Bob Perham also with an accordion. There's Kathy Wilson, Tommy Smith, Mrs. Smith, Tommy's little brother, Robert, and Tim Allord. I glance back at Mike, still in the foyer, wearing a wry smile. So this was his secret.

Mama's got a big sign that says *USED CRUTCHES FOR SALE, 100% OFF*, and she's waving it back and forth. And there are my crutches, leaning against the wall behind her, like they're the guests of honor.

Johnny and Bob strike up the beer barrel polka on their accordions. Someone hands me my *Stella* guitar, and I join in on the song. Lois and Kathleen try to dance in the dining room, but there is hardly enough room for all the people, let alone for dancers.

After the song, Helen brings out a big tray with wax paper cups filled with Coca Cola, and passes them around. Mama bangs one of my drum sticks on the bottom of a pan. She wants quiet so she can make a speech. God! I hope she's not going to embarrass me!

"I want to make a toast to my son, John Patrick Reilly, also known as my Little Nudnik. Three years ago, he had a little argument with a car. Well, the car was a total wreck, but he survived. And now, here is my little Nudnik, ready to take on the world."

Oh damn! I just knew she was going to say something embarrassing.

She raises her glass, and everyone does the same, and then they take a sip. Just then, Johnny and Bob start in on *Shake, Rattle, and Roll*—the popular rock 'n ' roll song from *Bill Haley and the Comets*. I join in on the drums on this one, banging my sticks on the bottom of the cooking pot that Mama had brought out. The whole gang joins in the loudest and most off-key singing you ever heard. Mama claps her hands in time to the tune. Everyone else dances in place, shaking back and forth, swinging their hips in the shameful manner that got Elvis banned from TV.

Get out in that kitchen and rattle those pots and pans.
Get out in that kitchen and rattle those pots and pans.
Well roll my breakfast, cause I'm a hungerin' man.
I say shake, rattle and roll

Used Crutches Party. Standing L-->R: Lois St Croix (partial), John Andrews, Cathy Wilson, Ruth Ann Smith, Tim Allord, Jill St Aubin, Tom Smith, Mike Wilson (partial). Seated: Johnny Bober (accordion), Bob Perham (accordion), Helen Reilly, Pat Reilly (guitar).
Foreground: Robert Smith, Mrs. Smith. Large sign in background says: "Used Crutches for Sale—100% off." Mama probably snapped this picture.

59.

A Hangover

The last week of August is my last chance to get drunk before I start college. Mike Wilson drives Johnny Dreer and me towards the town of Romeo in his mom's Willys. Our destination is his mom's cottage, where we will be all alone for the weekend. But there's one small hitch. Not one of us is twenty-one, the legal age for buying alcohol; I'm eighteen, and Johnny and Mike are seventeen. We decide that since Johnny is the only one of us with chest hair, he should be the first to try to buy some beer.

"Open your collar," says Mike. "So your chest hair shows."

Johnny fumbles with the buttons.

"That's great," I say. "You could easily pass for twenty-one."

Mike stops the Willys in front of *Freddy's Beer and Party Store*. Johnny gets out, expands his chest by holding a deep breath, and struts up to the store, with a military bearing. A few minutes later he comes out, shrugging his shoulders with his empty hands pointing up.

"They asked me for proof. I said I forgot my wallet at home. But there I was, holding my wallet in my hand so I could pull out the money to pay him."

Mike flips a coin, catches it in his right hand, and slaps it onto his left wrist. "Call it, Sir" he says.

"Heads," I say. Mike uncovers the coin, which shows a tail.

"Looks like I'm next," he says.

We drive two blocks to the *Get and Go* store, which has a sign in the window promising COLD BEER TO GO. Mike strolls in. After a few minutes he walks out empty-handed. Now it's my turn.

Mike drives another two blocks and makes a U-turn, bringing us directly in front of *Tony's Bar*. I stroll into a smoky, dimly lit room and walk up to a long bar that curves around at one end. Tall round bar stools line the bar at which are seated three old guys wearing baseball caps. The side of the room is lined with booths with more old characters sitting there. The juke box is thumping out a country tune. The bartender walks up to me. I just know that everyone in the place is staring at me, wondering what this teen-ager is doing in their bar. I try my best not to make myself look guilty by shifting my eyes around to all the old codgers.

"What can I do for you?" asks the bartender.

"I'd like a six-pack of Stroh's", I say in an easy tone that says I do this all the time.

He reaches around into a cooler with a sliding cover and pulls out a six-pack of beer cans, which he plunks down on the counter in front of me.

"Anything else?"

I quickly do the arithmetic in my head: six cans divided by three guys—that's only two each. "Better make it two more six packs."

I walk out of Tony's with three paper bags under my arms, loaded with beer. "Open the trunk, Mike," I say. "We've got beer tonight."

We pull up to Mike's small cottage. I cart in two six-packs, and Mike carries the third. We put the beer into the refrigerator in the room that is kitchen, living room, and bedroom. The one other room is a screened porch, which serves as the overflow bedroom. The table is littered with magazines, pop bottles, dirty napkins, plastic forks, paper plates, and miscellaneous junk. Mike scoops all this into a trash can so we will have some space to play poker later on. The sink is full of dirty dishes. Bunk beds on one wall are in their usual mess, with moth-eaten covers in disarray and dirty sheets pulled out of their mattresses. The bunks are each double beds, so together they sleep four. Counting the two single beds on the porch, plus the couch, this place sleeps seven. Any more than that have to sleep on the floor, which they usually do in sleeping bags.

I stroll down towards the lake. On the grass, just before the dock, is an old wooden rowboat that Mike waterproofed by hammering oakum into the cracks between the boards. The boards on the dock are mostly split, and a few are missing. It takes a little care to avoid the empty spaces. Like many of the thousands of lakes found in Michigan, this one is big enough to have several cottages with docks on it, big enough to fish for perch, big enough to swim off the dock, and still small enough to easily row across the narrow part in only ten minutes or so. I have come here many times on my crutches, but I have never seen Mrs. Wilson here, or any other adult, for that matter. This place has become a great hang-out for teen-agers ever since Mike's dad died.

The kids who come here don't cause really serious trouble, even though there seldom is any adult supervision. There's never been a serious mishap here, unless you count the time last summer when Dick Tomak almost drowned. On that day I was sitting in the bow of the old row boat, facing the stern—a position where I could use one oar like a canoe paddle. Paddling the old rowboat was one activity I could do since I wasn't allowed to go in swimming because of my crutches. I was positioned about thirty feet from the dock and from a huge rubber raft tied to it, making a raised platform that was just right for diving. Each kid in turn climbed onto the raft and dove into the water, letting his momentum carry him to the boat without having to take more than one or two strokes on the way. Everyone successfully did this maneuver, except for Dick.

"Go on Dick," some of the kids were calling out. "It's your turn now."

"But I can't swim," he replied.

"You don't need to know how to swim. You can just glide to the boat. Didn't you see how everyone else did it?" someone shouted.

Dick climbed on the raft, and stood on the edge, first looking at me, then towards the others, who were sitting on the dock.

"Go on Dick. Don't be a chicken."

Suddenly Dick plunged into the water, made an awkward glide, and surfaced halfway between the boat and the dock. I could immediately see that he was in trouble as he clumsily thrashed about, trying to keep his head above water. I picked up an oar and tried to paddle to him, but the heavy boat was pointed in the wrong direction and wouldn't respond to my efforts to turn it around. Dick's head slipped below the surface, and once again he surfaced, sputtering and gasping. Just then, Don Sansoterra made a clean dive that propelled him to Dick's position. He flipped Dick on his back, grabbed his chin with one hand, and paddled with the other back to the dock. Don helped Dick up on the dock, where he stood and looked around at the faces staring in stunned silence at him. He seemed confused, like he didn't understand what was happening. In fact, the whole bunch looked that way.

Dick moved his lips in silence, like he wanted to say something, but couldn't get it out, like maybe he wanted to thank Don for saving his life or to make a vow never to do something so foolish again. But instead of talking, what came out of Dick's mouth was the lyrics of the popular song much played on the radio and juke boxes.

"Everybody razzle dazzle!"

That broke the silence that seemed to grip all the kids, who then began to applaud and laugh and join in on the tune. That episode became known in our teen folklore as the *Tomak Razzle Dazzle* incident.

I walk back up to the cottage, open the torn screen door and walk to the kitchen table. Johnny counts out piles of plastic chips, which we will purchase at the rate of one penny per white chip, five cents for the reds, and ten for the blues. Three cans of Stroh's are on the table, each with two triangular-shaped holes where Mike had used a church key to open them. "Gimme three bucks worth, Johnny," I say, peeling three singles from my wallet.

At nine o'clock we start with five card draw. I play cautiously as usual, throwing in my hand when I think it's weak. By the time I've finished my first beer, we've played probably a dozen hands, mostly just shuffling the chips back and forth from one guy's pile to another.

After my second beer is done, we three are getting a bit louder in our jokes, and I find myself taking more risks with my cards, staying in even when I have a bad hand with the hopes that the others will have something worse. Mike's pile looks decidedly bigger than ours.

After three beers Johnny makes a big raise drawing four cards. I stay in with three nines, upping Johnny's raises. When we show our cards, Johnny has pairs of tens and sixes, and Mike has three Jacks, and he rakes the pot into his now giant pile of chips. "Thank you Sirs," he says, with a crooked smirk.

I'm into my fourth beer, when I have to buy two more dollars worth of chips. Johnny has already bought three dollars worth. Mike just keeps raking it in.

It's midnight when I finish beer number five. Mike has most of the chips, and Johnny and I are low on money to buy more. We decide to let Mike keep all his winnings. Although he's had as much beer as we have, he seems to be the only one able to count the chips and divide up the pot. Mike ends up with ten dollars, Johnny gets a dollar fifty, and I get fifty cents. But who cares—it's much more fun making loud jokes and rude noises.

We carry the hilarity outside. By now Johnny's face is as red as a beet, like it always gets when he is excited—something he says comes from the Indian blood he gets from his mother. He starts a war dance, and Mike and I join in, hooting and hollering as we dance in a circle. I try to do the *Fluffy Dance*, which I learned before my accident when I was in the Indian dancing society *Heokawacheepee*. But my bum leg gives out, and I end up on the ground. I try to get up, but the ground starts spinning, making me fall back. Mike and Johnny continue to dance in a circle around me. Johnny makes a hooting sound while he slaps his hand over his mouth. His other hand holds his sheath knife with the five-inch blade.

"Let's scalp Reilly," he says as I get half way up. But the thought of getting scalped makes me break into more laughter, and I fall back to the ground. Johnny swishes the knife in big circles in the air as he spins and hoots.

"Okay, Johnny. Let's put the knife away," says Mike, as he embraces him with one arm and works his free hand up Johnny's arm, up to the knife.

As Mike and Johnny do a kind of dance, I crawl back to the cottage and up the steps. I find my way to the cot on the porch, flop onto it, and pull the covers over my head. This maneuver does little to stop the cottage from spinning.

I wake up feeling that a long time has passed. The cottage is no longer spinning. It's pitch black. I hear snoring coming from the bunks in the cottage. The air is oppressively hot, making my face sweat profusely. My stomach tells me to go outside. I stumble out the door and lay on the damp grass. I feel so sick that I want to die, right here, right now. Wave after wave of nausea hits my stomach, making me retch, puke, roll, cough, and fall back on my face. The nausea passes. I crawl on my hands and knees back to my bunk, trying to avoid the puddle of throw up.

I awaken to the sound and smell of percolating coffee and sizzling bacon. My head throbs, and my mouth feels like it's filled with cow manure. I stumble to the inner room, and look in at Mike, who is working at the wood stove over a black skillet. Johnny sits at the table, looking like death warmed over.

"Rise and shine, sir. Breakfast is ready," Mike says, in an annoyingly cheerful manner.

"No bacon for me, Mike. I'm really not hungry. I'll just have the coffee."

I go back to my cot, sit on the edge, place my head in my hands, and think a little prayer. *Oh God! I've learned my lesson. Let me recover from this, and I promise I'll never drink again.*

Part III

The Freshman

♫♫♫♫

60.

The Freshman

In September I enroll as a freshman at the University of Detroit. After reviewing my dismal high school transcripts, they send me to the head of the Physics Department, Dr. Harman, who is supposed to be my advisor. I stand at attention in front of his desk for what seems like eternity while he goes on with a lecture. I haven't spoken more than two words in the last half hour. He's been trying to convince me of the superiority of physicists over all other classes of people, especially engineers. I look at the stuffed leather chair along side the desk, and think about sitting there to relieve the pain that has been steadily building up in my right foot—a persistent problem since I've been off crutches. I have to endure this boorish man as part of the initiation rites for enrollment at the University of Detroit. I had explained to him that I tried to register in the Engineering College, but they wouldn't accept me until I had made up three High School math courses that I was lacking. I explained that I didn't take all the usual high school courses because of my accident. I told him that I signed up for evening classes at the Cass-Tech High School and had already started my twice-weekly classes in geometry there. Until I finish taking the required high-school math courses, I have to enroll in the College of Arts and Sciences at U of D. So I listed my intended major as *Physics*, even though my real goal was *Electrical Engineer*. That was over a half an hour ago. Ever since then he has been talking non-stop.

"Suppose one has to design a bridge. Do you know how an engineer would do it?" asks Dr. Harman. I don't answer, hoping that if I keep quiet, it will shorten this trying lecture. "Well, I'll tell you how," he continues, as if he didn't really expect an answer from me. "He would look up formulae in books, and come up with a design—the same design that engineers have been using for ages. But a physicist—now he's a real scientist—he would do it the right way. He would calculate the stresses in all the members of the bridge. He would take into account the wind loads and the traffic on the bridge. He would understand corrosion and fatigue. He would appreciate why a bridge is built a certain way. He would know enough to alter the design to accommodate special loads, or aesthetics. You see, he's a scientist, but the engineer is just a crank turner. Do you see the difference? Now, I ask you, do you still want to continue with this foolish notion to become an engineer?"

"Yes, Dr. Harman," I answer defiantly. "I want to be an engineer—an electrical engineer." I suppose I could get him to shut up by agreeing with him, by saying that I now realize the errors of my ways, and that now I want to be a physicist. All I really need from him is his signature on the stupid paper so I can be accepted into the College of Arts and Sciences and get on with my business to eventually qualify for the College of Engineering. But it's not in my nature to lie, and I don't bow down to assholes.

"I see that you're thickheaded. You'll understand what I'm talking about when you get into your studies. I'll sign the paper accepting you into the College of Arts and Sciences with a major in physics." He signs the paper with a flourish. "Good luck to you young man. Remember my advice."

"Yes, sir. I won't forget. Thank you."

My next stop is the University Book Store, where I purchase a pile of books with the money Mama gave me. It's amazing how expensive it all is: Twelve dollars and fifty cents for *College Chemistry*, plus another six dollars for the Lab manual; nine for *The Public Life of Christ*, eight-fifty for *English Composition;* eight for *American Government*. And I already paid six-fifty for my geometry book at Cass Tech., plus their enrollment fee. Tuition here is twelve-fifty per credit hour. And then there was the Student Activities fee, Registration fee, and Administration fee. So far I've shelled out two-hundred twenty dollars which is two-hundred and twenty more than what Mama can afford. I could have enrolled at Wayne State, where the tuition is half of what it is here. But there was never any question about what college I would go to. U of D is a Catholic university run by the Jesuits, and I won't get contaminated by Protestant ideas here. It's also the school that Daddy went to for two years.

At the book store they give me a little red beanie with white *U of D* letters. This I stick in my pocket; I don't want to look like a jerk, like the other pimply-faced boys with their dopey-looking red beanies. I catch the Livernois bus towards Six Mile Road, where I will transfer to another bus. I make sure that *College Chemistry* is on top of my stack of books so that the other passengers can see that this in no ordinary bus rider; this is a college man. I try to ignore the admiring glances that are cast my way.

I get off the Six Mile Road bus at Schoenherr. I can now wait a half hour for the Schoenherr bus to come along, or I can walk the ten blocks to Pinewood street. Either way I will have to be standing or walking. I decide to walk and look over my shoulder for the bus. After five blocks, the pain in my right foot is so great that I can hardly go on. I want to sit on the lawn in front of one of the houses on Schoenherr, but that would only make me look conspicuous. Rather than do that, I limp the final blocks to Pinewood. At home it is a great relief taking off my shoes. My right foot is so swollen that I couldn't get the shoe back on, even if I wanted to.

In the fourth week after I enrolled at U of D, Frank Koczot, my friend from Explorer Scouts, picks me up each morning at seven o'clock—just enough time to pick up the other car poolers and make eight o'clock classes. I meet him on campus at five in the afternoon three times a week to be driven home. The other two days I take the Livernois bus towards downtown for my geometry classes at Cass Tech. It was Judy Wilson who told me that Frank's car pool had room for one more. What a relief to ride like this! I didn't think my foot was going to hold out with riding the busses. The only hitch riding with Frank is the formaldehyde smell from the dead cat he and Joann, another car-pooler, share for their comparative anatomy class. They take their cat home every day in a plastic bag so they can do evening study on it. It's kind of sickening to see the skinned cat, and even worse to smell it all the way home. But I don't complain about that. It sure beats standing on the bus with a painful foot. And I find Frank to be a great mentor helping me untangle the mysteries of Chemistry.

I eat lunch in the Student Union—a dingy room in the basement of the Chemistry building. The ceiling is lined with leaky pipes, so you have to avoid the spots where they have placed trash cans to catch the water. The stand-up benches throughout the room are covered with litter, as is the floor. Once each day, someone comes in with a giant barrel on wheels—just like the street cleaners used to use when I was a child—pushed by a sleepy-looking student. He pulls a snow shovel out of the barrel and proceeds to shovel up the giant mounds of trash that have accumulated everywhere.

My report card comes in the mail in June. But I already know the bad news from the postings of grades that are on the walls outside of every department. I got a *D* in chemistry, a *B* in Rhetoric, and a *C* in Government and a *C* in Theology. The letter that comes with my report card says that since my grade-point-average falls below two-point-zero I am now on probation. I can't understand it. I went to all the lectures and even took notes. I studied at least an hour a day. I got together with Frank to help me with my Chemistry, but he had some smart-alecky question like "Did you study the book?" Well, of course I studied the book, or at least I skimmed through it, only skipping over the hard parts, which I didn't think you had to know anyhow. But I did get an *A* in geometry at Cass Tech. Unfortunately, U of D doesn't count those high school credits in my average.

Next semester, I plan to add a fifth course in Freshman Mathematics, and to continue with my high-school math at Cass Tech. Maybe if I'm lucky, I can get off probation.

61.

The Settlement

Mama finally gets word from Charlie Earl about the insurance settlement on my accident. "Five hundred dollars, and I thank the Holy Mother for it."

"But Mama, five hundred dollars? For being laid up for almost three years, four operations, the wheel chair, the body cast, years on crutches, home schooling, not even an apology from the driver who hit me—it's all worth five hundred dollars?"

"That's all Charlie said he could settle for."

"But he came here every few months, sat right in that chair with his briefcase and all his papers, saying he was working diligently on the case, that everything was going fine, that we would get a settlement when all the medical bills came in. Now he tells us five hundred dollars. That can't possibly even cover the hospital bills."

"That's right, Pat. The hospital wants over eight thousand dollars that the medical insurance didn't cover. But Charlie said there were no witnesses to the accident, no one to say he was running a red light. The driver said he was going with the green. And you told the police you didn't know the color of the light. So they settled out of court for five hundred dollars."

"What are you going to do with the money?"

"I'm going to turn it all over to Dr. Maguire. He told me I could pay him whatever I could afford, and he'll consider the bill settled. So this is what I can afford."

"What about the hospital?"

"I've been paying the hospital twenty dollars a month— that's all I can manage. They'll just have to wait for the rest. I trust in God and the Holy Mother to find a way to settle this debt."

In a few weeks Mama gets a summons to appear in court as a defendant in a suit by Saratoga General Hospital. She decides to go there without benefit of counsel, without Charlie or any other lawyer. "The Holy Mother will be my attorney," she says.

She comes back from her court appointment with a big smile.

"What happened, Mama?" I ask.

"I sat there at a table in from of Judge Sheridan, just me against those lawyers from Saratoga Hospital, with their brief cases and fancy suits, shuffling their papers on the table. I explained to the judge that I am a widow supporting my three children. I explained about all the bills we've incurred from this accident. I showed him my pay stubs and told him I was paying Saratoga Hospital twenty dollars a month. I told him my only assets are our home and furniture, and Saratoga can come and take all the furniture if they want it, just leave me the home is all I ask."

"How did the judge react to that?"

"He gave a lecture to those lawyers. He said Saratoga is a city hospital, not a money-making concern. It's there for the public benefit. He scolded them for hounding this poor widow lady. 'I order you to forgive this debt. Case closed!' he said."

"You mean we don't owe any more money?"

"Not a cent. I hope this will be a lesson to you. Trust in God and the Holy Mother, and all your needs will be taken care of."

Now the pressure is off. We are out of debt, Kathleen is away in Biloxi, I'm holding up my grades at U of D, Helen is doing fine going to Saint Anthony's and working at Burler's dime store on Seven Mile Road. Mama has a new job in the office at Detroit Tool. I had thought that once Kathleen had moved out and wasn't any longer around to fight with Mama, that she would improve. But Mama doesn't improve.

62.

Black Coffee

She is no longer Helen, but Julia, with a new life, and a new husband, Jack Reilly—a shy, handsome man, with curly hair and soft brown eyes, who knew her only as Julie. They met while working at an auto factory where she made springs for new cars. They were married by Father Swift without publication in Jack's home parish of their marriage banns—the announcements of a pending marriage that every Catholic is supposed to publish on four Sundays before the actual event. We can't publish them at my home parish, Holy Trinity, said Jack. It's my mother. She doesn't approve of Julie because she's Polish. So the old priest had the banns published instead in his own parish and in Julia's. The wedding ceremony was held with only two others in attendance: Frank and Josephine Rochaviak, their friends from work who would serve as witnesses. They were married on the second of February, nineteen thirty-five—she was twenty years old, he twenty-five. She wore the simple ring that Jack had purchased at the five and dime. The Rochaviaks gave them ten dollars to get started. It all seemed so simple at first. She would live in a small flat on her factory wages, and Jack would live at home with Mother Reilly. But she never had a period after the marriage—three months now. They will have to find a way to tell Mother Reilly.

*   *   *   *

Late one Friday night in the fall of nineteen fifty-five, I head for my bedroom to get ready for bed. As I pass the door of Mama's bedroom, she calls to me in a mournful voice I fear portends an attack. I walk into her bedroom to see her sitting on the edge of her bed, wearing her tattered blue night gown, looking sleepy.

"Oh my dearest son," she says in a dopey, dreamy voice, as she waves an empty bottle. "It's my sleeping pills. I took the whole bottle. Now I just want to go to sleep."

"How many did you take?" I ask, fearing the worst.

"I don't know. It was at least half a bottle," she answers and then flops down on the bed, pulling the covers over her head.

Jesus Christ! Mama's tried to kill herself, I think as I run out to the living room where Helen is watching television.

"Helen, we've got a big problem. Mama took half a bottle of sleeping pills. We've got to do something."

Helen's eyes open wide as saucers. I can see the look of panic spread across her face. "Oh God! What happened? What do we do?" she says, as she stands bolt upright.

"I don't know. She just told me she took them. The medicine bottle's empty. Help get her out of bed, and I'll call Doctor Johnson."

We race to Mama's bedroom where Helen shakes Mama from side to side. I set the little pointer to *J* on Mama's flip-up directory and take the phone to the limit of its long cord into the dining room. I can hear Helen pleading with Mama to get out of bed and Mama protesting in a dreamy, childish voice. I dial the number for Doctor Johnson.

"Hello, Doctors' answering service," says a woman's voice.

"I have to reach Doctor Johnson. It's a matter of life and death. My mother just took an overdose of sleeping pills."

"I'll have the doctor call you right away," says the voice. "Hang up now and stand by the phone."

The few minutes seem like an eternity. Helen keeps urging Mama, who keeps on protesting that she wants to go to sleep. The phone rings.

"Hello. Is this Doctor Johnson?"

"Yes. This is he."

"This is Pat Reilly. It's my mother. She's taken all her sleeping pills. She says it was at least half a bottle."

"Well, what the hell do you want me to do about it?" he says, angrily.

"I don't know, Dr. Johnson. I don't know what to do. I'm afraid she might die."

"Just keep her awake. Have her call my office in the morning to make an appointment." I hear a clunking noise followed by dead silence that tells me he has just slammed down the receiver of his phone, but it feels like I got slammed in the face. I hold the telephone receiver for some time, staring at it in shock, then place it in its cradle.

"Doctor Johnson says to keep her awake. Try to get her to the living room," I say to Helen as I put the phone back on Mama's dresser. "I'll put on a pot of coffee."

In the kitchen I measure out coffee grounds into the reservoir of the coffee percolator. I hear bumping and stumbling noises that tell me Helen is getting Mama to the living room. I put in an extra handful of grounds for good measure, put the pot on the stove, and go to the living room where Mama is lying stretched out on the couch.

"Helen, we can't let her go to sleep. We've got to walk her around," I say, remembering the scenes in the movies where someone who had taken an overdose of sleeping pills was saved from death. "And we'll give her lots of black coffee."

Helen and I grab Mama under her arms and pull her to a standing position. Mama cries out in a voice that sounds like a drunken little girl, saying she wants to go to sleep. As we march Mama around in a small circle in the living room, I think about Kathleen, away in Biloxi. I want to call her, but what could she possibly say to help us?

After an hour of pacing, it's hard to keep going. We keep pouring black coffee into Mama. Helen and I chug-a-lug coffee too, hoping that it will keep us awake as well. Mama keeps trying to lie down on the couch, but Helen and I pull her up to a standing position each time. We decide to make a game out of the pacing, so we march in time, pounding our feet to the rhythm of our song, trying to get Mama to join in.

I love to go a wandering,
Along the mountain track.
And as I go, I love to sing,
My nap sack on my back.

At the three-hour mark, it seems like it's impossible to go on any longer. I want to sleep so bad. The black coffee doesn't seem to work for me, and we've run out of songs. We decide to take fifteen minute shifts. One will pace with Mama, while the other rests on the couch.

At the four hour mark, it is impossible to keep Mama on her feet. She keeps flopping down like a sack of potatoes on the floor where she tries to sleep. Helen and I work together once more, each of us holding up Mama under one arm.

At the five hour mark, Helen and I are both exhausted. We let Mama take a rest for twenty minutes. When we resume our pacing, it's almost impossible to get her back on her feet. We decide it's too risky to do that again.

At the six-and-a-half hour mark we've gone through two and a half pots of coffee. I pull the shade of the living room window to see the sky starting to light up. The clock says six fifteen. The dawn is breaking.

"Helen, I think we can let Mama sleep now. And we can get some rest too."

"Oh, what a relief," sighs Helen. "That'll give me a couple of hours to sleep before I start work Burler's. You lucky bum, you don't have to work today."

"Yeah, I know, Helen, and I'm really sorry."

We drag Mama back to her bedroom, plop her on the bed, and pull a thin cover over her already sleeping figure. Helen says she'd rather sleep on the couch than in her bedroom with Mama.

I sleep in late on Saturday. Helen is gone, working at Burler's. Mama sleeps in past noon. She gets up and makes a pot of coffee, shuffling in her slippers, like this could be any old Saturday morning.

"What happened last night, Mama?"

"Did something happen?"

"Yes, you took an overdose of sleeping pills."

"Oh, go on with you. I wouldn't do that."

"But you told me you took at least half a bottle. The bottle was empty when I checked."

"Oh my no. I might have taken one or two pills; that's all that were left. You've got this all blown out of proportion," she says with a waive of her hand, like she's shooing flies.

"But that's what you told me. You said it was half full."

"I must have been tired, or maybe you heard me wrong. Just forget about it. We'll have no more talk about this."

63.

Kathleen Returns

In the spring, after my nineteenth birthday, Kathleen comes back from Biloxi to start the next part of her life. She is engaged to Frank Dinan, an upstanding Catholic, she says, who has just been discharged from the Air Force and is looking for work. "Can he come stay for a little while with us, just until he finds work here in Detroit?" she asks Mama.

"Of course," says Mama. "I'll be glad to help my future son-in-law," and we set about switching the bunk beds from the girls' bedroom with mine. Frank will take the upper bunk in my room, and Kathleen and Helen will sleep together in my bed in their room.

Helen and I tell Kathleen about Mama's deteriorating condition, about her increasing drinking bouts, about her overdose of sleeping pills. We three decide to pay a visit to Doctor Johnson.

We meet with Doctor Johnson in his office. We tell him of the sleeping pill incident, of Mama's gradual decline, including the disastrous month-long treatment that he had placed her on a few years ago, of Mama's attacks as far back as we can remember, of the many nights she has been drunk recently. All the while, Dr. Johnson remains silent. He stares intently at each of us as we speak, his mouth pulled down in what looks like an angry grimace. Finally, when it seems we have placed the whole sorry mess before him, he speaks.

"And just what do you want from me?"

"You're her doctor. We want you to know what's going on." Kathleen says. "You're the one who's giving her pills, but she uses them to try to kill herself. She says you recommended that she drink beer in the evenings to help her sleep, but now she's drunk a lot. We think something is going very wrong here."

Dr. Johnson's face turns red as a beet, and anger spills out of his mouth. "Well, let me tell you something, young lady," he says, shaking his finger at Kathleen. "I have been treating your mother for some years, and I think I know her problems quite well. I have to honor the sanctity of the patient-doctor relationship, and I'm not at liberty to discuss her case. But I can tell you this. Your mother has had a hard life. There is nothing wrong with her that couldn't be helped by a little love and understanding from her difficult and ungrateful children."

He folds his arms, in a gesture that looks overbearing and defiant. His mouth makes a thin angry line. His body tells me he has said his piece, and will say no more. Helen and I look at each other in stunned silence. I feel ashamed. Of course he's right. I am difficult and unloving to Mama. I only try to get away from her every chance I get.

Finally, Kathleen breaks the silence. "Thank you, Dr. Johnson. I think we have gone as far as we can with you." We leave in awkward silence.

Two weeks later Frank Dinan shows up. He is a tall, handsome Irishman, with fiery red hair and a quick smile. Everyone immediately likes his easy, friendly manner. Mama makes a nice dinner, and we break Frank into family antics by pulling the *passing routine*. Mama sits on his left, and passes the serving dishes to her right, and Kathleen on his right passes the dishes to her left. That leaves Frank in a muddle, trying to juggle serving dishes that come from both sides. We all break into laughter, as Frank catches onto our little prank.

Frank is quickly accepted as a member of the family. Kathleen and Frank act like two people in love, Mama treats him like a second son, Helen loves to joke with him, and she encourages him to tell stories about his experiences, and he takes interest in my school work and ambitions in electrical engineering. When Frank's sister comes from New York to visit her future family, Mama fixes up the couch for her to sleep on. "There's always room for one more," she says.

After the second week of Frank's stay, Kathleen gets a job working on the switchboard of a car dealership, but he hasn't found work. After the third week, Mama circles adds in the *Help Wanted* section of the Detroit News, and tosses him the paper. After the fourth week, her mood turns to simmering anger. "It's finding a job, or out you go," she says, with a brittle edge to her voice. "I'm giving you one week."

Mama takes to slamming doors, acting like she's seething with anger, ready to explode at any moment. Helen and I fear Mama going into a rage, smashing dishes against the wall, or going into an attack. Kathleen and Mama shout abuses at each other. Frank talks to me of his distress and puzzlement at Mama's behavior.

I can see our family is about to come apart at the seams. I don't know how to stave it off. If only Frank and Kathleen had some money, they could get married and move out before Mama explodes. I want to help them, but I'm a student, without a job. As I ponder this dilemma, an inspiration comes to me. I'll sell my blood to the Red Cross—a pint each week. I look up the number of the Red Cross in the phone book.

"Where do I go to sell my blood?" I ask the voice on the line.

"Why would you be selling your blood?"

"I need some money, but I don't have a job. I'm a college student."

"Do you know the type of people who come down here to sell blood?'

"No sir, I don't."

"Well, just get that idea out of your head. Don't even think of it. Find some other way to earn some money," says the voice, angrily.

As I am despairing of our family crisis ending peacefully, Frank gets a hot prospect from an ad in the Detroit News. He says he needs a white shirt for an interview. "Go ahead, take one of mine," I say, and off he goes to the interview. He comes back, with a set of brochures. "I got a job selling an insulation and building material." He shows me brochures that extol the virtues of *Celotex*, the new miracle product for the building industry. I try to express interest in this great product, but I am wondering: What kind of future is this? How much scope is there in a job selling Celotex? What is my sister getting into with Frank Dinan?

Frank borrows the rest of my white shirts, which he needs during his first week of employment. He takes dinner with the family, and sleeps in the upper bunk bed in my bedroom. The tension with Mama is still thick and ugly. On the second week of his employment, he receives a paycheck and moves out to his own apartment. After the third week he hightails it to New York with all my white shirts. The engagement is broken off. Mama is delighted to get rid of a no-good, free-loading bum. Kathleen is relieved too, having found out about the many lies Frank told her about his education and background. Helen is sad, because Frank treated her like a sister; I am glad he is out of our lives, but I wish he had first returned my shirts.

64.

Speedway 79

On a beautiful June morning I report for work at the *Speedway 79* gas station on Six Mile Road and Conant. The small building has a peaked roof, like the gingerbread house in the story *Hansel and Gretel*. There's a single bay for car repairs attached to the gingerbread house. On the driveway are two pumps: a red one for *REGULAR*, and a blue one for *HIGH TEST*. Inside is an office where a guy only a few years older than me, sporting crew-cut hair, sits in a wooden swivel chair with his feet up on the desk. The concrete floor is stained and cracked. Cans of various fluids line the shelves along the back wall. In the middle of the room is a kerosene stove. At one end of the office is a door leading to a tiny bathroom.

"Hi! I'm Pat Reilly. I'm supposed to report here for work."

"Glad to meet you. I'm Steve Harrison," he says, pulling his feet from the desk and extending his hand. I'll get you started in just a minute. First you have to put on this uniform. They sent it over for you." He hands me a folded blue shirt and pants, and he motions towards the bathroom.

I go to the bathroom and unfold the shirt. Over one pocket is a logo saying *Speedway 79*; over the other pocket is an oval-shaped patch saying *Pat*. Both the shirt and pants fit. Apparently they got my size right from the questionnaire I filled out previously. One week ago I was finishing my second semester at U of D, just barely off academic probation. Now I'm a working man. It's a good feeling.

Steve shows me around the station. "This is where the money goes at the end of the shift," he says, pointing to a heavy-looking safe behind the desk. "We don't do any car repairs here—only tire repairs." I feel greatly relieved. I don't drive, and I hardly know which end of the car has the motor in it.

"I'll get the first few cars," he says, "until you get the hang of it. Then you can do it."

Within a few minutes, a blue Buick pulls up. Steve speaks to the driver and then goes to the pump and turns a crank. "You have to do this before every sale. It zeros out the previous amount."

He unscrews the car's gas cap and inserts the hose nozzle. He explains how you know when the tank is nearly filled by the sound of the gas bubbling up the filler pipe. After the tank is filled he washes the front and back window. Then he lifts the hood and checks the water, oil, and battery fluid levels. He goes up to the driver, takes some money, and pulls a rolled-up wad of bills from his pocket to hand some change through the open window to the driver. The car then drives away.

Soon another car pulls up to the pump. "Three dollars," says the driver.

"You have to be careful when they ask for an exact amount," says Steve. You can never stop on the exact penny. If you're under a little bit, the customer will complain that he got a short gallon. If you go over, we have to make up the difference when we go off shift. A couple of pennies over on every car, and you owe a few bucks by the end of your shift. Even a fraction of a penny adds up."

As the numbers on the pump dial get near three dollars, Steve eases up on the pump regulator, then he suddenly releases it. The final number ends up somewhere between three dollars and three-and-a-penny.

We go on like this for a few more cars. As he works, Steve tells me how he got out of the Marines a few months ago, how Speedway 79 is a great company that has lots of stations all over Detroit and offers good chances for advancement to a station manager—something he hopes to work up to some day. I don't tell him that I want to be an electrical engineer, not a gas station attendant, that this is only temporary for me so I can pay my way at college night school next semester.

After servicing a few more cars, Steve says that I am now an expert pump jockey. He hands me his wad of bills, and a handful of change.

"Here, don't get this mixed up with your own money. You're in charge now."

Then he walks off. Just like that. Here I am, running a gas station all by myself, with a lifetime total of one hour's experience. I stare in amazement at the diminishing figure of Steve Harrison, who walks up Six Mile Road and disappears into a beer joint a block-and-a-half up the street. I stick the wad of bills and change in my pocket.

After a few minutes, a car pulls up to the pumps. The driver asks for two dollars worth of gas. I remember everything that Steve did. But when I release the pump handle, the pump shows a dollar ninety-nine The customer's not going to like this. I give a tiny squeeze and let go, causing the dial to show two dollars and two cents. That's going to cost us something. I collect two dollars without a hitch. I then do five more cars, also without a hitch.

Car number seven drives up. Will my luck hold out? After pumping the gas, I lift the hood and check the fluid levels, just like Steve did. The driver gets our of the car.

"I need some oil in my air cleaner. It's an oil-filled air cleaner," he says.

"I'm sorry sir, but I'm new here. I don't know where it goes."

"That's the air cleaner, right there," he says, pointing to a thick circular object as big around as a pizza in the center of the motor. "You have to take off that wing nut."

I unscrew the nut in the middle of the pizza.

"Now pull that thing off."

I grab hold of the circular thing, wiggle it back and forth a little, and pull it straight up. That exposes a much smaller circular hole, about the size of a cup, with a slanted disc in it.

"In there. Oil goes in there," he says, pointing to the hole.

"How much does it take sir?"

"Oh, I'd say about a quart."

I grab a can of oil from the rack beside the pump and insert a spigot with a cutter blade into the top of the can, the way Steve showed me.

"In there, sir?"

"Yep. That's it."

After the glugging sound of the oil stops, I check to see if the can is empty. "Yes sir, that'll do it," I say, proud that I have successfully handled my first mechanical task.

The customer pays me, takes the change I give him, slides into the driver's seat, and reaches for the ignition key. But instead of the motor starting up, it makes an awful groan, like when a battery is nearly dead. Several more groans come from under the hood.

"Won't start," says the customer. "Something's wrong."

"Let's look under the hood," I answer, not having the foggiest idea what to look for.

I raise the hood and study the motor. I jiggle the pizza a little to be sure it's fastened correctly and look over the motor for something obvious. As I stand there, scratching my head, Steve sidles up to me. *Thank God for the Marines*, I think.

"Anything wrong here?" he asks.

"The customer's car won't start," I say. I explain what I did with the oil in the air cleaner, where I put the oil, how much I put in.

"Holy shit!" he whispers. "You just put a quart of oil in this guy's carburetor. Better let me take care of this."

Steve asks the customer to let him get behind the wheel. Then he pumps the gas pedal several times. He turns the key, but again the motor only groans. He repeats this procedure a few more times. A giant cloud of black smoke spewing from the tail pipe announces that the engine has finally caught. Steve guns the engine, making the dark cloud even bigger. He keeps his foot on the accelerator, and the cloud continues to grow, now filling the whole Speedway 79 driveway and half of Six Mile Road. He drives the car to the side of the driveway and gets out—the engine still running, the black smoke still spewing. "We'll just have to leave the engine running, Sir," he says, "until all the oil is burned out."

Steve and I go back into the station while the customer nervously paces up and down the driveway. Maybe it's because of the dense smoke that no new customers show up. After about ten minutes, a lady walks into the station.

"Who's in charge here?" she asks, with a brittle edge to her voice.

"I am, ma'am," says Steve.

" I live three houses down the street. I just hung my wet laundry on the line, and all that black smoke is ruining it. You've got to do something to stop it."

"Don't worry, ma'am. I'll take care of it, right away."

Steve goes up to the customer and talks with him. Then the customer gets in his car and drives it out into traffic. I stand at the street side, watching in relief as the car proceeds up Six Mile Road, leaving a trail of thick, oily, black smoke that entirely fills the street.

After the end of our shift at four-thirty Steve shows me how to do the accounting. We take a clipboard out to the pumps and write down the little numbers at the bottom of the pump face. Then we subtract these from the numbers that were written down at the beginning of our shift. We add up all the money that we collected during the day. It comes up a dollar twenty cents short. "We have to split that," says Steve. "That's sixty cents out of each of our pockets. Be more careful tomorrow when you do the pumping."

I find a seat on the Six Mile Road bus headed towards Schoenherr. Soon the bus fills up with riders. I spot a standing elderly lady and offer her my seat, wondering if she's one of the old ladies who gave up her seat when I was on crutches. As I stand holding on to the pole with my gritty hands, lurching from side to side in synchrony with the other passengers, I turn towards the center of the bus so the passengers can see my uniform with its *Speedway 79* logo and *Pat* patch. These things speak of a working man.

65.

Doo Wop

In the summer of nineteen fifty-six Bob Perham, Johnny Bober, and I decide to sneak into girl scout camp. Johnny drives us to a place outside Detroit and parks his car near a gate that announces *Metropolitan Girl Scout Camp*. I carry my guitar and join Johnny and Bob past a *NO TRESPASSING* sign. As we climb a little grassy knoll, we receive quizzical stares from several girls. After an introductory vamp on the guitar we start singing one of our original songs: *That's What You Do To Me*. Pretty soon a crowd of girls forms around us.

My heart starts pumpin'
And my feet start a jumpin'.
My knees start knockin'
Cause the whole room's a rockin'.
When the sky starts fallin'
You'll hear me callin',
That's what you do to me.

You make my head go spinnin' round,
My temperature goes up and down.
I don't know if it's night or day,
Cause baby that's why I act this way.

Doo wop, doo wop, doo wop, ACKAWAK!
Doo wop, doo wop, doo wop, ACKAWAK!
Doo wop, doo wop, doo wop, ACKAWAK!
That's what you do to me.

When we get to the *Doo wop* part, the girls make giggly, screamy, swoony noises, like we were some sort of celebrity stars. But we're just three guys with more nerve than voices or brains.

Bob says: "And now girls, here's our number one most popular song, the one that gets the most requests. It is called *Exlax* ," which brings up a gaggle of snickers and giggles—everybody knows Exlax is the chocolate candy-flavored laxative. We sing it to the music of Elvis Presley's song *Black Slacks*, which has a line that goes something like: *Black slacks, they're really slick. When I put 'em on I'm raring to go.*

> *Well..., when I get a pain or a tummy ache,*
> *I don't care 'cause you know what I take.*
>
> *Exlax, a little round pill,*
> *Exlax, you can't stand still.*
> *Exlax, take it cool Daddy-O,*
> *When I take a pill I'm rarin' to go.*
>
> *I went to a blast the other night,*
> *They gave me something that gave me a fright.*
> *I tasted something as smooth as silk,*
> *And you can guess what was in my milk.*
>
> *Exlax, it's real slick,*
> *Exlax, won't make you sick.*
> *Exlax, I'm the cat's meow,*
> *When I gotta go I really know how.*

As we finish that song and get ready to start another one of our specials, a matronly lady breaks through the ring of girls.

"What are you boys doing here?"

"We're part of the entertainment ma'am," says Perham. "We were told by headquarters that we're supposed to appear here."

"Now don't be giving me the blarney," she says. "This is a girl scout camp. No boys are allowed. So I'll be thanking you three to just skedaddle."

We turn and leave, to a chorus of complaints from the girls.

As we walk back to the car, Bob gives me a punch in the arm and says with a snicker, "Hey Reilly, did you see that blond chick in front making eyes at me?" He rolls his googely eyes.

"Perham, you were seeing things. It was me she was making eyes at," and I give him a shove back.

In the evening we meet at Roller World. Round and round we go as organ music plays a drippy song. A lot of the kids from our bunch is here—Mike Wilson, Judy Wilson, Johnny Dreer, Bob Perham, Tom Smith, Butch Stone, Johnny Bober and Dick Tomak. I stick close to the rail, which seems to be the place for slow and wobbly skaters like me. Suddenly, a sharp push from behind causes me to completely lose control of my already tenuous balance, and I end up in a spin which lands me flat on my face. I try to roll to an upright position, but stumble back to the floor. A ring of skaters has already formed around me. Dick Tomak and Mike Wilson kneel beside me, trying to help me sit upright. A sharp pain just above my left eye prompts me to rub it with my fingers, which quickly become blood-stained. Shit! I'm in no mood for another accident.

A man pokes through the crowd and kneels down beside me.

"Are you okay son?"

"I think so. I'm just a little woozy. Give me a chance to catch my breath."

"That's one sorry eye you've got there. You're bleeding like a stuck pig. Here, press this towel to your eye."

"I think I better get to Saratoga Hospital to get my eye patched up."

"How many kids in your bunch?"

"I think it's about nine, sir."

"Well, have one of your friends stop in the office. I'll give you and your friends some coupons for free pizza, compliments of Roller World."

We are crammed into two booths at Singing Sam's, gorging ourselves on four large pizzas, compliments of Roller World. I've got four stitches in my eyebrow, compliments of Saratoga

General Hospital Emergency Room. Bop Perham leads everyone in song, as they raise their Cokes in my direction.

> *Here's to Reilly, he's true blue,*
> *He's a drunkard through and through.*
> *So set him up a bumper, set him up today,*
> *He wanted to go to heaven, but he went the other way.*

Dick Tomak says he woulda killed the sumanabitch who pushed me, but no one knew who did it.

66.

Greener Pastures

At the end of August, Mr. Wolfe, my company supervisor at *Speedway 79*, gives me a new work schedule: six AM to three PM two days a week, from noon to nine PM another two days, and three PM to midnight another two days, making a six-day work week that makes going to night school impossible. So it's with no regrets that I give Mr. Wolfe my resignation, sign up for night school classes at U of D, and go to greener pastures at *Rehbine Welding* on Eight Mile Road. There I won't have to work outside when the winter comes, like I would at a gas station, and I have regular hours that let me go to night school at U of D.

Rehbine's does heat treating and brazing of metal parts used in Detroit factories. It takes two men to work each of the three furnaces, and one man to work the fourth. I shovel the metal parts from a giant pile onto steel benches alongside my furnace—forty pounds of metal per shovel-full. My partner and I trade off jobs; one puts the steel parts on a moving steel belt that slowly creeps into a long furnace, and the other squirts the parts with a brazing compound. The parts come out the other end, brazed and tempered by heat. For this I get a dollar-eighty an hour; overtime pays two-seventy.

At first I thought this would be a crummy, boring job. But it turned out to be great. I even like the heavy shoveling, which I use as weight-lifting exercises. I expand my chest and hold a deep breath, pile a load onto the shovel, and swing it in a smooth arc onto the metal bench next to our furnace, making a loud clattering noise with each shovel full. And when the sweat drips down my face, it proudly announces: *this is a man doing a real man's work*. At one point, one of the guys at another furnace says, "Slow down, Reilly. You're gonna set a new standard on furnace speed, and we'll all suffer." And so I slow down. You've got to keep peace in the family.

Billy Lee is my furnace partner. He's a tall lanky guy from the hills of West Virginia. He has a series of tattoos on his arms. One is of a highly distorted naked woman, with her body all twisted, and one boob looking like it's growing out of her shoulder, and the other non-matching boob sticking out in another direction. "Me and the tattoo artist got drunk before he did that one," he explains. In another place, there are some tattoo letters that are crossed out by tattoo Xs. "Had a girl friend's name there, but we busted up," he says. On one of his biceps is a snake coiled around a dagger. "Got that one when I was in the army. Must have been drunk," he offers.

When they first paired me with Billy Lee, I was disappointed to get stuck with an uneducated hick like him. But I soon discovered that he makes up in experience what he lacks in education. The repetitive motions of our job give us plenty of opportunity to sling the bull and tell jokes to each other and to the other guys at the furnaces alongside ours. And, when the belt gets loaded up and we wait for a space to work its way up for another load, I work on my singing technique, doing operatic arias, Elvis impressions, and crazy songs that I compose.

Our most hated job is the one from Holley Carburetor. That one comes as a huge bin of thousands of little widgets that look like a swan's neck and head, with a body composed of a little round cylinder with a gear stuck in. These are the smallest parts of all the jobs we work on. And, since the parts are so small, you have to stick one in each space in the belt's mesh. If you leave empty spaces, the belt will be under loaded, which will make the temperature inside the furnace rise to levels that ruin the heat treatment. To properly pack the belt, the belt man has to work like fury to keep up, and the paste man has to get into a fast repetitive action and still squirt just the right amount of paste in exactly the right place on the little swan's body.

This is not an easy task. It takes real concentration to keep up with the belt, and to keep doing it for the three hours that a typical Holley job takes. You're so busy all the while, that it's hard to keep up the cock and bull stories. After an hour of on a Holley job, the belt starts to hypnotize you, and then all sort of strange things happen. Every once in a while, it looks like the belt starts to go backwards, and then suddenly it lurches forward, causing the belt man to miss a spot, or to double up on a mesh, or causing the paste man to squirt his load in some strange place. And sometimes it seems like the lights get dim, like you're in a dream, and then suddenly you wake up to find the stuff on the belt getting away from you. On this job, the belt man has to constantly lean forward against the drum that the belt goes over, which lets the wire mesh wear the front of your jeans to shreds. The belt can play other tricks on you. "Gives me a perpetual hard on," says Billy Lee.

Two old-timers in their late fifties, Tom and Andy, work furnace number one for the grand salary of two dollars an hour—something I can aspire to if I spend half my life busting my ass here. Tom, who speaks in a thick Scottish brogue, is no dummy. He gives me problems that can only be solved if you have mastered calculus—a mathematics discipline he still remembers from his younger days, and which I have yet to encounter at U of D. I wonder what brought such a smart guy to a dead-end job like this. Maybe it has something to do with the way he mutters to himself all day, occasionally shouting out and gesturing to the empty air, driving Andy crazy in the process. "He got shell shock in the war," is Andy's explanation for Tom's odd behavior.

Furnace number four is operated singly by a colored man named *Duke*, who takes the really big loads with extra heavy parts. As he works with his shirt off, his skin glistens like oiled ebony, his pectorals and biceps bulging like the statues of the Greek athletes, his stomach looking like a washboard. Maybe if I shovel enough metal, I can look like Duke some day.

While Billy Lee fills the belt with parts, I have a little lull in my work, so I take the opportunity to treat Tom and Andy to a little harmonica playing. I do a rendition of *Turkey In The Straw*, shuffling my feet in a little dance as I play the notes in rapid succession, while Tom and Andy clap their hands in time with the music. Then I do the vocal part:

When I was in Boston, I walked around the block,
And I walked right into a bakery shop.
And I pulled a donut right out of the grease,
And I handed the lady a five-cent piece.

She looked at the nickel, and she looked at me.
This nickel is no good said she.
There's' a hole in the middle, it goes right through.
Said I there's a hole in your donut too.
(Shave and a hair cut — two bits!)

I get the other guys to join in the singing at the top of their lungs. I don't figure this is going to annoy the bosses in the front office. But annoy them it does. The shift boss, Mr. Baker, comes charging out of his office, marches up to me, probably figuring that I am the ring leader, and says, "What the hell are you so damned happy about Reilly?" I reply with my rendition of *I Got Plenty of Nothing*, in a basso-profundo style. I guess that annoys him all the more, because he says, "Get the hell back to your furnace," and he gives a couple of turns to the wheel that makes our belt go faster, stomps back to the office, and slams the door.

In October I use ninety dollars of my earnings to buy a junky nineteen-fifty Mercury. It sounds like a tank and looks like one too. As I pull up to the service station to get the faulty brakes fixed, the brake pedal goes to the floor, and I crash into the side of the station, putting a big dent into the station's metal facade. The battery keeps needing a charge, and one or another of the bald tires gets flat with the slightest provocation. It may look and sound like junk, but it's mine, all mine. I've named her *Ole Betsy*.

Billy Lee invites me to his home for a Thanksgiving Day dinner. Ole Betsy takes me to an address in a trailer park on Twelve Mile Road and Ryan Road. The trailer is a tiny affair— just one bedroom, a bathroom, a little kitchen, and a small living room. Billy introduces me to his wife, Sarah, who holds an infant baby "This here is Ryan," says Billy. "This boy ain't gonna end up like me. He's gonna make something of himself." But Sarah adds, "I'd be proud if he turned out like you, Billy Lee."

Sarah has got the table loaded with turkey and all the trimmings. Billy says grace. "Oh Lord, we thank you for all your blessings, for our good home, for baby Ryan, and for our friend Pat Reilly." After dinner, I play harmonica, and Billy and Sarah dance with baby Ryan.

I feed the furnaces at *Rehbine's* with tons of metal, and work up gallons of sweat in the hot factory. "Just wait till the heat of the summer," the old timers warn me, "when the temperatures inside get up to a hundred and ten."

But in January, long before the hot weather hits, I decide to go back to day school for the spring semester. From the money I earned at Speedway Seventy-Nine and Rehbine's, less my expenses and the room and board money I've given Mama, I've got a little over Seven Hundred. With three-hundred going to tuition books, and fees for seventeen credit hours, that would leave over four-hundred to cover my personal expenses during the semester. So what will I do when the money runs out? *Don't borrow trouble*, Mama always says. I'll worry about that next summer.

I go around to each furnace, and say good by to all my friends. To the Duke, and to Tom and Andy. Billy Lee's eyes glisten when we shake hands, and I hand him a wrapped gift of an outfit for baby Ryan. In the front office, Mr. Baker says, "I sometimes thought you were going to drive us nuts, Reilly. But now I'm going to miss you and all your singing. Good luck to you in college." He gives me a hearty handshake and a big smile.

67.

A New Fender

I'm taking six courses at U of D; Helen is a senior at Saint Anthony's High School; Kathleen is a switchboard operator at Deringer's Chevrolet; Mama works in an office at Detroit Tool Company.

My friends at U of D call me the garbage man. I bring baloney sandwiches for lunch, and I eat every scrap of food that my friends leave from their own lunches or dinners. I'm not ashamed of my reputation as a garbage man, which prompts my friends to offer their left-over scraps of food rather than dump them in the trash. This helps me stretch my meager budget and to fuel myself for a busy day.

I start my days with eight o'clock morning classes, I study in between and after classes in the library or student union until eleven o'clock at night. On Friday nights or on weekends, I'm either studying, or else on a date with girlfriend or on some social excursion with my friends. These activities let me avoid the nut house as much as possible.

My birthday is coming up in a few weeks—just like it does every March nineteenth—two days after Saint Patrick's day. I'll be twenty years old. My sister, Helen, asks me what I want for my birthday.

"A Fender guitar," I tell her, thinking I might as well ask for the moon. "That's what Little Joe Messina uses on the Soupy Sales TV show. But it costs a hundred and twenty-five bucks There's no way you or I can afford that. Maybe you could just get me a guitar pick."

The week before my birthday, Helen insists she wants to see the guitar that Joe Messina plays—the one I have been dreaming about. We drive together to Grinnell Brothers Music Store near Gratiot and Grand River. I lead her into the display room filled with guitars of all descriptions, and to the lacquered white beauty that looks like none of the others. I pick it up off the stand, and reverently glide my fingers over the shiny finish. The salesman finds a chord, and plugs one end into the guitar, and the other into an amplifier. "Listen to this, Helen," I say, playing a few chords and some licks I picked up from Little Joe.

"You look like that guitar belongs with you, Pat. I want to do something for you," she says, with a sly smile. "I'm going to buy it for you for your birthday."

"You'd buy me a guitar? For my birthday? But there's no way you can afford it, Helen, on the money you make at Burler's—sixty cents an hour. Why, it would take you the rest of your life to pay for this."

"Don't worry, Pat. I can pay for half of it right now from my savings. And the rest can go on lay-away. I can have it paid by June, and after that I'll graduate from St. Anthony's and have a good job."

Guitarist Pat Reilly is one of the talented musicians aiding the Players in "Paint Your Wagon."

I never dreamed that my little sister, Helen, would be to one to answer my prayers. How long did it take for her to save for this, working after school and on weekends in a lousy dime store on Six Mile Road? And what does she have to give up so I can have this wonderful gift?

I played my new Fender in the school's production of the play "Paint Your Wagon." This picture appeared in the school's paper *The Varsity News*.

68.

An Engagement

Kathleen's love life continues like a television soap opera. She dates Bob Swanson, a kind and gentle man whose love, besides Kathleen, is electronics, and he is employed in that field. I think that both Kathleen and I have hit the jackpot with this guy, and I hope she will become serious about him. But serious she's not. A few days after Christmas, she tells me the latest chapter in her love life. Bob Swanson proposed to her on Christmas day, but she turned him down and broke of their relationship. She was not ready to settle down. She says it was her thirtieth proposal of marriage, counting the many she received in Biloxi, mostly from Air Force men. Kathleen keeps track of such things.

After Christmas, at the start the year of nineteen fifty-seven, Mama fills me in on a surprising development with Bob Swanson. Unbeknownst to Kathleen, Bob met privately with Mama to pour his heart out and seek her advice. Mama tells me the details.

"I love your daughter," Bob had said. "But she turned me down. I need your advice. How can I win Kathleen's love?"

"Bob, I would love to have you as a son. And Kathleen thinks highly of you. But there are two impediments, as I see it, to your relationship with her. You are not a Catholic, and you are just too stable, to the point of being boring."

"But what can I do about that?" he had asked.

"First, you need to take instructions to become a Catholic, and get baptized in the church," Mama had advised. "And secondly, you've got to be more exciting. Do something outrageous to sweep her off her feet. If there's a puddle of water, take off your jacket and cover it over the puddle for her to walk over. Tell some jokes; sing some songs; act nutty; be spontaneous; be exciting."

In April, just after my twentieth birthday, Kathleen has some surprising news. Bob Swanson, who she hadn't seen since Christmas, suddenly, out of the blue, asked her to join him at Saint Raymond's for an important event on a Sunday at two o'clock, after the last Mass let out. Intrigued, she went to a two o'clock Baptismal ceremony of two infant babies, and Bob Swanson.

Soon afterwards, Kathleen tells me the latest news. "I started dating Bob again, and I've accepted his marriage proposal from last Christmas."

"What changed your mind?"

"I realized that he is intelligent, kind, steady, and good to his parents. I just didn't know what to do; I was in despair, not knowing how I was ever going to get away from Mama. I closed my eyes to pray, asking for God's guidance. When I opened my eyes, I was staring right into the green eyes of *Tony-the-tiger*, the stuffed animal Bob had given me before Christmas. Tony's eyes seemed to be saying: this is a decent man, a steady man, one who will never drink or run around on you, one who comes with a fifty-year warranty. The next time I saw Bob, I told him that if his offer from Christmas was still good, I wanted to accept it."

"What did he say?"

"He ran out to his car, came back with an engagement ring, and got down on his knees, and proposed again. I was never before so touched. We're going to be married in August."

Pat, Kathleen, and Bob Swanson, spring, 1956.
They were married in August of that year.

69.

Tough Times

I'm out of school for the time being, out of money, and in desperate need of a job. But times are tough in Detroit, which is having one of it's periodic recessions. My buddy, Frank Koczot, needs a job too, not just to pay for college next September, but to support his high school sweetheart, Verne, who he plans to marry in August. We decide job hunt together so we can share gas expenses. Frank has a driving technique that saves gas. When we encounter a hill, he turns off the motor at the top and coasts to the bottom. Just as the car loses momentum, he switches on the ignition and snaps the clutch to restart the engine. We go all over the city this way, looking, asking, and finally begging for work—any kind of work—sweeping floors, anything. But jobs are scarce, and half of Detroit is unemployed.

After three weeks of job hunting, we resort to a more desperate method—the *hands of God approach* where we pick a stretch of road lined with businesses and shops, switch off the ignition, and let the car coast to a stop. We then inquire about a position at the business closest to our resting place. But God doesn't provide much help because we always get the same answer. *Sorry guys, but times are tough right now. Try applying in a couple of months.*

Frank finds a cushy job working in the office of the Metropolitan Gas Company, where he wears a white shirt and a tie and sips coffee all day long in a nice clean office while I continue job hunting on my own.

Just when I am despairing of ever finding employment, I try my luck at *Target Tool and Die*, which is run by Mr. Lehman and his partner Tony Burr, who interviews me. Tony offers me a dollar an hour—way below the usual scale, even for unskilled labor. He explains that as soon as I can make accurate measurements with the instruments in the shop, I'll get a twenty-five cent an hour raise, another twenty-five cents when I can operate the hand tools, twenty-five cents for each metal-working machine I learn to operate, and so on. "As you get more and more skills your salary will keep rising," says Tony. "There's no limit."

At first, I'm the only worker here, excepting Tony and Mr. Lehman. I start off doing simple work, like sweeping floors, oiling the machines and cutting metal on the band saw. At first I can't even use a hand file properly—my legacy of growing up in a home bereft of tools. Even sweeping the floor takes more skill than I realized to satisfy the high standards of Mr. Lehman. "The shop enemy is dust, my boy," he says, and explains how to sprinkle the entire shop floor with water before sweeping and how to push the broom so as not to raise dust that will get into the precision machines.

After one month, I can use most of the hand tools in the shop and can read the calipers, micrometers, and layout instruments. "How about my twenty-five cent raise?" I ask Tony.

"We're on a tight budget," he replies, "You'll get a raise as soon as we get on our feet."

One by one Target hires skilled workers—highly experienced and usually well-paid out-of-work machinists who come here to work at slave wages, with promises of good times ahead. No matter how much the production hums, the good times never seem to come when payday rolls around. The other shop guys start to grumble and complain.

When I learn to operate the grinder, I ask for my twenty-five cents. When I learn to operate the shaper I ask again. When I learn to lay out metal from shop drawings I ask again. I prove my worth as the only guy in the shop who can help the other machinists by applying trigonometry to work out dimensions from shop drawings. When I go solo on a milling machine I ask again. Always the answer is the same: *Good times are just around the corner.*

One morning I start work to find the shop in disarray—tools thrown around, windows broken, collections of nuts and bolts spilled out of their storage bins. Mr. Lehman puts me to work cleaning up the mess. I hear about what happened during bitch and moan time at a lunch break in a local diner. Pete, the underpaid and now-fired lathe operator, came into the shop last night and smashed it up real good, much to the admiration that all the guys express at the lunch break. It seems that Pete was unhappy about the unrealized promises of salary increases— always just around the corner.

Mr. Lehman gives me the job of picking up long bars of raw steel from a supply house a few miles away. The only hitch is that he expects me to use my own car. I'll admit that my old Mercury is a junker, but it's my car, and I resent having to tie greasy bars to the door handles—the only way I can transport the material. I have a little talk with Mr. Lehman.

"I'm sorry, Mr. Lehman, but I'd rather not use my car any longer to pick up materials for the shop."

"What's the problem?"

"The stuff spreads grease on my car, and scratches the finish."

"Do you have any other suggestions for how we'll get the materials? You know we don't have a shop truck."

"Sure, Mr. Lehman, I know that. It's not like I'm not willing to do my part. If you let me drive your car, I'd be glad to pick up the metal."

Right about now Mr. Lehman is probably having a shit fit, but he can't possibly show it. He's thinking of me driving his fancy white Cadillac to the supply house and coming back with it full of scratches and grease. He's thinking what an insolent little shit I am. But I don't care.

"Just don't worry about it. I don't want you using my car. I'll have them deliver, even if I have to pay extra," he says, with a scowl.

When the work slows down at *Target Tool and Die*, I get loaned out to Cheap Joe Wyker, the skinflint who owns *Nu Era Sheet*

Metal next door. Joe offers me a dollar an hour. I'll bet Mr. Lehman told him what cheap wages I'm willing to work for. How am I ever going to save for college like this?

I thought the work was dangerous at Target, but it's nothing compared to the sheet metal shop, which is full of razors—sharp edges of sheet metal sticking out from every table and bench and from the piles of metal on the floor. I get particularly scared when I help unload sixteen-foot long sheets of metal from the delivery truck that comes each week. For that operation, Joe sets up a wooden ladder on the flatbed truck. Two guys climb on the truck, pull one sheet at a time off the stack, and start feeding it down the ladder, which acts like a sliding ramp. Two other guys on either side of the ladder grab the metal and give it a sharp pull to get it sliding. My job at the bottom of the ladder is to guide the metal onto a stack. The leather gloves I wear seem to offer little protection against the possibility of getting an arm or leg slashed by the fast-moving guillotine.

Saturday is just like any other day at *Nu Era Sheet Metal*, except this is the day Cheap Joe usually has his two kids here to help out—his ten-year-old daughter, Lisa, and his eight year-old son Carlie. Carlie is assigned to put trash and metal scraps into bins outside. Lisa is supposed to work with me on the slicer. I don't like the idea at all. The slicer is at the end of a long table, on which is stacked a pile of twelve-foot long sheets of metal. It is set to cut a certain length when a sheet of metal is slid through the blades. Lisa is supposed to stand on one side of the slicer, peel off the top sheet, and push it through the blades. My job on the other side of the blades is to set the sheet, and to slam my foot down on a lever that makes the slicer come down like a guillotine. The two workers usually get into a rhythm for top efficiency: *peel, push, set, slice—peel, push, set, slice*, in the cadence of a slow march. But every time I mash down on the foot lever, I imagine delicate little fingers getting sliced off, so I slow the cadence way down, and check the blades each time. After fifteen minutes, Lisa suddenly stops her job, and puts her finger to her mouth.

"What's the problem, Lisa?" I ask.

"I cut my finger," she says, her eyes welling up with tears.

"Go tell your dad," I say.

She goes to the front of the shop, where Joe is working on a crimping machine. I continue with the slicing operation, but I have to leave my position at the slicer to feed and push each sheet and then go back to operate the foot pedal. It's much slower this way. After a few minutes, Lisa comes back with a bandaid on her finger.

"What did your father say?"

"Daddy says to keep working, but to be more careful."

I feel my anger rising. "Just wait here. I'll talk to your father."

I leave my station and go to Cheap Joe's position at the crimping machine. I don't know if I can control my anger.

"I refuse to work with your daughter."

"What's the problem, Reilly?"

"The work is too dangerous for a child. She's already cut herself on the metal. A lot worse can happen. If you insist on putting your daughter to work here, you'll have to bear the responsibility. But I want no part of it. I will not work with her any longer."

I've said my piece. I just stare Cheap Joe straight in the eyes. He looks dumbfounded. His eyes shift around the shop, like he's wondering if someone else heard all this. He's probably thinking he'll tell me to take his orders—or else! "Go work the slicer solo," he says softly. "I'll put Lisa outside with Carlie." He looks away, as if to avoid my intent stare.

On the Monday after the Lisa incident, I'm working on a crimping machine. I decide to replenish the pile of cut metal on the table beside the machine. I walk over to a stack on the floor, crouch down, and work my fingers under a six-inch pile. The stack is too heavy to just pick up, so I swing it in a big arc up to the nearby table, just like I've done a thousand times before. Only this time something new happens. Something hits against the back of the joint on my left ring finger. I place the stack on the table, and watch the blood drip out of my knuckle onto the floor. A sinister sheet sticks out of the stack that was already on the table—another razor to catch the unwary. I wrap a handkerchief around the finger, but it quickly becomes stained red. I go to Joe, where he's working on the riveting machine.

"Joe, I think I did a number on my finger. I sliced it real good."

"Christ, Reilly, how the hell did you do that?"

"I caught it on a piece of metal as I swung a stack onto the table. I think I'm gonna need some stitches. I'm thinking I ought to go to Saratoga Hospital."

"No. You can't go there. There's a clinic on Eight Mile Road. It's the one I use for my insurance." Joe gives me the directions.

I drive to the clinic, all the while trying to keep the handkerchief tight so the blood won't drip on my pants. At the clinic, the procedures are simple: I pick a number; I wait my turn; the nurse hears my tale of woe and looks at the finger; she cleans the finger with a swab; a guy in a white outfit puts in several stitches; I get a tetanus shot. I drive back to Joe's with my finger in a splint and wrapped in white gauze and tape.

As I walk back to the crimping machine, ready to resume my task there, Joe is fuming. He lights into me, shouting in a loud voice that can be heard by all the guys in the shop. He raves about my carelessness, about how he has to cover my wages while I was at the clinic, about how it gives him a bad name to have guys injured on the job. He goes on and on for another five minutes, fuming, fussing, shouting, cussing. I listen passively, without saying a word.

At five o'clock, the shop is in the process of closing. I wait for all the guys to file out so there's just me and Joe left. I reach into my pocket, pull out a dollar fifty, and slap it on the table next to Joe.

"Here, Joe—a dollar fifty. I figure that's what you've got coming. You pay me a dollar an hour. I was gone about an hour and a half when I went to the clinic. That makes a dollar fifty. Now don't say you're out any money on my account."

Joe clenches his teeth in an angry snarl. His face turns bright red. "Reilly, you sonavabitch! You pick up that money, or you're fired."

I stare him straight in the eyes, pick up the money, and walk out of the shop, without a word. But I'm satisfied he got my message: *Joe, you are a cheap skinflint.*

Just three days after my little accident, Joe swings up a big stack of metal from the floor. I hear him cry out.

"Shit! Shit! Goddam Shit!"

I look over to see blood dripping from the back of one of his finger joints. There's a razor sticking out of the pile on the table where he swung his stack. Joe reaches into his back pocket, pulls out a big red bandanna, and wraps it around his finger.

"Just keep working. I have to go to the goddam clinic," he says to no one in particular, as he walks out the shop door.

Three hours later, Joe walks back into the shop with a giant white bandage wrapping one of his fingers. The whole shop is silent, wondering what comes next. I stand at the crimper, where I have been working all week. Joe goes back to the riveter. The shop stays as quiet as a morgue. Finally, Joe breaks the silence.

"Okay, Reilly. You can laugh now."

"Oh no, Joe," I say in my most sincere voice. "I wouldn't want to laugh at someone's misfortune. I think what happened to you is a real shame, and I'm really sorry." But all the time I'm thinking: *God! What a wonderful world this is.*

Frank Koczot on his High School graduation (June, 1952)

70.

YWCA

Julia — the name makes her feel reborn. She tells no one of her terrible past when she was Helen. Life was supposed to be better with her new handsome husband, Jack. She didn't anticipate that he would be out of work, and that they would have to scrape by on her meager factory earnings, or that she and Jack would move in with his mother on Marantette Street. Mother Reilly doesn't hide her contempt towards Julia for trapping her Jackie into marriage — and to a Polack at that. Her pregnancy only makes matters worse. Jack's frail brother Edward is easy to love; his shy, quiet sister Lillian is kind to her; and his beautiful vivacious sister Helen Marie, who lives with Aunt Margaret in Grand Rapids, treats Julia like her own sister when she comes to visit. The problem is with Mother Reilly, who considers her an intruder. I'm a poor widow lady, says Mother, and I can't afford to be supporting every stray cat and dog that comes my way. If her child is a girl, Julia will name her Kathleen, after Mother Reilly's name, and after the name of Mother Reilly's own mother. Surely that would encourage Mother Reilly to love and accept her.

         *   *   *   *

Kathleen got married in August—one month ago. That should mean one less stress for Mama, now that she and Kathleen were no longer engaged in America's second great and not-so-civil war. Helen loves her new job with Capitol Airlines; I'm still working at Nu Era Sheet Metal and doing well in my night school classes; Mama keeps working as an office manager at American Tool Company. Our house should be peaceful now. But it doesn't happen that way. Mama continues to be on edge, bursting into angry fits at the slightest provocation. Her drinking seems worse than ever, and on this night Mama gets sloppy drunk while Helen's friends, Gertie and Beverly, are in the living room with Helen. That's when Mama staggers in, wearing the despicable tattered robe of hers that makes her look like a deranged, drunken tramp. She pontificates on moral purity, asking them embarrassing questions about their personal lives, as if she was in some shape to lecture them about morality in her slobbering condition.

I don't know why she acts up like this in front of Helen's friends; she's always on her good behavior in front of my friends and Kathleen's, who have never seen her drunk or having an attack. But for some reason that I simply can't explain, she lets herself go when Helen has her friends over.

After Mama goes back to her bedroom, Helen apologizes to her friends, and asks them to leave.

On the next night, Helen and Mama are in the living room. " I have to get up before you tomorrow," says Helen. "I'd like to set the alarm for six-o'clock, and then reset it for a quarter to seven, which is the time you had it set for."

"I don't want you resetting my alarm."

"But Mama, it's the only one we have in our bedroom. How am I supposed to get up for work?"

" Why do you have to rely on me for everything. You're working. Why don't you buy your own alarm."

"All right, I'll buy my own alarm. But I need one tonight. Why can't I just use yours? Why do you have to be so mean?"

"Don't you give me that sass," shouts Mama, now exploding into fury. She slaps Helen across the face, again and again. Helen backs up from the living room to the kitchen, while Mama pursues her, slapping her all the while.

The scuffle dies down as quickly as it begun, and next thing I know is that Helen is in her bedroom packing her suitcase, and Mama is down in the basement. Helen says she won't live here any more. She wants me to drive her somewhere, so I wait in the living room on standby.

Why does Mama take her anger out on Helen like this? Helen seems to take the brunt of Mama's problems, while

Kathleen and I could always find ways of escaping them. Kathleen could always stand up to Mama, and in recent years, she has had plenty of boyfriends with cars who could take her away from the house when Mama got weird. And now that she's married, she has her own life, and she's out of the nut house. For my part, I usually can get away when I need to. From the time I was sixteen years old and up on crutches, one or another of my buddies had access to a car, and I found plenty of occasions to get out with them. Now I have my own car—an old Chevy that I bought for two hundred and fifty dollars—my wheels to freedom and independence. I work during the day and go to school at night. In the evenings I study in the school library or hang out with my friends. That usually leaves Helen to put up with Mama by herself.

Helen always was the good daughter, while Kathleen was the fighter, and I was the budding scientist with plenty of freedom. Being a good daughter must be a heavy burden when Mama goes nuts. It's natural for Helen to want to find her place in the world since graduating last June from Saint Anthony's High School. She started work at Capitol Airlines as a reservation agent after going to airline school.

It's Helen's nature to be loving and generous toward everyone, especially Kathleen and me, even though we don't always deserve her kindness. I think of all the times that Kathleen and I excluded her from our adventures because she couldn't keep up. I think of all the teasing I've done, of the rough games we played at her expense. I think of how much she wanted affection from Kathleen and me, but we would just run away from her. I think of the time when she was laid up with rheumatic fever and she told Mama that she thought Kathleen and I didn't love her, how Mama tried to encourage Kathleen and me to be kinder to Helen. Mama was always the source of affection for Helen, and now that source has gone crazy.

I feel sad and scared for Helen. She doesn't deserve this. How can she manage if she leaves home now? It has been a little over two months since she graduated from St. Anthony's, and she doesn't have the money or experience to make it on her own.

Helen walks into the living room carrying a suitcase. One suitcase. Everything she needs to get a new start in life is in there. Her possessions in one stinking little box. She's not crying. Her face looks determined.

"Let's go, Pat."

I hold the door open, letting her get ahead of me down the cement steps, crossing the sidewalk to my Chevy. I open the trunk, take the suitcase, and place it in. Helen slides in the passenger seat. I open the driver's side door and slide behind the wheel.

"Where do you want to go, Helen?"

She looks at me quizzically, like she hadn't anticipated this question, hesitating while she ponders the answer.

"I don't know. I don't have the foggiest idea. I only know that I can't go back there. Do you have any ideas?"

"Do you have any friends you can stay with?"

"I don't know. Nobody who has her own place. And I don't want to pile in on one of my girlfriend's parents."

"Let's think this through, Helen. Where would you go if you were a stranger in town with no place to stay? I know. You'd go the YWCA. They have a branch downtown where they take in boarders. What do you think of that?"

"Sounds good to me. Let's go."

We drive down Gratiot, to down town. We pass Beaubian, then Brush. I'm bringing Helen here, on a Sunday night at ten o'clock, to a part of town that most mothers wouldn't want their daughter to be in alone at this time of night.

We swing onto Woodward Avenue, pass the Fox Theater, and stop in front of a gray brick building with a sign announcing with vertically arrayed letters: *YWCA*. The streets are dark and nearly deserted.

"You go in, Helen. See if they can take you in. I'll wait here in the car. There's no parking here."

Helen leaves the car and walks into the building. After a few minutes, she comes back. "They have a room for me. It's cheap, and this place is not too far from work. I'm going to stay here until I can make other arrangements."

"How much money do you have, Helen?"

"I think about ten bucks, maybe."

I check my wallet. "Here Helen. Take this twenty. It's all I have. You might need it."

I open the trunk, and set the suitcase on the sidewalk. Helen and I embrace. Then she picks up her suitcase and walks bravely into the YWCA, without looking back.

Helen at the reservations desk of
Capital Airlines (1960)

71.

Ballistic Missiles

Christmas will come in a few days. Kathleen is married, and Helen now shares an apartment with two of her coworkers at Capitol Airlines. It's just Mama and me at home, and I try to avoid being home as much as possible. Business has picked up at *Target Tool and Die*, and I'm back to work there. I still get a dollar an hour.

I'm going around the shop oiling the machines. This isn't as simple a job as one might think. You have to know where all the oil points are on each machine and how much oil to put in. And each oil point takes a different kind of oil, which I dispense from five different cans. Mr. Lehman is real particular about using the right oil. At the moment I'm applying oil to the shaper ways—the guides that the huge shaper head slides back and forth on. Mr. Lehman watches me from a few steps away.

"Reilly, you stupid asshole. What in the hell do you think you're doing?"

"Oiling the ways, Mr. Lehman."

"I ought to kick you in the balls, you dumb shit. Don't you know you're not using *way oil*?"

"I'm sorry Mr. Lehman," I say, now standing up and looking him straight in the eyes. "If I made a mistake, I'll wipe off the oil, and start over. But let me tell you, sir, you have no right to speak to me like that. I do my best here, and I want to be treated with respect."

"You uppity little snot. This is my shop, and I'll talk to you any way I damn please. If you don't like it, you're fired. Just get your things, and get the hell out of here."

I get my jacket and walk out. As I drive home, I wonder how I'm ever going to get enough money together to go back to school—the new semester starts in just three weeks, and how I'm going to pay for my expenses and help out Mama. I'm out of a job and nearly out of money, and right before Christmas.

In early January I fill out a job application at *Chrysler Missile* on Mound and Sixteen Mile Road. I have to fill out a questionnaire that asks nearly two hundred true/false and multiple guess questions, many of them like: *I sometimes hear voices; everybody is out to get me; I hated my father but loved my mother; I am often depressed; I would like to kill somebody.* For most of the questions, it is easy to figure out what answers they are looking for. But some are tricky, for example: *I have never stolen a thing in my life, not even a pencil.* If I answer *true*, they won't believe me; if I answer *false*, they might think me a thief. What is the correct answer to that one?

In another week I start my new job at Chrysler Missile. I'm called a *Specifications Writer*, but I'm not quite sure what that means. Like the other workers in my group, I keep lists of parts that go into the *Jupiter* and *Redstone* missiles that Chrysler makes. The group next to ours keeps lists of the same parts in books that are organized a little differently from ours. All these groups are in the Specifications Department. In the grand center of the sea of desks is an area filled with file cabinets where they keep drawings of all the parts. Each guy here has his own category of parts that he keeps records on, including changes that are made to the parts. Occasionally, I make a little draftsman's sketch on the drawing showing the change.

The actual missile construction goes on in Huntsville Alabama, so I'm really not sure what the purpose of this plant is. It's a huge factory, which has tall ceilings to accommodate the missiles they once built here, areas containing enormous machines, chemical treating pools, and machine shops. But most of this machinery is silent, and the main activity is a thousand people keeping records of each other's records.

You have to understand the deal here. Chrysler works on what they call a *Cost Plus* contract. That means that Chrysler's profits are a percentage of what they spend. Get the picture? Everyone else does.

My work area consists of an acre of desks all jammed together, except for aisles where people are supposed to walk. The ceiling is about twenty-five feet high, just perfect for shooting paper clips in ballistic trajectories from my paper clip launcher, which is calibrated with little tic marks for angle settings that are accurate and repeatable enough to shoot a paper clip nearly to the ceiling and have it drop on any desk I please. Right now I have it set for the desk of Fussy-Freddy, the guy who works right behind me. He's a grumpy, anti-social, fussy guy who wants everything just so.

The launcher is set up in the front drawer of my desk, and my body shields it from Freddy's view. The missile is a bent-open paper clip, and the propellant is a rubber band, on which I pull the clip to a precise distance and then let it go. Now it will be exactly two and one-half seconds to target time, just enough time for me to put away the launcher and spin around in my chair to talk to Freddy.

"Freddy, I wonder if you have a record of this part number," I say, pointing to an entry on the list in my hand. Freddy looks at me, but before he can reply, a paper clip drops from above and bounces right in the center of his desk.

"What the hell is that?" he says, looking annoyed. "These damn things have been dropping on my desk all day."

Beautiful! I have perfected the world's first ballistic paper clip launcher. That's the beauty of working here at Chrysler Missile. You get plenty of time for creative work.

Time and a half, that's what I'm getting for ballistic paper clip development. Today is Saturday and I'm working overtime. We get paid time-and-a-half on Saturdays, and double time on Sunday. Although we can work all the overtime we want, and lots of the workers get overtime checks that are bigger than their regular pay, there's hardly any work to do. It's not that I like doing nothing. I even try begging my supervisor, Bruce Tite, and his supervisor, Mr. Lange, to give me more challenging work. I say I would keep up with all my lists, but I would like to add to my tasks the work the engineers here do. "Just keep up your lists," I am told. "You're doing just what we expect of you."

One of the first things I have to learn at Chrysler Missile is how to take a crap in peace. The men's bathroom that serves our area is up a long flight of metal stairs to a module somewhere in the stratosphere of the building. The first time I went there, I encountered a big, smelly, dingy room with commodes lined on opposite walls, and with newspapers and magazines strewn all over the floor. Since each commode stall lacked a door, your business could get the attention of the entire row of guys lining the opposite wall. Some guys might be sleeping or reading a newspaper which would shield his face and afford some small modicum of privacy. A guy across from you might try to start up a conversation, or someone else might be telling jokes. And, just when you were at a critical part in your business, some joker would come to your stall, root around in the newspapers at your feet, and ask: "Reading this one, buddy?"

I soon discover the executive bathrooms in the administration building adjacent to ours. There, the bathrooms are clean and brightly lit. And, best of all, the stalls have doors. By dressing in a suit, white shirt, and tie, I can blend with the executives in the administration building, roll into one of their bathrooms with no questions asked, and revel in the experience of my own private stall, where I can sit, read, meditate, contemplate, snooze, get my creative juices going, or just do my business.

One of my creative inspirations is a grasshopper sanctuary that I keep on my desk. It's a gold fish bowl that cages what has to be grasshopper paradise right here on earth. There is a little mossy area for lounging, and a grasshopper size swimming pool with a miniature diving board. It also has what looks like tiny palm trees. A little sign says *Arnold,* which is the name of my pet grasshopper. I experimented with various foods, and found that Arnold just loves lettuce.

On Friday I return from a short trip on the other side of the plant where I had visited my buddies, Frank and Don, who work in the Engineering Department. As far as I can tell, they keep records of part numbers and drawings like we do in the Specifications Department. As my desk comes into view, I see that something is amiss—some sort of structure has been added to my desk.

As I get closer, I see that it is a miniature gallows. Someone has made a tiny platform with an open trap door. There is a pole over the hole, with a string tied to the end, and at the end of the string hangs Arnold—dead as a doornail.

"Who the hell did this?" I demand, not thinking this caper is a bit funny. Jerry Charbenau and Al Woloczyk are snickering, shoulders shaking, trying to hide their stupid smirks. They're just the types who would pull a stunt like this.

"You guys had no right to do this. This is not the least bit funny. Don't you realize that was a living creature?" Jerry and Al keep on snickering. Those cruel bastards!

At five I leave for night school without the my usual *See you Monday* or other Friday quitting-time small talk.

On Monday I'm still burning from the Arnold incident. I go to my desk where I place a cup of the cardboard-tasting stuff that comes out of the coffee machine. Jerry and Al are hunched over their desks, looking busy. I sit at my desk and open the center drawer where I keep my pencils. There's something odd about the top left-hand drawer where I keep my pads of paper. Tips of weeds and grass stick out from the edges of the closed drawer. As I give the drawer a jerk open, something happens that makes my heart skip. A cloud of insects emerges from the drawer—a flying, jumping, crawling menagerie of grasshoppers. Soon they are hopping on desks and on the floor all around the area.

"Jeeesus H. Christ!" cries Bruce Tite. "What on earth are you doing, Reilly?" Charlene, our typist, cries out with little *eeks*, and quickly moves away from her desk. Fussy Freddy lets out a string of curses while trying to brush the little critters off his desk. "What the shit is going on?" someone calls out a few desks away. Jerry and Al keep their noses pointed at their desks.

"Honest to God, Bruce! I didn't have anything to do with this. It's some sort of conspiracy," I plead, convincingly I hope. That night, as I drive to U of D night school, I can't help laughing all the way. I'm thinking, *Chrysler Missile—is this a great place, or what!*

Some of the folks from Chrysler Missile throw a dance party. Al Woloczyk (standing) Frank Lentine (accordion) Pat (Guitar), Charlene (Frank's girl friend, and secretary at Chrysler Missile), Lyn (my girl friend, and eventually my wife). (1959).

72.

Licensed Practical Nurse

I come home from night school to find Mama sprawled out on the couch, looking tired as usual after a day's work as the office manager at American Tool. This time she looks not just exhausted, but confused.

"I can't take it there any more," she says. "The pressure, the dirty jokes, the bosses flirting with the women. They want me to put false entries in the books. Today something happened to me. I heard a buzzing sound, and the lights seemed to go dim. The darkness and buzzing appeared to be closing in on me and vibrating in and out. I couldn't think straight, so I came home."

"Mama, you've got to get away from that place. Find another job."

Three weeks later Mama announces that she quit her job and signed up for nursing school.

"All my life I've wanted to be a nurse," she declares. "I passed a high-school equivalency exam with flying colors. They've accepted me in nursing school to start in the next class."

Mama goes to school during the day, and comes home with piles of books and papers that she spreads on the dining room table. Occasionally, she asks me to help her with some anatomical drawings because Mama can't draw much more than little stick figures for people. It's supposed to be a one-year program, which will lead to her becoming a *Licensed Practical Nurse*. Mama likes to stress *Licensed*, as though that makes the certificate more special.

Nothing is said about how the bills are going to be paid, and I assume it is my responsibility from now on. My earnings at

Chrysler Missile are nearly triple what I was bringing home from Target Tool and Die. Every week I cash my paycheck and give fifty bucks to Mama. I try to save what I can so I can go back to day school, but I just can't seem to save enough.

Mama hasn't had an attack or been drunk since she started school.

73.

Snake Music

No Duncan Hines on Dakota Inn.
Bop! Bop! Bop! Bop! (Bongos)
Cause they won't let us bring our bongos in.
Bop! Bop! Bop! Bop!

Frank Lentine plays bongos, Don Afeldt is on maracas and wood block, and I take a break from the flute-a-phone as we perform our spontaneously-created heart-felt song of denunciation on the sidewalk just a few doors down from *The Dakota Inn*, where just minutes ago we were requested to leave, presumably because some jerk there doesn't appreciate snake music. Talk about outrageous!

How can a place like The Dakota Inn fail to appreciate our musical talents? They will never get a listing in the *Duncan Hines Restaurant Guide* if we have anything to say about it. To understand this outrage, let me explain something about this place. Dakota Inn is a boisterous hangout for people who like to sing and drink beer, the clientele consisting mostly of college kids as well as some over-the-hill folks in their 30s and 40s. People sit at long wooden tables where waitresses in *Swartzwald* costumes serve pitchers of beer that typically have a lifetime of about five minutes. There is an old rinky-tink piano at one end, and lyrics of a German drinking song are painted on the wall: *Ist das nicht eine Snitzelbank? Ya, das ist eine Snitzelbank!*, along with accompanying illustrations. I hid my bongos underneath a jacket, and when the place started to warm up, I handed them to Frank who pounded out a Calypso beat while Don and I stood on the table, I playing flute-a-phone, and Don shaking maracas and directing the whole place to join in on *Jamaica Farewell*:

Down the way where the nights are gay
And the sun shines daily on the mountain top.
I took a trip on a sailing ship
And when I reached Jamaica, I made a stop. But I'm...

Sad to say, I'm on my way.
Won't be back for many a day.
My heart is down, my head is spinning around.
I had to leave a little girl in Kingston Town.

The whole place was rocking. Folks were banging out rhythms with silverware on the tables—like nothing Dakota Inn had ever experienced before with their usual *Snitzelbank* songs. After *Jamaica Farewell*, just when we were planning to get into *Day-0*, a plump, sniveling waitress in her cute little *Wiener Schnitzel* outfit came up and said, in a loud commanding voice: "Ve do not permit bonkos hier. Pleess ve ask you to leaf."

That is not the reaction we are used to getting. Usually we walk into a joint, sit down, order a beer, and start playing music after a style which Don has christened *snake music*, because some numbers I do on the whistle, which Don calls a *flute-a-phone*, bring to mind the music of a snake charmer. The usual result is that the management sends over rounds of free beer, and keeps us thus supplied for the rest of the evening. We are regular performers at *Strosnider's* in East Detroit, where Frank sometimes plays the piano to our Calypso and Latin numbers, and even the old-geezer-on-pension customers appreciate our snake music, which usually includes singing and choreography.

Frank, *AKA Mafia*, on snake-music bongos, is a short guy with thick glasses, tightly curled hair, and the map of Sicily engraved on his face. He smokes a pipe, which he draws on with great vigor whenever Don and I are about to prove one of his many ridiculous opinions dead wrong. After I met Frank in a night-school physics class we began to study together and soon became friends. It was through Frank that I learned about an opening at Chrysler Missile where he worked.

Frank plays accordion in his band, *The Blue Jays*, which, besides himself, now consists of: his brother, Sam (*il Pazzo*) on tenor sax; his younger brother, Mike (*il Giovanne*) on drums; Jimmy (*il Stanco*) on trumpet; and on guitar (no applause please) Pat Reilly (*il Allegro*). The *Blue Jays* give me a great way to have fun and earn money too. We play at weddings and parties, and I usually earn ten or fifteen bucks at one of our gigs.

Frank's father died when he was just 13—my age when Daddy died—and his family, which consists of his mother, the band guys Sam and Mike, and his sister *Rose*, is struggling to get by. So we have a lot in common to talk about besides music. His mother is the quintessential *Mama Mia,* who, every Sunday afternoon after the customary rehearsal of the *Blue Jays*, makes a huge early dinner to which I can usually wrangle an invitation. She is so Italian that she even makes her own macaroni, rolling the dough around a jack straw, which she then pulls out, leaving the essential hole-in-pasta. Her delicious custard-filled pastry balls are a delight, but there is a risk in eating one. Some of them have a rolled-up anchovy right in the middle, which will give you the shock of your life when you bite into it. The trick is to try to figure out how to avoid the ones containing these little *bombe*.

Once I peeked into Mama Lentine's bedroom. There, on a table taking up half of one wall, was a shrine the likes of which I had never seen before. There were icons of the Virgin, and a whole rack of lit candles in little red glass holders, pictures of saints, rosaries, and holy medals. She makes Mama look like a heathen.

I met Don, the snake music maraca man, soon after joining Chrysler Missile, where he worked in the Engineering Department with Frank. He too was going to night school at U of D, taking courses leading to a major in English, which are probably so easy in comparison to Engineering courses that anyone with half a brain can pass them. Don't get me wrong. I have no doubt that Don has a whole brain, albeit one that is twisted and highly abnormal. He is a tall, slender guy who looks like he is either in deep thought or is about to break into a big smile. He shares with me a love for jazz, and we use every chance we get to hear performers like Dave Brubeck, Theloneos

Monk, Oscar Peterson, and Miles Davis. We often hang out at jazz joints, like the *West End Cafe*, an after-hours coffee house in downtown Detroit where jazz musicians appearing at various clubs in the city come from two to six AM on Sunday mornings to participate in jam sessions, waiting their turns on stage in a phone booth which serves as a holding tank for the next soloist.

The things I like most about Don are that he is totally honest—both about himself and about others, he is open to all kinds of views, and he asks probing questions that force you to think about your deeply held beliefs and prejudices.

Don is about to recite poetry, while I accompany him on bongos and he plays maracas to punctuate the lines that have especially deep meanings. He is doing a recitation at the *Bohemian Caverns*, a coffee house that has chess boards on the tables and features jazz and other forms of creative art, like Don's recitations. Don reads from one of the works of Diane Di Prima;

> *Bob bopa Dop boba Dop bopa Dop dopa (slow bongo beats)*
> *There is no way out of the spiritual battle (determined reading)*
> *There no way you can avoid taking sides (voice rising; bongo beat a little louder)*
> *There is no way you can not have a poetics (vocal emphasis on "no way" and "not")*
> *no matter what you do, plumber, baker, teacher (loudly recited; Bongos give fast roll, stopping with the end of recitation. Meaningful pause.)*
>
> *Bopada dopada Bopada dopada Bopada dopada Bopada dopada (bongos picking up; maracas shaking in time.)*
> *you do it in the consciousness of making*
> *or not making your world. (each word carefully enunciated, maracas and bongos keep time)*
> *you have a poetics: you step in to the world*
> *like a suit of ready made clothes (very fast roll on bongos and shaking of maracas)*
>
> *Bob bopa Dop boba Dop bopa Dop dopa (soft, slow bongo beats)*

or you etch in light (recitation done in nearly a whisper)
your firmament spills into the shape of your room (voice and
bongos rise in volume)
the shape of the poem, of your body, of your loves (voice and
bongos continue to rise)

A woman's life/ a man's life is an allegory (recited very loud,
bongos reach a crescendo and stop suddenly. Silence. Don looks
the spectators directly in their eyes, one by one, letting this
message sink in)

DIG IT!!! (shouted fortissimo, bongos rising to furious roll and
crescendo, frantic shaking of maracas—silence)

Applause. Utterances of affirmation: *That's really deep, man!* or
Heavy! Don takes a bow, and sits at the table where I have been
playing bongos.

I act like these lines have some deep meaning that explains
the very essence of life itself. But I'll tell you the honest truth: I
don't have the vaguest idea what Don's poetry means. It's all
part of the *Beatnik* role I like to play. My mustache and goatee
help my persona, and seem to attract elderly women who come
out of the blue and strike up conversations, but makes quite
nervous many others who mutter things like: *What in God's name
is this country coming to?* What a great time to be alive!

Our performance now is at the outdoor band shell at Belle Isle
where, tonight, the Detroit Symphony Orchestra failed to
schedule their usual Saturday night concert. In the front row a
man in tattered clothes drinks out of a bottle held in a paper bag.
Towards the back a couple are locked in serious embrace. A few
other people sit in the middle—families keeping their little kids a
good distance from the front row, and a few other confused
souls who expected an evening of Tchaikovsky. What they are
getting is the essence of snake music. The three of us sit at the
front edge of the stage, legs crossed in the lotus position. Frank
plays bongos, Don is on maracas and wood block, and I'm on

flute-a-phone. After an instrumental rendition of Day-O, we break into a vocal.

Work all night on a drink of rum.
Daylight come and me wan' go home.
Stock banana till the morning come.
Daylight come and me wan' go home.

Don and Frank stare at me, and break out laughing. I suppose the verses put them into ecstasy.

Come mista tally man, tally me banana.
Daylight come and me wan' go home.
Come mista tally man, tally me banana.
Daylight come and me wan' go home.

Before I can get into the next verse, I feel hot breath on the back of my neck. I turn to stare into the nostrils of a horse, on which sits a Park Ranger.

"Having a good time, boys?"

"Yes officer," says Don. "We thought we'd fill in for the Symphony tonight."

"That's okay boys. Just make sure you behave yourselves," says the man on the horse, as he jerks the reins, and trots away.

I can't count the many times Don, Frank, and I have had late night sessions where we discuss matters personal, universal, and cosmic. Usually one of us gets a session started with the invitation: *Want to do some snake music tonight?* We three understand that to mean an invitation to a talk session, whether serious or frivolous, starting off playing snake music, but always ending with a deep discussion that goes late into the night. Some of the questions we have discussed with great gusto are:

Does God exist?
What did the philosophers Aristotle and Aquinas say about God?
Is reality knowable?
How can I deal with my unstable mother?

Why was my father so uncaring?
Why am I so screwed up?
Can I truly love both the Big One and Small One?
How can I deal with my sexual urges?
What is a spiritual life?
What is the meaning of sin?
Do individuals have free will?
What is important in life?
How can we change the world?
Is war a necessary condition of mankind?
Will marriage screw up my life?
Does the play "Don Juan in Hell" describe Don Juan's reality or fantasy?

When we attack this last question one night at Don's home, we three having been lubricated with an adequate supply of Budweiser, and with Frank as usual holding on to an untenable position, Don and I, with the enjoinder *Lets beat the shit out of him,* have to abandon our verbal powers of argumentation and resort to physical persuasion to get our point across, during which altercation Frank's glasses get crushed. And even that fails to persuade the thick-headed dolt.

Pat (flute-a-phone), Don (maracas & wood block), & Frank (bongos) play snake music (1959).

74.

Big One, Small One

Bunny sits beside me as I drive home from a party. She occupies the center of the seat, allowing me to drive with my right hand around her and to shift and steer with my left hand. Left-handed shifting is a feat I am quite proud of, considering that the gear shift lever is on the right side of the steering column. She suddenly spots something that makes her sit upright, knocking my arm askew.

"What's that?" she demands, pointing to the sun visor above the windshield, where, sticking out of the visor is a pair of leather gloves, just the size to fit small hands, like those of the Small One. "Whose gloves are those?" she asks, grabbing the gloves for closer inspection.

"Oh, those—they belong to one of my friends."

"I think I've seen those gloves before. Don't these belong to Lyn Bielat?"

"Um... yeah. Those are her gloves. How did you know that?"

"You're dating her, aren't you!" she asks, accusingly.

"Well, yes Bunny. We do date."

"Oh my God!" she cries, as she buries her face in her hands, sliding over to the right side of the seat. "I'm so embarrassed. How long have you two been dating?"

"Oh, I don't know for sure. Maybe a couple of months."

"I feel like a fool."

"Gee, Bunny. I'm sorry. I didn't mean to upset you. But we talked about it. Neither of us wants to go steady."

"We're in the same carpool in Judy Wilson's car—the three of us. Didn't you know that? We drive to U of D together every day. And these past few weeks I've been telling them all about my boyfriend, Pat Reilly. I told them about last Saturday, when we went to that joint, *The Snake Pit*, with your buddies Frank and Don. How you were playing guitar, Frank was playing accordion, and Don was on bongos. I told them how you guys stood on the table and got the crowd to sing those calypso songs. And while I went on like a fool, Lyn just sat there, like a bump on a log, keeping her mouth shut."

"Gosh, Bunny, we did have a good time, didn't we?" I say, thinking this will place it all in proper perspective.

"And I blabbed about the flowers you gave me for Valentine's day a couple of weeks ago. What did you give her?"

"Uh ... Flowers. I got her flowers too. But they weren't the same kind as yours."

"I bragged about that too. I'm so dumb. She's smart, isn't she. Not a dummy like me. I don't even take classes. I'm just a secretary in the Purchasing Department, doing office work."

"Don't worry about it, Bunny. You're special to me."

But my words don't seem to mollify Bunny, who rests her head in her hand, and goes silent. I think I'm in some kind of mess. But I don't know where I went wrong. We're not going steady—that was always understood. No strings attached. We're both free to date others. How did I get into this fix?

It was Bunny whom I dated first. So in a way, she ought to get priority treatment, shouldn't she? I met her through Judy Wilson, Mike's sister. Bunny was working at U of D, where Judy also works. She turns heads with her five-foot ten-inch frame, long wavy brown hair like in a shampoo ad, and beautiful figure. That and her gentle and cheerful disposition attracted me. We have great fun on our dates. She not only tolerates my antics, but actually enjoys them, getting into the swing of singing and hell raising till the wee hours of the morning.

But things got complicated last November when I received an invitation to the *Sadie Hawkins* dance at U of D. Sadie Hawkins day was dreamed up by Al Capp in his comic strip *'Lil' Abner*, where, in the town of Dogpatch, once a year on Sadie Hawkins day, all the town's single women chase the eligible men, and each poor guy has to marry the woman who catches him. According to the strip, this event was cooked up by a wealthy Mr. Hawkins of Dogpatch who had an ugly daughter who couldn't get married any other way.

Inspired by that comic strip, many schools have a Sadie Hawkins dance where the girls invite the guys. I received in the mail a formal invitation from the dating committee at U of D that said: *Mr. Patrick Reilly is hereby invited to be the guest of Lynette Louise Bielat for the Annual Sadie Hawkins Day dance.* And enclosed was a little card that let me check one of two boxes: *acceptance, yes* or *no,* and a note that instructed me to return the card to the dating bureau.

This invitation caused me a lot of worry, and I put off an answer for a several days. The big problem was that Lyn was always Mike Wilson's main girlfriend, and he had been in the army for the past year when I got the invitation. How could I possibly date my buddy's girlfriend? That was one of the topics in a late-night talk session with Don and Frank. After going over all the complications and possibilities, I decided that I would be doing my buddy a favor by accompanying his girl friend in his absence. It would be strictly platonic—no monkey business. But it didn't work out that way, and monkey business happened.

On Sadie Hawkins night Lyn picked me up for the dance in a car driven by her girlfriend Sharon, who also had a date. She gave me a corsage, which she pinned to my lapel, and we drove to the Veterans' Memorial Hall downtown, where they had a big band that played till midnight. Afterwards, we went to a restaurant, with the girls picking up the tab. When we drove home, it seemed innocent enough to put my arm around her, which did not violate any platonic principal. And when she snuggled up to me, something made my heart go faster. Was it was that her tiny five-foot-two-inch frame fit so nicely under my arm? Or the soft fur jacket she wore? Maybe it was her pretty face, bright and sparkling eyes, and cupid lips. I couldn't resist one little kiss. It turned out to be not so little after all.

After that, I started dating both Bunny and Lyn weekly— the Big One and the Small One, as Don calls them in our regular snake music talk sessions—one on Friday night, the other on Saturday or Sunday.

I soon came to realize that Lyn was really special in a lot of ways. Maybe the big test came on our fourth date, when Don, Frank, and I triple-dated to the musical play *My Fair Lady*, which was playing at the Fischer Theater. Frank was fixed up for his first date with Lyn's girlfriend, Shirley, and Don was to go with his girl friend, Carole. None of us could possibly afford the price of a ticket. However, Frank's uncle Max, the head usher at the Fischer, had agreed that we could come free with dates. Our cost of admission was that we three guys were to usher before the play. After the play started, we and our dates could take unoccupied seats.

On the big night each of our dates were dressed like they were queens of the ball. Don, Frank, and I made a big deal about how we had connections at the Fischer and could get in for free. We didn't want to tell our dates about the ushering part. Somehow, that would work itself out.

Arriving at the Fisher Theater, Uncle Max greeted us, and Frank made the introductions. Uncle Max showed us into the lobby, without any tickets being requested, which must have impressed our dates. "Frank, you take the right upper balcony, Don you take the orchestra section, and Pat, you take the left balcony," he said, gesturing. "And you girls. You can go behind the candy counter."

The girls looked at each other with astonished looks. "What are you talking about?" retorted Shirley.

"The candy counter. I want your girls to sell candy."

This provoked expressions of displeasure, such as "Like hell," and "Hey, this is my good dress and I'm not about to ruin it behind the candy counter," and "No way, buster."

Uncle Max, sensing that he had an unexpected rebellion on his hands, calmed our dates with: "Well, you girls can just sit in the back row until the guys are finished. They'll get you later."

A little later, Lyn and I sat in the sixth row, having missed only ten minutes of the play. The music and acting that night were wonderful. "Those were my favorite songs," Lyn said afterward," without a trace of anger or upset about being asked to be the candy girl. "I've listened to the record so much that I have most of them memorized." However, Frank didn't fare so well with Shirley, whom he never saw again.

Another test came the first time we were caught in a rainstorm while out driving. My junker Chevy has a little problem with the windshield wiper that needed Lyn's help. The wiper motor doesn't have enough power to get the wipers to the up position, but, if they are already up, it has enough strength to flop them down when you turn the wiper control to *off*. I came up with an ingenious engineering solution to this problem. I had tied to one wiper arm a rope that went through the partially opened passenger window. The operation worked like this. I pull the wiper control to *on*. Lyn yanks the rope, which pulls both wiper blades up. I pull the wiper control to *off*—the blades flop down. We keep repeating this operation, as long as it keeps raining. I guess I was impressed, not because Lyn had the coordination for us to work as a team, but because she was such a good sport about it.

Lyn really proved that she was a good sport with the *cops-and-bongos* caper that we often laugh about. We used to park after dates in front of her house for late-night romantic interludes. But her mother put a stop to that by switching the porch light on and off, as if to say: *You two better doing stop performing that questionable behavior for the whole neighborhood to see.* So we complied by moving our romance sessions to the end of Annot Street in the deserted parking lot of a factory. One night, as we were testing our will to avoid the near occasion of sin, we saw in the moonlight a slowly moving cop car with its headlights off. From where it stopped some distance away a figure emerged and stealthily crept up to the driver's window of my car, from whence appeared a flashlight beam that seemed to accuse: *Aha! Caught you in the act, didn't I!* He shone the beam first on me, studied my goatee and mustache, then studied Lyn, and then the back seat, taking an interest in the bongos and other instruments there.

"Hey Charlie," he shouted to his partner. "Come on over here. You've got to get a load of this."

Charlie came along side to observe the spectacle that so enchanted his partner.

"Hey man! Are you some kind of beatnik?" He asked, gleefully.

"Am I some kind of beatnik?" I echoed. "I'll show you what kind of beatnik I am."

With that, I stepped out the car, and pulled out a pair of maracas from the back seat, and demonstrated how they are played.

"I'll ask you to play these," I said, handing them to Charlie. "And here's something for you," I said, as I produced a pair of claves, which I demonstrated with rhythmic clinks and handed them to the other cop. I handed the bongos to Lyn. "Okay, hit it Lyn," I prompted, getting Lyn to start up a bongo beat that I had taught her. "Now you guys join in," I said, and I started with a Calypso tune on the flute-a-phone.

I suppose an observer might have thought the scene a bit unusual. In a moonlit parking lot at the end of Annot Street were two cops swinging and shaking to calypso rhythms while they played along with a goateed flute player and a petite bongo girl to the sounds of *Jamaica Farewell*. After that, we switched to *Never on a Sunday*, and the rhythms continued. We finished the number in a flourish of bongo beats, maraca shakes, and flute licks. "You've got rhythm—no question about it," I said.

"The guys back at the station are never going to believe this," said Charlie, handing back my maracas.

"We'll mosey along now," said his partner. "We expect to patrol this area again in another two hours. No one will bother you. Have fun, you kids."

Any girl who dates me has to be prepared for sometimes weird capers like this and cheap dates. It's not that I'm naturally cheap—I'm poor. Like Frank and Don, I'm trying to pay for school personal expenses. And like Frank, my father is dead, and I need to help with the household expenses, which leaves little money for entertainment. But our imaginations seem to be boundless in coming up with ideas for cheap ways to entertain ourselves, like a hay ride someone organized through a farmer friend, parties at homes and halls where we often provide musical entertainment, sing-alongs, free concerts, and, of course, our own performances in local bars that tolerate snake music, and provide us with free drinks. After some of these cheap dates, we treat our girlfriends at the local White Castle Hamburger establishment, where burgers can still be bought for eighteen cents.

Although I seem to be attracted to Lyn more and more, I don't want to lose Bunny. I hope this glove discovery won't put a monkey wrench in our relationship. I pull up to Bunny's house. Bunny stays quiet. She opens the car door, exits with a polite "see you later," and slams the door. Damn! Not even a good night kiss.

Pat and Lyn Bielat (The Small One). ≈ 1959

75.

Last of the Inheritance

Kathleen, Helen, and I sit at one side of a table in the law office of Barron, Beranek, and Newton, situated in a tall building on Woodward Avenue in the heart of downtown Detroit. Everything about this place says that it was built on money— and lots of it. The table, long enough to hold a banquet, is made of beautiful mahogany with a glossy luster that makes the surface look almost like a mirror. From the big window I can see the Detroit River just beyond some tall buildings. The two men sitting on the other side of the table wear expensive-looking dark blue suits. The one who introduced himself as Mr. Barron wears a ring that identifies him as a Mason—a member of an organization that we Catholics are told epitomizes the very essence of evil. A second man has a note pad made of extra long paper. A secretary brings in a tray of coffee cups and passes them around. We take a little time to get the cream and sugar the way everyone likes it. Despite the coffee, polite introductions and sincere smiles, I don't think these people are going to act on our behalf.

Mr. Barron arranges his papers, making the stack perfectly squared up. "As you know, we called you here to settle your grandmother's estate. She died on September second, nineteen fifty-eight, just four months ago. According to her will, her estate was to be divided among her children: Lillian, Helen Marie, and Edward. Your uncle Edward passed away on August fifteenth, nineteen fifty-three. Estate law dictates that his inheritance goes to his brothers and sisters, and that includes your father, who is also deceased. Therefore, your father's share passes to his descendants, which are you three." He pauses to let this sink in. "When we apportion his share to his children, the amount comes out to three thousand, five hundred, and sixty-two dollars for each of you."

My head spins with this information. Something from Daddy—an inheritance that could finance the rest of my college education. Maybe I could even go to day school. But I have a funny feeling that Mr. Barron hasn't finished his story—that somehow the money is not going to materialize.

"The only surviving recipients of your grandmother's estate are your aunts Lillian and Helen Marie. Your aunts do not feel that your grandmother intended for you to share in her estate. Otherwise, she would have included you in her will. Therefore, your aunts are contesting the adjudication of this will." He pauses, letting us absorb this disappointing news. "Your aunts feel that your are entitled to nothing at all. But they are willing to make a generous offer to settle the estate: one-thousand dollars for each of you."

Mr. Barron carefully lays an official-looking piece of paper in front of us. "Here is an agreement for you to sign. It provides for the settlement and has you promise that you will make no further claims on this estate. The agreement is contingent on acceptance by the three of you."

I look at Kathleen, then at Helen, both of whom look puzzled. We remain silent.

"These are your choices," Mr. Barron continues. "You can sign this paper and receive one thousand dollars each, or you can choose to fight us, which would involve hiring a lawyer to represent you. And I can tell you that we will vigorously resist any efforts on your part to make claim to this estate. You could spend a great deal of money in this fight, and end up with nothing. And quite frankly, you deserve nothing. This is a very generous offer from your aunts. I'll let the three of you talk this over if you wish."

Mr. Baron and his assistant leave the table and exit the room.

Kathleen, Helen, and I talk over what we have just heard, but I have a hard time keeping myself focused.

"I don't know what you guys think," says Helen, "but I think Aunt Helen and Lala are being generous. Mr. Barron is right. Grammy didn't intend for us to have anything. I'm willing to sign."

"It's fine with me," adds Kathleen. "I sure could use a thousand bucks. I have no problem with the settlement. What do you think Pat?"

I think that this is no generous offer. This is my father's inheritance. Something he can now contribute to us after having neglected our family when he was alive. Something the law says belongs to us. And our stingy aunts want to take it away. It's unfair. I think of the difficulty of hiring a lawyer and fighting. It would be messy—we would be fighting our own aunts. And how could I possibly find time to pursue a legal battle?

"I don't like it, but I'm willing to sign," I say.

Kathleen goes to the receptionist and informs her that we are finished discussing the matter. "We will accept the agreement," she says.

76.

Mama's Graduation

This past year has been one of the best. I've got a thousand bucks socked away, I'm making good money at Chrysler Missile, and I'm chipping away two courses each semester in night school. And the year has been good for Mama too. She has been going to and from her nursing classes like the excited school girl she has always wanted to be, keeping the dining room table piled with books and papers, talking enthusiastically about diseases and nursing techniques, copying anatomical drawings from her text books, and generally all abuzz about nursing.

One day at the end of February is one of the proudest day of Mama's life. She receives a certificate that announces:

Certificate of achievement issued by the Detroit Board of Education, in cooperation with the Office of Vocational Education, the Detroit Public Institute hereby grants Julia Rogoza Reilly, who has successfully completed the course in one-year trade preparatory course in practical nursing. Filed January 24, 1959.

Mama gets her first job as a nurse at Saratoga Hospital. Imagine that! The place where I spent so much of my teen years; the place that tried to sue Mama for nonpayment of my hospital bills. They've given her a job in pediatrics, and she is ecstatic.

I wonder if Helen's departure shocked Mama enough that she decided to get her life together and start nursing school. I wonder if her great achievements will marshal the end of her attacks. Her best achievement is that she hasn't been drunk once since she started nursing school, hasn't had a single attack, and hasn't once cornered me for chair talk. I think Mama is cured forever.

Mama on her graduation, February, 1959.

77.

The Last Attack

It all happened to Helen, not Julia. But still the voices won't go away. Filthy whore! No good bitch! Julia tries to quiet them. She smashes a plate of oleo against the wall, leaving a creamy blob that oozes towards the floor. She screams out Shut up! Shut up! and smashes another plate against the wall. But that too fails to quiet the voices. She doesn't hear two-year-old Helen Therese crying in her crib, nor does she notice six-year old Kathleen and four-year-old Patrick hiding behind the bedroom door, hugging each other in terror. Now, she is in bed. The darkness closes in, making a buzzing sound. Jack. My dearest darling Jack. Come to me. Hold my hand. She tightly clasps his hand, transferring its hot sweat to his. She starts coughing and gagging. Please, get me a throw-up pan, Jack. She makes more gagging sounds, but all that comes out is a string of drool. She flops on the pillow and takes his hand again. I'm such a failure. No good failure. No you're not Julie, you do the best you can. The best I can. My best is a failure isn't it. Just relax, Julie, everything will be okay. Try to go to sleep.

*   *   *   *

It has been three months since Mama finished nursing school and has been working at Saratoga. I continue to work at Chrysler Missile during the day and attend classes at night. On this particular night, like so many in the past, I quietly tiptoe up the stairs leading to our flat on Schoenherr Street where we moved a year ago, trying not to wake Mama. It's nearly midnight.

I hardly spend any time at home any more, except to sleep. Usually I get up early in the morning and go to work. I buy my meals in cheap restaurants. I go to classes, and study in the library or the student union. On Saturdays I go to school to study, and on Sundays I first go to Mass, and then back to school. When I'm not working, going to classes, or studying, I'm out on a date or with my buddies. Nowadays Mama and I hardly ever cross paths. But I'm afraid she might be working herself up to another attack, so I've got to be extra careful not to stir her up.

She hasn't had an attack for more than a year. But I'm afraid one is coming. I could see the signs a couple of weeks ago, when I came home one evening and found not a single glass dish in the house. Not a plate, not a cup, not a saucer—everything gone. "I got upset and smashed them all," Mama had said, without any sense of apology or shame. Amazingly, there was not a single glass shard anywhere in sight. Apparently Mama had cleaned up the whole mess after her rampage. The following Saturday she and I went to Montgomery Wards and bought an entire service for six, including drinking glasses, plates, saucers, cups, and serving bowls with one hundred ten dollars, paid for out of my inheritance. She didn't speak about what caused her tirade, and I was too afraid to bring up the subject, fearful that any talk of it might stir her up again.

The kitchen light is on. As I pass by Mama's bedroom, I hear a series of moans. "Oh my dearest darling son. Come sit with me."

I walk into her bedroom. The light that filters in from the kitchen reveals Mama lying in bed. She gasps in slow, deep, chortling breaths. "What is it Mama?"

"I'm having a bad time. I need you to sit with me. Please sit down." A chair is already set up by her bed side.

I know just what this means. Mama wants me to sit up with her for an attack, until God only know what hour while she goes on and on about things I've heard it a million times before, and I don't think I can stand another minute of it. I've done my duty, paid my dues, had my fill of attacks.

"I'm sorry, Mama. I can't sit up with you tonight. I've been up late studying. It's already past midnight. I have to get up early to go to work, and I have exams tomorrow evening. I can't afford to sit up with you all night. It's always the same. You talk and talk about what a failure you have been, and you want me to listen to you for hours. But tonight I can't do it. I have to get some sleep and be fresh for my exams tomorrow. I'm afraid you'll have to have your attack by yourself tonight."

My own words surprise me, and apparently Mama too. She suddenly jerks off the covers, sits bolt upright and snaps on the light beside her bed. She stands, facing me, full of fury. "What do you mean? How dare you talk to me like that?"

She dashes to the dresser and grabs a stack of papers. "Look at this. Just you look at this," she says, shaking the pile of papers in my face. Her face is contorted with anger. "The phone bill. The gas bill. The electric bill. Who do you think pays for all of this? Don't you dare give me that insolent back talk." Her lower jaw juts out. She clutches the papers like she is trying to choke the life out of them. Her hand is trembling.

She looks me straight in the eyes. Usually Mama's gaze pierces right into my soul. After all, she can read through my lies by looking directly into my eyes. But tonight something different happens. Instead, my gaze pierces into her soul. I can see everything so clearly. My eyes are saying: *Mama, you faked this. It has always been a fake, hasn't it! All these years. All these attacks. You could turn them on and off any time you wanted, couldn't you!*

Mama doesn't answer my gaze. Her face goes slack. She doesn't speak, but just shrinks, right there before my eyes. Her jaw isn't rigid any more. The anger is gone. She keeps getting smaller and smaller. Still I gaze deep into her eyes. Mama turns away.

"I'm really sorry, Mama. I wish it didn't have to come to this. It's a bad time for me. I'll say goodnight to you now.

I turn and go to my bedroom. I don't feel upset, I don't feel afraid of Mama's attacks, and I don't feel afraid of chair talk. I just feel tired. Sleep comes the instant I lie down.

78.

An Unwelcome Opportunity

It all started with the efficiency goons sent by the government to poke their noses around the various departments at Chrysler Missile. The department heads sent strict word to all employees: keep busy at all times, don't leave your desk unless it's lunch time, and no shenanigans. Overtime has stopped dead. So too has all the fun here. I stopped flashing an orange peel at the gate as proof the guards were too inattentive to notice the discrepancy from our regular orange identification badges, I stopped meeting Frank and Don in the parking lot for snake music, I dismantled my ballistic paper clip launcher, no more insect sanctuaries, no more studying for my U of D courses, no more joke sessions around the cardboard-tasting-coffee machines, no more plant-wide hoaxes—just the boring task of trying to look busy on little work. I even stopped spending time in the toilets in the Administration Building. The interlopers have completely ruined this place.

No matter how busy everyone tries to appear, the layoffs spread around the plant like the black plague. No one knows whose turn will be next to catch the dreaded disease of unemployment. And once you catch it, you're as good as dead, because it's almost impossible to find a job in Detroit. People talk with fear and dread. *Did you hear that they are going to lay off fifty percent of the work force? Did you hear that just yesterday three guys got the ax in the records department? Maybe the lucky ones are the first laid off— those ones have the best chance of finding a new job. Did you know that even supervisors are getting axed?*

On Monday, one day in July of nineteen fifty-nine, Charlene tells me that Mr. Lange wants me in his office. He is a big shot, which entitles him to have his desk surrounded by four walls about seven feet high, painted drab green like the rest of the plant, and containing a row of glass windows so he can stand up and look out over the troops to see who is screwing off. He motions for me to sit in the chair facing his desk.

"I'm sorry to be the bearer of bad news, Pat," he says, as he hands me a pink envelope. The outside is stamped *Administrative Confidential.*

"I don't know what to do," I tell my girlfriend, Lyn. "It's registration time at U of D. I spent the last four years finishing my first two years of pre-engineering, and the next step is a big one—three years of hard-core engineering courses by full-time day school. It's going to take me forever to do it by night school. I could do it much faster in regular day school on co-op, where I would alternate every three months between school and work. I think that Mama could get by on her own income, now that she's a nurse at Saratoga Hospital. But I don't know if I could earn enough to get by myself. I have only seven hundred-fifty dollars left from the inheritance that I didn't give to Mama. And I don't know if I could handle full-time school. Electrical engineering courses are really tough. I'm not even sure if I could get up in the morning to make eight o'clock classes."

"Of course you can do it. Didn't you start getting A's after you borrowed my economics book for your course in night school?" she says with a chuckle. "See what a good influence I am on you. And as far as the money is concerned, why don't you try day school. The worst that could happen is that you would have to take out a student loan. As for getting up in the mornings, I'll give you a wake up phone call every morning."

"I don't know. It's such a big step. The biggest one I have ever faced."

The time has come for me to once again perform my role as the job applicant from hell. I really don't want a job. My objective is to appear ready to take a job, but to put on such a bad impression that no one in their right mind would want to hire me. To hedge my bets, I enrolled in engineering day school and filed for unemployment compensation at the same time. The rules of unemployment are that you must actively look for a job. Either you follow the leads they may give you, which have been zilch so far, or else you have to ask for a job at two companies every week and give them proof of that. My real hope is that I can keep from getting a job so I can go to school and collect unemployment at the same time.

So far I've been lucky. Every business that I have visited either has not had any openings, or else they have declined to offer me a job. But now Chrysler threatens to mess up my life by inviting me to interview for a job, and, would you believe, at the Missile Plant—the same place that laid me off just three and a half weeks ago. Engineering day school starts next week—just days after I am eligible to start collecting unemployment.

I sit at the desk of Mr. Murphy, an energetic man with a bald head and a bushy walrus mustache. He puffs excitedly on his pipe. I wonder what he thought of the limp handshake I gave him when we first met—my first bad impression. I neglected to shave—bad impression number two. I am wearing a sport shirt, without a tie—bad impression number three. He has been going on about what a great place Chrysler Missile has become.

"You wouldn't recognize this place. We laid off forty per cent in the past few weeks. We now expect to become a leaner and meaner operation. Some of the actual shop work is going to come back here. We expect this plant to become a vital center of engineering and fabrication. This is going to be a terrific place to work. And the job opening you are applying for is an exciting one. You will be doing liaison between the Engineering Department and the fabrication shops, making sure that the work is performed up to our standards. It's a great opportunity for a young man like yourself."

Mr. Murphy stops his agitated presentation, obviously waiting for a reaction from me. I wait a bit, thinking how I'm going to start my response.

"Thank you, Mr. Murphy. I appreciate your speech and that you want to give me an opportunity. I have learned something since I was laid off three and a half weeks ago. When you're down and out, everyone says they want to give you an opportunity. They think that since you're out of a job, you'll take any crummy offer that comes along. But let me tell you this. I'm not desperate, and I'm not interested in an opportunity to move down. I'm looking for an opportunity to move up."

I fold my arms defiantly and stare him straight in the eye. But I feel guilty as hell. This actually sounds like a neat job. And I really like Mr. Murphy. But I can't turn back now. School starts in just three days, and I really need to collect unemployment.

Mr. Murphy's face turns bright red; he produces giant clouds of smoke from his pipe. He slaps his desk with the palm of his hand and jumps to a standing position.

"Move down! What the hell are you talking about, move down?" he demands, pacing back and forth along side his desk. "This is great career opportunity, and you don't realize it. Damn it, young man. You remind me of my son. Pig headed! But you've got the right background for this job, and you know something? I think you've got the right personality too. I don't want some weak, sniveling school boy in this job. Those shop guys are tough, and they'll try to push you around. I need someone who has the guts to stand his ground. I think you will be just perfect for this job, and I'm going to recommend you for the position."

I reach for Mr. Murphy's extended hand, feeling embarrassed. I want to say *I'm sorry I spoke to you like that, Mr. Murphy. I'm really not like that. You see, it's all an act. I would be honored to work for you.*

"Thank you for the interview," I say, this time shaking his hand firmly.

A few days later, I get a formal offer of re-employment at Chrysler Missile. I decline the job, thereby forfeiting my claim to unemployment compensation. This means I won't collect a cent from Michigan Unemployment. I feel relieved to be spared the guilt of carrying out a sham.

I start the next part of my life as a full-time student of Electrical Engineering at the University of Detroit.

79.

A Final Word

There are neither happy nor sad endings—but only beginnings.

JOHN P. REILLY, son
Mrs. Julia Reilly of 181:
Schoenherr, is the reci
ent of the Institute
Radio Engineers Award f
outstanding service at tl
University of Detroit, Rei
ly, a 1955 graduate of N
tivity High School, is
senior electrical engineering student in the U. of D.
College of Engineering and
Architecture.

Upper row: Pat & Lyn wed (Sept. 1, 1962); Pat graduates from University of Detroit (June, 1962); Ken, Alan, Pat, Lyn, Maureen at Falling Waters, Pennsylvania (1976). Middle row: Lyn with our first-born, Kenneth (June, 1963); Pat plays flute-a-phone (1997); Lyn, Kathleen (Swanson), Pat at our home in Maryland (1998). Bottom row: Pat with first-born, Kenneth (June, 1963); Pat receives Institute of Radio Engineers service award (1961); Pat, Ken, Maureen, Alan, Lyn)1983).

End Notes

Chapter 10: The Skeleton Building. I later learned that a boy had died after falling down the elevator shaft of the skeleton building. After that a fence was erected it to keep kids out. For many years afterwards I had nightmares of falling off the skeleton building.

Chapter 11: Mama Runs Away. No one asked any more questions of Mama, or ever spoke of her trip to East Rochester again. For the next ten years she got a Christmas card from a woman who signed herself Joan. The card always carried the same note: "Dear Julie, I thank God for putting you on the train with me to Rochester. I will always keep you in my prayers. God bless you and your family."

Chapter 13: Grand Rapids. I never found out what happened to the shell in Uncle Bert's gun. But for years to come after that trip to Grand Rapids, I feared that someday an article would appear in the newspaper that Bert Maloney of Grand Rapids, Michigan blew his head off while cleaning his gun.

More than 50 years after my Grand Rapids adventures, having lost contact with the Maloneys, I was able to track down Dick and Pat Maloney and their families, then living in Minneapolis. After a few words of greeting, I asked Dick: do you remember the Vernor's incident? He immediately replied: "You mean when we peed in the bottle?" Of a life time of experiences that might be stored in our memory banks, why do such really stupid capers remain so vividly lodged in the male brain? On July 15, 2001, not after I visited Pat and Dick in Minneapolis, Dick died of emphysema. I was grateful to Pat and Marylyn Maloney for making this reunion possible.

Chapter 15: Mama's Education. After I was grown, Mama liked to play the word game *Scrabble.* We always made her spot us 50 points. She usually made some protest about that, but accepted the terms and won anyhow.

Chapter 17: The New Palace. To my lasting amazement, neither Helen nor I ever got punished for the spitball caper. The only times Mama ever spoke of the event was with amusement, as if it was all part of a great joke in which she played a role.

Chapter 19: The Musician. I later learned that those missing harmonica notes were deliberately left out so the chords would come out right. And much later, when I had children of my own, I learned how to restore those missing notes, and create others too by *note-bending*—a special technique used in playing the *blues-harp.*

Chapter 22: The Will. While writing this memoir, I obtained a copy of Aunt Margaret's will. It wasn't exactly worded the way Daddy reported it, although it must have felt that way to him. It had a provision excluding him from a share in her estate with the stipulation: ... *John Reilly shall not share in the division for the reason that he is better situated financially than the other children of said Catherine Reilly.*

Chapter 27: A New Friend. Many years would have to pass— graduation from college, and a career path in Bioelectricity— before I could understand how my electric shocker worked. But at the age of 13, there would be plenty of time to experiment with this new concept that Jerry introduced to me, and plenty of chances to cause all kinds of mischief with it.

Chapter 33:A Letter to Grammy. Grammy sent photocopies of Mama's letter to many of the relatives on Grammy's side of the family. That created irreparable rifts between Mama and many of Daddy's kin. Among those, Cousin Nell and Uncle Salem (mentioned in Chapter 4) remained good friends who were loving and helpful to us for years to come. My sister Kathleen maintained a connection with Aunt ("Baby") Helen, and Lillian (Lala), and cared for Lillian in her old age.

Chapter 39: An Attack. Mama smashed that radio several more times in screaming rages over the following year. Not knowing why it angered her so, I patched it up each time, except for the final time, when she smashed it to smithereens. In later years I think I came to understand what it symbolized to her. It was a gift from Daddy, purchased on credit at the last minute before some special event—birthday, wedding anniversary, or Christmas—which he left for Mama to scrape up the money to pay the bills that followed. Perhaps those bills symbolized to her Daddy's lack of affection, which she craved deeply.

Chapter 41: Gene. Gene did get killed, but not the way I expected. In 1958, when he was 22, he fell off the boat he had purchased along with three other buddies. Gene, still not a swimmer, slipped beneath the surface and drowned.

Chapter 49: Mike. Twenty years later, Mike and I played chess when I visited him in Phoenix, where he lived with his wife and family. I didn't tell him that I had been playing chess during lunch periods at work, or that I had studied *Modern Chess Openings*. When I check-mated his king, I opened the door of his house and shouted "Check mate!' so the whole neighborhood could hear of my victory.

Mike married Pat Malloy—his girl friend from Detroit. They settled in Phoenix where the had four children. While they were still young, Mike left his family, eschewing serious responsibilities, choosing instead a life as an alcoholic drifter. Eventually he lost all contact with his family, and became homeless and indigent. He died from throat cancer—probably a result of decades of cigarettes and alcohol—leaving behind acutely saddened children, who only became aware of his location and condition near the very end. Those children carried scars they acquired from years of abandonment. Those scars could not be assuaged by late-in-life reconnections. In his final days, while Mike was still in a coma in a Phoenix hospital, I played harmonica at his bedside while his sister, Cathy, sang some of the old songs.

Chapter 52: A Radio Hoax. The next day after playing the hoax on Lois, Dick and I let Mike know he had also been the victim of a hoax for the past two weeks. Although he took the joke without rancor, no amount of persuasion would entice him to practice Morse code with me again, nor would he talk about getting a Ham license.

Chapter 53: Mama's Treatment. Mike continued to attend Mama in private chats during her treatment. More than forty-five years later, while Mike was hospitalized with throat cancer, we spoke about our boyhood remembrances. He recalled the many times he sat with Mama. "Can you recall what she talked about?" I asked. "Yes, I can," he replied in a whisper by placing his finger over the hole in his tracheotomy. "But I can't talk about it. It was just between me and her."

Chapter 55: Mama Gets Courted. Mr. Mansfield called Mama a few days later to apologize. He said all the kids scared him. He expected to spend a quiet evening with her at our home, not to take her out to dinner as she thought. She neither saw him nor heard from him again. As far as I know, it was the last date with any man that Mama had.

Chapter 60: The Freshman: Frank Koczot married his high school sweetheart, Laverne Shraeder, in 1956. After a stint in the army, he landed a position researching microbiology at the National Institutes of Health in Bethesda, Maryland, a suburb of Washington DC. I began my career at the Johns Hopkins University Applied Physics Laboratory in 1962 after marrying Lynette Bielat (The Little One in Chapter 74), and we lived only a few miles from the Koczots. Our families maintained a close friendship ever since. Frank acquired a fatal infection, and died on September 17, 2012. I was honored to have been asked by his widow, Verne, to give the eulogy at his memorial service.

Chapter 65: Doo Wop. Johnny Bober, Bob Perham, and I continued to perform popular songs and original numbers at every opportunity and wherever folks would gather. But it was Bob who showed the greatest talent, as he sharpened his wit and performing style. He joined the navy at the age of 19, and would display his new repertoire and polished singing style when he came home on leave. Bob was on naval maneuvers in a sub-hunting airplane off the coast of Washington state when a torpedo on the wing exploded, sending all aboard to their deaths. He was only 20 years old. The world lost a very funny guy that day.

More than twenty years later, when Mike and I met in Atlanta at the home of his sister, Judy, on the occasion of the wedding of one of her boys, he confessed that it was he who pushed me at Roller World. And another 20 years elapsed when I sent Mike drafts of some of these memoirs while he was in the hospital under treatment for throat cancer. "Make sure you say it was accidental," he prompted in a whisper while plugging the hole in his tracheotomy with a finger. "I meant to help your progress with a friendly push that just went bad."

Chapter 67: A New Fender. My Fender guitar served me well over the course of many years, in sing-alongs, parties, and gigs with several bands. Every time I used it, I was reminded of the generosity of my little sister, Helen.

Chapter 68: YWCA. In a tacit agreement between Mama and me, we never spoke of the incident that led Helen to leave home. Helen didn't come back, and she did manage on her own quite well. She eventually forgave Mama, and, in later years, became her best friend.

Chapter 72: Licensed Practical Nurse. I often wondered if Helen's departure shocked Mama enough that she decided to get her life together and start nursing school.

Chapter 73: Snake Music. More decades later, even while I began writing this memoir, we continued to get together for snake music during one of my periodic visits to Detroit. Our discussions continued on into the night, just like 40 years was only yesterday. Frank never stopped defending all the wrong positions.

When Don was 72 years old, he fell from the top of a stair case and suffered brain damage from a blow to the head. He died of his injuries some months later. I played "What a Wonderful World" on the harmonica at his memorial service. Later in the evening, his wife, Janet, told me that they had made an agreement years earlier to have that song performed at his funeral. I still cannot get used to the idea of a world without Don Afeldt.

Chapter 74: Big One, Small One. I continued to date both the Big One and Small One, but eventually fell hopelessly in love with Lyn. After dating for three years, we married on September 2, 1962, three months after my graduation from U of D, and a little over one year after her graduation. Mike Wilson, then married and living in Phoenix, sent his good wishes to both of us. More than thirty years later, during a reunion at his sister Judy's house in Atlanta, I asked him if he ever held it against me for not only dating his girlfriend, but marrying her. "No Pat, he said. It was never a problem for me. We were on the verge of breaking up anyway. You just helped that along."

Chapter 75: Last of the Inheritance: Kathleen eventually inherited the small remainder of Aunt Margaret's (Ahnty Reet) estate from Aunt Lillian (Lala), for whom she cared in Lala's old age. Today, two of Kathleen's daughters-in-law wear the diamond rings inherited by Aunt Helen Marie (Baby Helen) from the original estate.

♫♫♫♫

Part IV

Epilog

♫♫♫♫

Pat

I finished my degree in Electrical Engineering in June of nineteen sixty-two, having graduated *Cum Laude* no less. Fortunately, in figuring scholastic averages for honors awards, the University of Detroit didn't count the first two years of classes for which I earned so many mediocre grades. My girlfriend, Lyn (who is the "small one" I introduced Chapter seventy-four), graduated the year before, and became a French teacher in Detroit's Ford High School. On many of our weekends together, her time was shared with her paper correction tasks, an activity in which I could sometimes assist her when she provided me with the answer key.

We married on September second, nineteen sixty-two, three months after I began my professional career at the Johns Hopkins University Applied Physics Laboratory in Maryland. We had three children, and, as I write these words, three grandchildren. We have weathered ups and downs, happy and sad times, love and anger, and remain married to this day. I will never forget the words of Father Lyons at a wedding ceremony: "Some say that love sustains marriage. But I believe it is the other way around. It is the marriage that sustains love." I have come to understand those words. The passage of time has deepened my love for Lyn, who continues to tolerate my antics, and support me in many ways.

As for my experiments with electric shock—that became a career path, along with other disciplines, including radar, sonar, infrared science, and environmental engineering. Of these disciplines, my enduring love was in the field of bioelectricity. Not only did I get to shock people as in my boyhood experiments, but I got paid for it, and could write scientific papers that got me on trips to interesting places. I wrote and had published three books on the subject, and get much satisfaction working as a consultant in the field of *Bioelectricity* during my retirement from The Johns Hopkins University Applied Physics Laboratory, where I worked full time for nearly thirty-seven years, and another thirteen part-time, during which time the Laboratory supported me in my work with professional groups involved in the development of exposure standards to electric currents and electromagnetic fields. As I put the final touches on the memoir (in the year 2012), I remain active in professional consulting, and development of standards.

Oh yes. Music. Our ten-piece band and vocalist *A Band For All Seasons* meet weekly at our house, and we perform in concerts, dances, and various functions. I also lead a four-piece jazz quartet: *JP Jazz*. I play guitar and harmonica in both groups. Don, Frank, and I would occasionally get together, reminisce, debate, and play snake music, until Don's untimely death in 20xx. On my trips to Michigan, I still see Frank and Bev Lentine, who often host Lyn and me at their home. Our intense discussions continue, but now without the support from Don I could previously count on to counter Frank's stubbornly held and illogical positions.

Mama

After I graduated from college and moved to Maryland in nineteen sixty-two, Mama continued to deteriorate. Numerous drunken phone calls over several years distressed me greatly. I eventually took to responding to these calls by saying: *I'm sorry Mama, but I don't want to talk to you while you're drunk. I'll call you tomorrow when you're sober.* I'm not aware of her having any more attacks after the final confrontation in *The Last Attack (Chapter*

77). It did appear that Mama could hold off attacks and drunkenness for long periods. Cousin Joyce (*Little Iodine* in the stories) lived with her for almost one year after I moved to Maryland, and not once did she see Mama drunk or acting in an unstable manner. But I suspect that Mama could hold off the demons only so long.

Mama retired from her nursing career at Harper Hospital at the age of fifty-nine and continued doing private nursing for a few more years. She moved frequently, and had a succession of landladies and roommates—all failed relationships I suspect. She made a number of what appeared to be deliberately failed attempts at suicide. Helen and Kathleen, who continued to live in the Detroit area, were called in on these. We considered them to be substitutes for her previous attacks, and didn't take them as serious suicide attempts—until the final one, which was nearly fatal. At that time she was living in a beautiful apartment complex for retired persons; the State of Michigan paid a share that allowed her to live on social security and her meager nurse's pension. During one of the regular nighttime checks, the floor monitor found her passed out on the floor in her apartment. This time she had consumed a potentially lethal dose of sleeping pills.

A rescue squad saved Mama from death, and she was committed to psychiatric treatment in a hospital for one month. During that hospitalization, the psychiatrist who was treating her called both Kathleen and Helen to attempt to find more background on Mama. The psychiatrist told them that Mama was deeply disturbed and that she had been sexually abused by someone close to the family as a child. She was amazed that Mama had survived so long and that her children were not themselves mental wrecks. I am thankful that her psychiatrist was more competent than Dr. Johnson, (his real name) who appears in several stories.

After Mama's discharge from the hospital, she lived an apparently stable life, without alcohol, attacks, or suicide attempts. She enjoyed writing poetry and knitting beautiful creations, including blankets that each of my three children still have and fanciful dolls and clothing which she loved to give to children.

During her final year, Mama's demons seemed to reappear. She destroyed the collection of poetry she had written and all the family photographs that her children so admired and coveted. Fortunately, I had years earlier made copies from some of the negatives I borrowed from her shoe box, and I possess the only two surviving pictures of Daddy ever taken after his own boyhood. A number of pictures from that collection appear in this book. In that year she wrote hurtful letters to her siblings. She also told one of her grandchildren the identity of the person who abused her as a child. I do not repeat the abuser's name in these memoirs since I am not sure of Mama's mental state when she reported it, and I lack independent verification. Aunt Mary, Mama's eldest sister, was the one who was best able to shed light on this matter. She once told me that her mother (*Ma* in the stories) was extremely brutal to all the children, but especially so to Mama. "Why did Ma single her out?" I had asked. Mary gave me a stunned look and replied with tears in her eyes, "I'll never tell. I'll take that to the grave." And so she did.

On the twenty-fourth of September nineteen ninety-four, just days before her eightieth birthday, Mama was discovered during a room check on the floor of her apartment, the victim a severe stroke. Helen made it to her bedside in the hospital as Mama began to lose her final moments of consciousness. She recognized Helen, who stroked her hair while Mama uttered her final words: *Forgive... forgive... forgive... forgive... for... for... for... for... f..f..f..f..f..f..f..f..f..f..f..f..f..f..f....*

Mama died a week later.

Kathleen

While growing up, my older sister was always my playmate, my confidant, my protector, and my bossy sister. Her position in the family and her personality made her the one with whom Helen and I conferred while trying to make some sense out of our often desperate circumstances—and also the one who was other times bossy and overbearing. Kathleen became a substitute mother before her time. She desperately wanted the family to work, but at the same time she met confrontations head on—traits which she continued to possess into adulthood. She had six children by her husband, Bob Swanson. Her urge to make relationships work often compelled her to take an active role in the lives of her children, her siblings, her friends and relatives, and all other's who came her way. I don't know what role her childhood experiences may have had in her selection of marriage mates and three failed marriages, or the succession of careers that never quite worked out.

I never doubted Kathleen's generous and loving nature. It was she who gave me a CARE package of miscellaneous household necessities to get me started in Maryland. It was she who helped Lala when she was old and friendless—a recluse in her increasingly dangerous neighborhood. It was she who always remained sympathetic and understanding not only to her family, but also to all who crossed her path—the elderly, the young, the sick, the handicapped, and the healthy.

As ever, she remains the eternal optimist, always knowing what must be done to make everything come out right. And as ever, she remains my lifelong dear friend.

Helen

My sister Helen lived independently after the events in *YWCA*. She continued to work as a reservationist for airlines and eventually became a world traveler. It was satisfying to see her taking many junkets that often included Mama as a guest traveler: to New York for an evening of theater; to Las Vegas for a foray into forbidden pleasures of gambling; to New Orleans for a visit to the French Quarter.

I don't know when Helen stopped being my little sister. Perhaps it began when she married Bill Pitts and had two children of her own. She became the office manager in a printing firm and my hostess during visits to Detroit, which were especially frequent after I got too close to the attractive force of genealogy and memoirs.

After Mama's hospitalization for psychiatric treatment, Helen came to accept and truly love Mama, the two becoming good friends. Mama was a weekly guest at Helen's home, where they often played *Scrabble*, and other word games. Although Helen and Mama were very close, it remained strictly taboo for Helen or any one else to ever talk about the past with Mama. But Helen was able to accept and love her unreservedly, something I could not achieve.

As I wrote this final chapter, Helen faced major surgery for lung cancer—the price for many years as a heavy smoker. I think of her often. We faced so many challenges together while we were growing up. She died of cancer in January, 2003, leaving a big empty spot in my heart.

Daddy

It might seem a bit strange to put Daddy in an Epilogue—after all, he died in Chapter thirty, long before my final episode. But he did develop in a way during the writing of these memoirs.

When I started writing these stories, I had hoped I might learn something about Daddy. Perhaps if I could learn what made Grammy the way she was, I could understand something of the kind of person he was, and how he came to be that way.

So I traced her genealogy and uncovered much information going back to the seventeenth century in Holland. I found an elderly cousin of his who remembered his uncle Jack (my grandfather), his cousin Jack (my father), and his grandfather John Reilly (my great grandfather), all of whom he could visit in a two-home plot they called *The Homestead* in the Irish section of downtown Detroit known as *Corktown*. When I found those homes, still in good condition today, I tried to imagine the environment in nineteen twelve, when Daddy was born. I tried to envision the relationship of four generations of Reillys who had lived in those two houses: my great-grandparents John and Matilda, my grandparents John Edward and Catherine, my parents John Lawrence and Julia, and my sister Kathleen. But no matter how much data I collected, no matter how much I learned about my ancestors and their circumstances, Daddy continued to elude me.

I should add something in his defense. My sisters remember and understand the negative things I recall about him. But they both have affectionate remembrances that I lack. Helen remembers happy occasions sitting on his lap, him playing the violin for her, and his joking ways. And Kathleen recalls the morning of the day he died, how he made unusually pointed efforts to get a good-bye kiss from each of his children.

As an adult reflecting on these events, I came to question why I found such difficulty in reconstructing an image of Daddy, except for a residue of negative memories. Still, I can recall that he was sometimes playful, and told us silly jokes. Although he raised his fist to Mama, he never hit her as far as I know. And while he swung his belt as us kids for misbehaving, I can never remember him actually connecting. Although he spent money we could little afford on alcohol, he did otherwise steadily bring home his pay.

I did not until recently give him credit for the strides he had made in dealing with alcoholism shortly before he died. While writing these memoirs, I came to understand Mama much better, and I see the impact she might have had on him. I know how powerfully strong and emotionally demanding she could be, and I can guess what Daddy's reactions might have been. Perhaps the worst that could be said about him is that he had some emotional weaknesses that he wrestled with. Had he lived longer, perhaps his strides to overcome alcoholism might have revealed some inner strengths.

Before I finished the final chapter in these memoirs, I came to an important realization: in the process of writing, I forgave Daddy.

Part V

The Ancestors

♫♫♫♫

Reflections

When I reflect on my family history, I am awed by the improbability of it all. Were it not for my ancestors John Reilly and Margaret Farley, who just before 1850 fled from the Irish potato famine, were it not for the desire to escape hardships and political upheaval that compelled Dominik Rogoza and Stanisalwa Gryniewicz to take their chances in a new land in the early 1900s, were it not for the journey from Holland of Frank Impens with his eight children and later his wife Catherine Voet to come to America in the late 1800s, were it not for a determined but troubled Julia Rogoza and a shy and uncertain John Reilly who decided to find comfort together, I would not be here to reflect on these events. These reflections make me feel tremendously privileged, not just for having an easier life than my progenitors, but for life itself.

I include here a brief account of my progenitors in the blood-lines of my four grandparents: Reilly and Impens on Daddy's side; Rogoza and Gryniewicz on Mama's side. Much of what I have to report is a result of my own research over the past few years. Unfortunately, very little of my ancestry was passed on to me by my parents, and I suppose if such information had been communicated to me when I was young, I would not have been interested or inclined to remember it. It seems to be an affliction of men of a certain age who, seeing the likelihood of many fewer years ahead than behind, get the genealogy bug when practically everyone knowledgeable has already passed on.

Reilly

In 1849 John Reilly and Margaret Farley, my great-great grandparents, gave birth to a son in Canada. They immigrated there from Ireland; it was probably during the great potato famine, although I am not certain of their year of arrival. The potato famine was a time of severe hardship in Ireland when a virus devastated the country's entire potato crop. The potato, which had been imported from the new world, had transformed the nutrition of the old world by becoming a staple in most diets, including that of the Irish. Unfortunately, the Irish had planted only one variety of potato, known as a "lumper." Why should they diversify when that one grew so well in the Irish soil? And who could divine that a disease would come along many years later—one having an affinity to the Irish potato—a disease that would spread quickly, and eventually turn nearly every potato in Ireland to mush before it could develop in the ground? With the loss of the potato crop and widespread famine, land owners were eager to get rid of their starving tenant farmers by placing them bound for the new world in "coffin ships," so called because fully twenty percent of the poor, sick, and starving souls who came aboard in Ireland met their final resting place at sea. Canada was a popular place to send these desperate souls since it was considered part of the United Kingdom, and that included Ireland at the time. Fortunately for me, John and Margaret made it to Canadian soil.

My discovery of our Canadian roots came as a complete surprise to me and my sisters. It was never mentioned by anyone to us in our childhood. We were simply told that Daddy was Irish on his father's side, the first immigrant came from somewhere in County Cork, and was Dutch on his mother's side, but it's the Irish side that really counts, so never mind the Dutch, thank you.

That Canadian immigrant Reilly was the fifth generation of first-born sons named *John* that I could link with myself. I don't know how much further the John Reilly chain goes. It was I who broke it, naming my first son *Kenneth Patrick* so as to avoid the confusion I experienced in a family with two Johns, and I wasn't about to saddle a son with pretentious Latin numerals after his name. Mama surprised me by expressing her displeasure at my effrontery in breaking the *John Reilly* chain. Why should she care? The Reillys were no kin of hers. I hope my ancestors forgive me this indiscretion.

The earliest John Reilly that I know more about than just a birth or death date was the Canadian-born one whose name first appears in the 1869 City Directory of Detroit, a bustling industrial city at the time, and just across the Detroit River from Windsor Canada. He was nineteen years old when he began his employment in Detroit as a glass cutter—a profession he would have until his death. The Civil War had ended only four years earlier, the North was enjoying prosperity, and Detroit was one of the leaders in economic and industrial development. It was a perfect time for a glass cutter to help fill the great demand for window glass in the rapidly growing city.

In 1872, four years after arriving in Detroit, glass-cutter John married Matilda Collins, who was also born in Canada of Irish parents. Detroit was booming at the time. Why, only the year before, J. L. Hudson's opened its first Haberdashery—a beautiful, towering five-story building whose exterior was graced with rococo filigree. Ask any old-time Detroit native about the significance of J. L. Hudson's, and his eyes will glaze over from nostalgic remembrances of Christmas shopping, Thanksgiving day parades sponsored by Hudson's, and birthday excursions with parents in their popular basement restaurant. In 1998, long after Hudson's had become at its tallest section a twenty-five story Detroit landmark, it was imploded into rubble by dynamite, as if to punctuate the demise of the once great city.

By 1885 John Reilly became the owner of a house in what is now an historic Irish section of downtown Detroit known as

Corktown—named after the many immigrants who came from County Cork in Ireland, as did his own father. It amazes me that the son of an Irish potato famine immigrant, employed cutting window glass, could scrape together enough money to buy what I found to be a fairly substantial house—certainly a nicer one than any I had lived in as a young child. By 1890, the glass cutter became listed in the City Directory as a "foreman" in a glass company, that had by then changed its name (and ownership, I presume) four times. His obituary of 1910 says he served for twenty years as manager of the glass company that had been acquired by the Pittsburgh Plate-Glass Company, and through a series of prior acquisitions had been known as Blitz & Sons, Farrand Williams & Company, and E. P. Earl.

When John and Matilda acquired their house in Corktown, they had five children and a sixth either just on it way, or newly born. The fourth child, John Edward (my grandfather) was two years old at the time. There were, altogether, seven children.

When he was sixteen years old, John Edward's name first appeared in the Detroit City Directory of 1894 as a "tinner," and he continued to be listed that way for another eight years. After

Obituary picture of John Reilly (1849-1910). Born in Canada of Irish immigrants, he came to the U.S. in 1869. He worked as a glass cutter, and established the "Homestead" in the Irish section of Detroit know as "Corktown."

that he was employed as a conductor on the street car lines that plied Detroit, and for a few years he tried his hand on the side as a portrait photographer in an enterprise known as "Reilly and Hart." He married Catherine Impens (Grammy) in 1907. John and Catherine lived with his parents for another three years, whereupon they moved to the house next door, which was by then owned by the Reilly clan. The two houses had different street addresses, one on Thirteenth Street, and the other on Marantette.

John and Catherine settled in their own house with their two children Lillian (Lala), then two years old, and new-born John Lawrence (Daddy). Not long to follow were two more children: Edward (Uncle Eddie), and Helen Marie (Baby Helen).

It took me some time to get the domiciles figured out, with the city renaming streets (*Thirteenth Street* became *Vermont* in 1904), and renumbering the houses (*259 Vermont* became *1799 Vermont*, and *47 Marantette* became *2021 Marantette* in 1920).

Children of John E. and Catherine Reilly Helen (age 1 1/2), Edward. (3), John L. (6), and Lillian (8). (Picture ≈ 1916).

Armed with these discoveries, I visited Corktown in 1999, fully expecting to find a shanty town for shanty Irish, which I supposed were my family's humble beginnings. I was quite surprised to find within the rotting corpse that is much of present-day Detroit, a nicely-preserved historical section, and those two Reilly houses were quite substantial structures—one in beautiful condition (the Marantette address), and the other under renovation and unoccupied.

Although the two Reilly houses had different street addresses, they were situated at the intersection of Vermont and Marantette such that they shared a common yard. An elderly cousin of my father's (Eugene Towle, son of Martina Reilly), whom I had discovered in my research, reminisced about visiting those two houses, which the Reillys were calling *The Homestead*. He recalled his Aunt Kate (Grammy), and his uncle Jack, as well as cousin Jack (Daddy). He recounted a story about Uncle Jack, who was an amateur boxer in his spare time. It seems that in one bout, his opponent, who had an instinct for any weakness, kept striking at Jack's jaw which harbored an aching bad tooth. It got Jack so angry that he challenged his tormentor to a gloves-off bout, which challenge was accepted, and Jack proceeded to dispatch him, to the cheers of all the spectators. Well, there it is, confirmation of the stereotype—the fighting (and drinking) Irish.

Corktown was indeed an Irish section of town. When I was a small child, Daddy made proud references to the *Irish confetti* of his youth—a euphemism for rocks and bricks that were visited by the Irish lads on foreign interlopers in the neighborhood. And he reminisced about a wake held, as was the custom, in a deceased man's home where the bereaved friends, after drowning their sorrows in liquid ablution, took the body out of the casket and held it in a standing position while everyone sang Irish songs. There I go again with those stereotypes!

Glass cutter John died in 1910 at the age of sixty-one of a sudden heart attack, up to that time having been in apparent excellent health. In that same year my father, John Lawrence, was born. Widow Matilda continued to occupy the Vermont house for another fourteen years. Matilda lived in her final few years with her daughter, Martina Towle. Her grandson, Eugene, gave Matilda his bedroom and bunked with his brother. "I was glad to do it," Eugene reported to me when we spoke in 1998. Three years after moving from the Vermont house, Matilda Collins Reilly died of stomach cancer at the age of seventy.

Soon after his father's death, John Edward became the owner of a small convenience store on Michigan Avenue, just a few blocks from the homestead. It was sometimes listed as a "confectionery" store, and sometimes as a "tobacco" store. The 1916 Detroit City Directory carries an ad that suggests the Reillys embraced the newfangled telephone:

> John E. Reilly, Dealer in cigars, tobaccos, fine confectionery, magazines and newspapers, Branch Laundry Agency, 455 1/2 Michigan Ave, Tel. Grand 686-W,
> h [*h stands for "home"*] 47 Marantette.

John E. Reilly (1878-1934) posing outside his store on Michigan Avenue (≈ 1915 @ age 37).

My sister Kathleen, after caring for our aunt Lala in her old age, eventually came into possession of her pictures. I love the one of John Edward, our grandfather, taken outside his store, stylishly decked out in a bowler hat and bow tie, hands on his hips in a cocky pose, looking proud as a peacock of his business. I am also struck by the sad countenance of Lala in all her childhood pictures. I think she had a head start on what I took to be a sad adulthood.

Pictures of Uncle Eddie taken when he was a young man show him as strikingly frail—just a bag of skin and bones, as Mama would say. I'm not sure when or why he became hospitalized. I described his condition as I recalled it to my friend Arne, a medical doctor. His diagnosis: advanced rickets, a condition brought about by vitamin D deficiency. What a stunning thought! During those years when he was kept out of sight as was the customary treatment of handicapped people in those days, my beloved uncle might have been cured with some sunshine and vitamin therapy.

L --> R: John L. (Daddy) & Edward Reilly (Uncle Eddie) approx. 1928. Edward would be 15 years old, and is already looking very frail.

John Edward died unexpectedly of a heart attack in 1934 at the age of fifty-six. When I figured in Daddy's death of a sudden, unexpected heart attack at age forty, it always seemed to me that I had inherited some sudden death genes. In fact, as a young man, I fully expected not to outlive Daddy. Well, here I am, putting the finishing touches on this memoir at the age of seventy-five, having survived prostrate cancer, and receiving treatment for high cholesterol, with a heart stent to treat coronary arterial blockage, but otherwise in good health, already having far outlived the oldest John Reilly I could find—thanks, I think, to the diagnosis of my astronomically high cholesterol, and available drugs to treat the condition. God forbid! I'm not bragging.

My parents, John Lawrence Reilly and Julia Rogoza (AKA Helen), met in 1934 while working at a factory making auto parts—he a floor sweeper and she an assembly line worker. The work was hard, the hours long, and the pay small, but any job was welcome in those hard times. Mama recalled handling sharp metal parts that cut into her hands, causing an infection in the fingers of both hands. I vividly remember the X-shaped scars on each of her fingers where a doctor lanced them to let the infection drain out. Those Xs spoke more strongly to me of her hardships in those days than any words she could have conveyed.

Because of Daddy's shyness, it was Mama who made the first date. Daddy kept his Polish girlfriend a secret from his mother, who said she couldn't abide Polacks and other low-class people. When they married in secret, they thought they could live separately without Mother Reilly being any the wiser. But soon after they married, Daddy lost his job, and Mama's soon-to-follow pregnancy and their inability to support that life style forced them to break the news to Mother Reilly, who could not avoid taking in what she perceived as a low-class, ignorant and pregnant daughter-in-law. That union completed the fourth generation of Reillys who lived in the homestead: John and Matilda, my great grandparents; John Edward and Catherine, my grandparents; John Lawrence and Julia, my parents; and Kathleen, my sister.

Impens

Impens, the family name of Daddy's mother ("Grammy), is the blood line that I can trace back the farthest and find the most documentation and living relatives, thanks to some good luck in my research and the Dutch propensity for keeping records.

Grammy's father was born in 1835 as Francis Lawrence Impens, formally known in the Latinized version on official records as "Franciscus Laurentius Impens." I suppose Daddy's middle name, Lawrence, was taken after his grandfather's name. Francis was the ninth of twelve children born of Bellerminus

Impens family (≈ 1915). L-->R: Margaret ("Ahnty Reet," 1874-1948), Catherine Voet (1844-1936); Francis L. Sr. (1835-1923); and Francis L. Jr. (1885-1965). Catherine & Francis Sr. are Grammy's parents.

Impens (1789-1840) and Sophie Bourgois (b. 1797) in Belgium near the border of Holland. Bellerminus and Sophie represent my common link with living relatives in Holland.

Francis's wife, Pieternella* Mattheusse DeBarr, died in 1873 giving birth to twins, who also died, leaving him with three other children: Charles Joseph (1866-1937), Amelia (1869-1942), and Johanna Sophia (1870-1949). He soon married his housekeeper, Catherine Voet (1844-1936). I went briefly astray from the genealogical path by Grammy's death certificate, in which Aunt Lillian (Lala) listed Grammy's mother's name as "Catherine Foote," until I came to realize that the Dutch pronunciation of *Voet* is very close to *foot*; it means just that in English.

Before coming to America, Francis and Catherine had five more children: Margaret (1874-1948), Lawrence (AKA Louis, 1876-1948), Adriana (1878-1907), Frederic Ferdinand (1879-1929), and Sadie (AKA Julianna, 1880-1972).

Pieternella Impens (Cousin Nell, teacher), oldest daughter of Charles Impens, and Salem Smith (Uncle Salem-- a metallurgist mechanic, and draftsman). These two were constant loyal and helpful friends throughout my youth.

---

* Cousin Nell, who is mentioned along with Uncle Salem (Smith) in Chapters 4 and 28, was christened *Pieternella*—surely after her grandmother, Pieternella (DeBaar) Impens. I regret not having the space to properly acknowledge them and the many other loving people who influenced our lives.

Sadie was later to become Sister Magdalene, a teaching sister in the Dominican order. She writes in her biography for the convent archives:

> Born on September 1, 1880, in Heinkenszand, Province of Zeeland, in the Netherlands... When but six weeks old I came to this country on the steamer Amsterdam. It took us eighteen days to cross the ocean. Our voyage was unpleasant and inconvenient since my parents were of the poorer class.... While still a young Religious one of my dear sisters died, and through anxiety for her eternal happiness I asked God to let me suffer until she entered heaven. Shortly after that I began to ail and continued suffering until in 1918 a serious operation was necessary. All hope for my recovery was despaired of, but in answer to the mighty prayers of our beloved Community, our dear Lord saw fit not only to restore me to health but gave me better health than I had enjoyed before my illness, so I have been able to fulfill my duties ever since...

Sister Magdalen

Francis was forty-five years old and Catherine was thirty-nine when they made the trip to the new world, a fact worthy of some marvel because of the considerable risks in so dramatically changing one's life direction, leaving behind family, friends, and trading the known for the unknown. I can only guess that, besides them being risk takers, life for them in Holland must have been hard enough that they would venture to a new land with seven children.

Francis settled in Grand Rapids, Michigan—a largely Dutch community where he supported his family by making wooden shoes with the tools he had brought from Holland. Catherine (1882-1958), who came to be called "Kate" and known to me as "Grammy," was the first born in America, followed by Frank L. (1885-1965). It amazes me that there was enough money in wooden shoes that a man could support a family of twelve in Grand Rapids, Michigan, through that craft. Well, maybe the living wasn't so great, because after five years of making wooden shoes, he took a job as a laborer in the local waterworks company, and eventually came to be a foreman there, and he held that position for the final twenty-eight years of his working life. After fifteen years of retirement, Frank died at the age of eighty-eight following an illness of one week. His death certificate lists the cause of death as "fracture of ribs; senility and shock, with chronic bronchitis as a contributing cause."

The first child born to Francis and Catherine was Margaret, who we came to know as our rich Ahnty Reet. I found it somewhat ironic that our rich aunt began her working life as a resident servant girl in one of the wealthy households in Grand Rapids. Some family secrets don't get willingly passed on but, nevertheless, can be discovered through diverse paper trails and persistence by a future researcher. Margaret did well to marry Irving Anway, a man who would rise from the ranks of upholsterer in a Grand Rapids furniture store to become the wealthy owner of his own furniture business. He died in 1936, leaving Margaret childless at the age of sixty-one.

Three years later, Margaret decided to use some of her acquired wealth for an ocean voyage to Holland to visit the town where her father once lived. While on the ship, widow Margaret met widower Philip Klenk, whom she later married. Apparently Philip was well-heeled enough through his ownership of fruit orchards in the vicinity of Grand Rapids that he too could afford a European trip. His four children were grown and on their own at the time.

That trip also resulted in the Rosetta stone for future American researchers of the Impens clan. Let me explain. While in Holland, Aunt Margaret sent her sister Johanna a post card with a picture of a street in the town of Heikenszand with a lovely windmill in the background, and an arrow pointing to a house, with the notation: "This is where you were born." Now fast forward fifty-three years to Pat and Marilyn Maloney who had acquired Aunt Margaret's postcard among other family mementos. You might recall the Maloneys from Chapter 13 (Grand Rapids), in which I recount my adventures with cousin Dick. Pat was his older brother. In 1989, Pat and Marilyn were on an auto trip through Holland when they decided to visit Heikenszand. They soon found the street shown on the postcard, the distinctive looking houses, the windmill in the background, and Francis Impens' former house. Although that house was under renovation and no one was living there, helpful neighbors put them in contact with local folks of the Impens clan, including one elderly gentleman who still made wooden shoes (utilitarian ones still favored by gardeners and other country folk, not the tourist variety sold to naive foreigners).

I have to continue on this thread. Some years after the Maloney's Holland trip, I discovered them to be living in Minnesota, and opened a dialog in which they sent me much information on the Impens clan, including living relatives in Holland. Right about that time I was invited to give a lecture at a scientific conference in Maastricht, Holland, a trip on which my wife, Lyn, accompanied me. We used a copy of the Rosetta stone to again locate Francis's house. My knocks on the door of number twenty-six Stationweg* were met by a Dutch woman who spoke no English. I tried explaining my connection with her house in fractured German, since I knew a little of that language, and no Dutch whatsoever. The worried-looking woman fetched a neighbor who spoke English, and I again explained my family's connection with the house, while the woman fidgeted nervously. "And what do you want?" he translated for me. "Nothing," I replied. "I only want to say hello to the person living here." This caused visible relief to the nervous woman, who graciously presented me with a book on the history of

---

* Also called "Elvis Presley Lane" according to a sign erected by a resident.

Heikenszand. I suspect she had thought I was trying to make a claim on her house with some ancient lien. As a result of the Maloneys' contacts, I also established wonderfully rewarding friendships with third cousins and their families in two parts of Holland, one in Ijzendijke (Christine and Fred Lamens, and their English-speaking children Michael and Martine), and another in Zeist, Wim and Ans *Imbens* (a corruption of *Impens* forced on Wim's grandfather by a thick-headed bureaucrat). It is my experience that once I establish one drop of blood in common with another person, I am often embraced as a long-lost brother.

Catherine Impens, my grandmother, was born into the Dutch community in Grand Rapids. I marvel at her father's ability to raise such a large family on the wages from the city waterworks. I look for clues for what might have shaped her own personality, but find nothing. I know nothing about her girlhood, how she met her Irish boyfriend from Detroit, and why she would marry him and settle in an Irish community.

"Kate" Impens
(Grammy), age ≈ 12
(picture about 1894)

I confess that I grew up having a poor image of the Dutch, who I reasoned were like Grammy—stingy and crabby. Those pictures of cute blond Dutch girls wearing their angel-winged hats, flowered dresses, and white aprons had to be some Dutch propaganda to cover up their real nature. Somehow I carried this negative stereotype even into adulthood. My subliminal prejudices were not dispelled until, at the age of nearly fifty, I began to work on an international scientific program under NATO, and had the opportunity to work with Dutch colleagues and attend meetings in Holland. To my surprise, I found the Dutch to be friendly, enterprising, and fair-minded, and their country to be well organized and rich in beauty and culture. Only then did I come to recognize my long-held prejudices—something I thought I could transcend. How many other childhood prejudices do I retain to confound my present thoughts and decisions?

Rogoza

Mama's parents ("Ma" and "Pa" to her) were both Polish immigrants. Her father, Dominik Rogoza, came from a town of Rogozisky, which is a little north of Vilnius (also called "Wilnius," or "Wilno")—the capital of what is presently Lithuania. I suspect his family name was derived from the town of his origin. Both Ma and Pa considered their origins as Polish, not Lithuanian, and Polish was their mother tongue, as well as that of their children. In fact, Mama didn't learn English until she started school where the nuns forbade her to speak Polish.

Dominik Rogoza and Stella (Stanislava) Gryniewicz on their marriage in 1908. She was 16 years old.

I'm not sure of the date of Pa's arrival in America. In 1908 he married Stanislawa ("Stella") Gryniewicz, a Polish immigrant girl only sixteen years old in Baltimore, Maryland, and it was there she bore her first child, Marianna (Aunt Mary). They soon moved to East Rochester New York, which then was a worker's magnet because of its busy "car shop" that made railroad cars of all descriptions—cars for freight, passengers regular and fancy, sleeping, and dining. Work must have been good in East Rochester, for two of Dominik's cousins, Anthony and Felicia, soon immigrated to America, and settled there.

I suppose the Rogozas made a decent living in East Rochester. They apparently could afford to rent what appears today to be a fairly roomy structure at 27 Taft street. But it would be their bad luck that Dominik would contract a disease of his kidneys, an illness that would leave him sick for an extended period and would take his life at the age of only thirty-one, leaving Stanislawa with five children: Marianna (Aunt Mary), who was nearly seven years old; Dominik (Uncle Lefty), who was five and one-half; Anastasia (Aunt Stella), who was four; Helen (AKA Julia; "Mama" to me), age two and one-half; and Edward, an infant child of four months. Ma placed her daughters, Mary, Stella, and Helen in an orphanage, and son, Dominik, in an adjacent facility for boys until she found a new mate, Albin Zalut, to take over the responsibility of family support. She kept her infant son, Edward.

Mama had only the most primal memories of her Pa— memories of love as seen through the eyes of a child of two years and seven months, Mama's age when Pa died on May 17, 1917. His death certificate says the cause of death was "Chronic Parenchymatous Nephritis." My doctor-friend, Arne, helped me with this one too. It was a disease of the kidneys, something Uncle Lefty recalled as a long illness. Arn said it could have been caused by a streptococcus infection which settles in the kidneys, although there could have been other causes. The body's defenses create an auto-immune response that destroys the tissue. The progression of the disease is very debilitating: the legs swell up; the victim becomes weak; and the body may start to digest muscle tissue to make up for protein deficiency caused by the condition. He was thirty-one when he died.

I wanted desperately to find more about Mama's life as a child. I hoped I could learn more from Uncle Lefty, the last surviving Rogoza among Mama's siblings. Unfortunately, my belated interest in him did little to endear me to him. I called him numerous times, wrote letters, and even tracked him down where he lived in a gated community near Orlando Florida. I thought we hit it off pretty well on that visit, even though he had rebuffed my prior phone calls with sharp admonishments not to visit. But he was congenial when we actually met face to face, and he seemed to enjoy filling me in on some of the family history.

A couple of years later I found him in a hospital in Florida where he had been placed after being found unconscious at his home. I showed him some old family pictures that I had brought with me, hoping to stimulate some reminiscences. What I got was an angry stare, and a clearly enunciated message: "I know what you're doing. You're trying to play psychology on me. You know that I'm the last Rogoza, and you're trying to get me to talk. Well, you don't mean nothin' to me, and I'm not telling you nothin." I looked into his face as he spoke those angry words, and saw Mama, whom he much resembled. His words were like icicles piercing my heart. Of course, he was right. I was trying to coerce him to talk. But was that so bad? I wondered. Was he reacting because of a hurtful letter Mama wrote to him in her final, dark year? Was it a case of dementia? Was he just ornery? Uncle Lefty died a month later, the last of the Rogozas in Mama's direct family. I did grieve his passing, even though I little knew him.

Helen (AKA Julia) Rogoza (Mama). The sign in the basket says "1928." That would make her 13 in this picture. In my experience, girls would dress like a bride for their first Holy Communion, but 13 is quite old for that occasion. This picture was most likely taken on her Confirmation.

Gryniewicz

A boat departed from a North Sea port at Breman, Germany on October 29, 1903. Among the immigrants on board were Julia Gryniewicz and her four-year-old son, Wladyslav. Their ID tags listed their point of origin as Cicioritaki, Russia. Julia was my maternal great-grandmother. They settled in Baltimore, Maryland.

I know precious little about Julia. I do know that another of her children—Stanislawa, Mama's mother—later made the journey from Europe to join her mother in Baltimore. It would have been before Stanislawa's sixteenth birthday, her age when she married Dominik Rogoza in Baltimore. Julia supported herself in Baltimore by selling newspapers until her death. Her son, Wladyslav, became a U.S. citizen in 1932, and changed his name to Walter Green at that same time. Walter's brother, Joseph, would also adopt the surname Green, apparently as a convenience for the many Americans who found *Gryniewicz* too much of a mouthful.

Stanislawa, who was also known in the U.S. as "Stella," gave birth to her first child, Marianna (Mary), on February 13, 1917, when she was but seventeen years old. Dominik, Stella, and Mary soon moved to East Rochester, New York, where Dominik worked in the "car shops," which made railroad cars. Dominik died on May 17, 1917, leaving Stella with five children: Mary (seven years old), Dominik (five and one-half), Stella (four), Helen, (AKA Julia, two and one-half), and Edward (four months old).

The family received support from the nearby town of Pittsford for a while, but I suppose Ma became desperate with her burden. Four months after her husband, Dominik, died, she placed all her children, excepting the infant Edward in an orphanage. The girls were placed in Saint Patrick's Orphan Girl's Asylum, now a residential treatment facility for dysfunctional teen-agers known as Saint Joseph's Villa. I obtained the records of the girls' admission thanks to the generous labors of Dr. Lustig, the present director of Saint Patrick's. But the facility in 1917 was only for girls I was told. I recounted to Dr. Lustig Mama's early memory of seeing her brother Dominik beyond a fence, within hailing and waving distance, but out of reach. "Could there have been an adjacent facility for boys?" I asked. That prompted Dr. Lustig to seek the advice of an elderly nun in retirement. "Yes," she recalled, "there had been an adjacent facility for boys, and it had a yard separated from the girl's yard by a wire fence." Dr. Lustig then searched for additional records, whereupon he found an archived book containing the records of Saint Mary's Boy's Orphan Asylum, and there was listed Dominik Rogoza.

I was able to clear up a mystery of what happened to Edward, Mama's brother whom she and her sisters remembered as having been burned in his crib under vague circumstances. The Rochester Democrat & Chronicle of January thirteenth, 1918 provided the details. Ma had left Edward in the care of a friend, a Mrs. Kerjes, who in turn left the infant, then nine months old, in the care of her own eight year-old daughter so she could do some shopping. While she was gone, Edward reached for a cloth covering a nearby table, and pulled a lighted kerosene lantern into his crib. The girl, who was absorbed in reading a story, did not notice his dire circumstances until the flames engulfed him. She ran out in fright just as her mother was returning. Mrs. Kerjes smothered the flames, but Edward's burns were so severe that he died later that evening. Edward's death always left a deep impression on Mama and her sisters, even though Mama was only three and one-half years old when the accident happened, and still in the orphanage.

Two months after Edward's death, six months after their admission into the orphanage, the Rogoza children were reunited with their mother and a new father, Albin Zalut, who had already settled in Detroit prior to the reunion. The short

courtship, and the fact that Albin was willing to support Stanislawa and her four surviving children suggests to me that he was already a family friend when Dominik died.

Stella Gryniewicz Rogoza's 2nd marriage to Albin Zalut abt. 1917 The flower girl is probably Marianna Rogoza (Aunt Mary)

The Zaluts were as prolific as were the Rogozas. After Anna came Joseph (AKA Jerry), Stanley, Joan (AKA Jenny), Lillian, Johnny, and Dolores. In her two marriages, Stanislawa Gryniewicz gave birth to twelve children, and except for Edward, all survived into adulthood, although Mama and her sisters would always get misty eyed when they mentioned their beloved brother Stanley, who was killed at the age of twenty-one during the World War Two invasion of the Pacific island of Tarara.

My next record of the family comes from the 1920 census, two years after the Zalut marriage, when the family was living in Detroit on St. Auburn Avenue at an address now covered by a freeway. The family had by then expanded by another child, Anna, who was one and one-half years old. I suspect living conditions were crowded in the Zalut household. The same address listed two other families besides the Rogozas and Zaluts—altogether twenty-one individuals lived at that address. The census listed two borders in the Zalut family unit in addition to the parents and children.

I did not know my grandmother, Stella Gryniewicz-Rogoza-Zalut (Babka), as a child. Mama was estranged from her, and we seldom visited the farm where she lived in Reese Michigan. On the rare occasions when we did go there (perhaps twice in my lifetime), I had a great fear of her due to the stories I had heard from Mama of the extreme abuse she had suffered at her hands.

When I look at pictures of Babka I am struck by how old she appears even as she continued to bear children. In one picture she appears as an old crone holding Lilli, who is not yet two. But she is only thirty-three in that picture and had yet to bear another two children. I search her face for answers to my questions. Babka, what made you so cruel to your children? Was it the drudgery of your own life? The poverty? Can these things transform a kind, happy girl into the kind of mother that Mama and her sisters remembered? Or were you already cruel and angry when you married at sixteen? What horrors took place within your household that would compel authorities to place your daughter—my mother—in a foster home when she was sixteen? Did you not know that you were supposed to protect your children? Did you know she had a brilliant mind? Would it have mattered if you did know? I don't get any answers—not from her image in the pictures, not from any documentation I could find, not from her other children who maintained a code of silence about these things.

Stanislawa Gryniewicz-Rogoza-Zalut. Aunt Mary dated this picture 1925, which would make Ma 33. She is holding Lilli, according to Mary.

I asked cousin Joyce about her impressions of Babka. "Like Ma Kettle," she said, referring to the character in the film *Cheaper by the Dozen*. "A crude, cranky old gal who cursed and spat as she smacked the chickens off the kitchen table with her cane. An unhappy person. An angry person."

Stanislawa Gryniewicz died in 1960 at the age of sixty-eight. Her youngest son, Johnny, acquired the farm.